SOCIAL MOVEMENTS IN AMERICA

SOCIAL MOVEMENTS IN AMERICA

ROBERTA ASH
DePaul University

MARKHAM PUBLISHING COMPANY / Chicago

MARKHAM SOCIOLOGY SERIES
Robert W. Hodge, Editor

Adams, *Kinship in an Urban Setting*
Adams, *The American Family: A Sociological Interpretation*
Adams and Weirath, eds., *Readings on the Sociology of the Family*
Appelbaum, *Theories of Social Change*
Ash, *Social Movements in America*
Cole, *The Sociological Method*
Edwards, ed., *Sex and Society*
Farley, *Growth of the Black Population: A Study of Demographic Trends*
Filstead, ed., *An Introduction to Deviance: Readings in the Process of Making Deviants*
Filstead, ed., *Qualitative Methodology: Firsthand Involvement with the Social World*
Karp and Kelly, *Toward an Ecological Analysis of Intermetropolitan Migration*
Laumann, Siegel, and Hodge, eds., *The Logic of Social Hierarchies*
Lejeune, ed., *Class and Conflict in American Society*
Zeitlin, ed., *American Society, Inc.: Studies of the Social Structure and Political Economy of the United States*

Copyright © 1972 by Markham Publishing Company
All Rights Reserved
Printed in U.S.A.
Library of Congress Catalog Card No. 76–190602
Hardcover Standard Book Number 8410–4046–9
Paperback Standard Book Number 8410–4045–1

To Henry, Renée, and Marshall

Acknowledgments

A completed publication depends on the work of a large number of generally unacclaimed persons, often women. I must first emphasize my indebtedness to the people who made this book possible in the most concrete and fundamental respects.

First of all, I must thank Nancy Ennis, copy editor at Markham, who struggled with my prose, left my meanings intact, and suffered through my footnotes.

Credit for the index must be given to Sonia Marschak, who accepted and carried out what proved to be a very deroutinizing task.

An army of babysitters and housekeepers contributed to my efforts and held back the rising tide of chaos in my household: Grace Lo Kwang; Francesca Pieraccini; Cynthia Meyers, who gave Michael his first thrilling glimpse of the primeval world of children; Laura Thompson; Susan Rogo; Cynthia Schroeder; Helen Hill; Augusta Harris, from whom I learned very much; and best loved of all Jacqueline Lower and her inimitable doggies.

I would like to thank my typists: Sue O'Brien, Betty Thomas, Marilyn Guth, Mary Ellen Bell, Linda Bell, and Karen Hartley, all of whom worked under absurd time pressure and didn't let me down.

My stimulating discussions with Miles Hoffman, of the University of Chicago political science department, forced me to refine my theoretical positions; Miles is responsible for introducing me to two works that had a profound influence on my writing—Louis Hartz's *The Liberal Tradition in America* and Michael Rogin's *The Intellectuals and McCarthy*.

David Street and C. Warren Vander Hill read the first draft and provided many helpful suggestions; as a matter of fact, this book owes its existence to David.

Richard Flacks, Ellen Trimberger and Morris Janowitz—not always in agreement with each other—supported me in a variety of subtle ways by generally validating my efforts and aspirations. So did Bob Ogden, the SESPA group, and (in anticipatory socialization) Bob Ross, in a more explicitly political way.

My students have had a major influence on my commitments and my ideas. It is hard to single out a few individuals, but special mention should be made of Jean Benward Tempel, Linda Thalberg Silverstone, and Susan Rosen (all formerly at Barnard) and —although I often disagreed with them—Morris Grossner (Columbia), Hank Donnelly (Chicago), and Joe Johnson (Chicago).

Finally, I would like to thank my colleagues and the administration at DePaul for providing me with time, with a favorable climate, and with stimulating discussions.

Chicago 1972

Contents

1	An Analytic Introduction	1
2	A Descriptive Introduction	29
3	The Colonial Era and the First American Revolution	47
4	From Perfection to Progress: 1781–1850	81
5	The Second American Revolution?	97
6	The Era of Unrest: 1865–1900	116
7	The Rise of the New Industrial State: 1900–1929	152
8	The Rise of the New Industrial State: 1929–1960	193
9	The Present	228
Appendix.	Classes and Class Coalitions: A Model of American Politics	252
Index		261

1

An Analytic Introduction

THE DEFINITION OF SOCIAL MOVEMENTS

A social movement is a set of attitudes and self-conscious action on the part of a group of people directed toward change in the social structure and/or ideology of a society and carried on outside of ideologically legitimated channels or which uses these channels in innovative ways.

This definition will be clarified in several ways. First, we will show how it distinguishes social movements from a variety of related phenomena. Second, we will explicate some postulates and assumptions that underlie the definition. Finally, we will consider differences in the degree to which a movement reflects its members' understanding of society.

Distinguishing Social Movements

There are four phenomena that are related to social movements but must be distinguished from them:

1. The definition distinguishes movements from movement organizations. Movement organizations are formally constituted and internally organized groups that frequently are the acting components of the movement. For instance, CORE and SNCC are movement organizations that were prominent in the civil rights movement.

2. The definition distinguishes movements from attitudinal change without action. Changes in attitude without action do not create a movement. We recognize that persons who are sympathetic to a movement but fail to undertake any action provide an important and possibly *necessary* support base for a movement but are not part of the movement itself. Similarly, an individual *weltanschauung* does not constitute a movement unless it is shared and associated with some overt behavior.

3. The definition distinguishes movements from premovement rebellious acts. A movement includes self-consciousness, that is, a conception of one's behavior that links it to the prevailing social structure or ideology. Thus, for example, the runaways and "street people" of the 1960s are part of a social movement; the juvenile delinquents and Labor Day rioters of the 1950s were *not*.

4. The definition distinguishes movements from changes initiated by a ruling class, an elite with political power, or an intelligentsia associated with such an elite. Neither Nixon's New American Revolution nor the Dodge Rebellion was a social movement. Nevertheless, the boundaries of the phenomenon are hard to identify, as the elite revolutions of nineteenth century Japan and twentieth century Turkey, the relationship between the Office of Economic Opportunity and militant urban ethnic groups that enjoy its sponsorship, and the New Deal suggest. These phenomena partake of movement characteristics but are not clearly movements; each indicates that an elite can influence social structure in innovative and even nonlegitimate ways.

Underlying Postulates and Assumptions

Some postulates and assumptions that underlie the definition must be explicated. First is the assumption that members of society distinguish between legitimate modes of action (those defined by law books, civics textbooks and organizational handbooks, for example), quasi-legitimate or customary channels created by informal practices, and wholly illegitimate means. Channels available to some groups are illegitimate for others. In a modern nation, for example, violence is a legitimate channel only for the nation-state; for all others, it is an illegitimate channel.[1] Social movements may involve wholly nonlegitimate action, the creation of new channels of questionable legitimacy, the innovative use of existing channels or even the demand that elites abandon their quasi-legitimate practices and stick to the "letter of the law."

Underlying this assumption is the more fundamental postulate that power is very unevenly distributed in any large society and that some groups hold power only to the extent that they can beg or steal it from groups that would otherwise monopolize it. Power may be defined [2] as the ability to carry out one's will regardless of opposition.

Our distinction between legitimate and nonlegitimate modes of action reflects the tenet that societies have prevalent ideologies that are symbolic systems of norms and values that explicitly or implicitly support the prevailing social structure. (By social structure we mean the combination of existing class relationships and distribution of power.) These ideologies include not only "official" norms but also a variety of informal regulations and personal rationalizations.

Understanding the Structure of Society

Finally, our definition suggests that there are differences in the degree to which individuals and groups understand the structure of their society. In this sense prepolitical or subpolitical movements can be distinguished from political movements; the former lack a secular analysis of the society, while the latter operate on the basis of such an analysis even if it is incorrect or sketchy. In some cases movements are based on very elaborate symbolizations of the social structure (as are many religious movements such as heretical late medieval Christian sects, Melanesian cargo cults, and the Ghost Dance movement); these are difficult to dismiss as simply prepolitical. In general, movements must be distinguished from premovement phenomena, lacking any analysis, be it secular or not.

Now we will outline a more general theoretical framework for the analysis of social movements employing only those assumptions absolutely necessary to the discussion of our definition.

A FRAMEWORK FOR THE ANALYSIS OF MOVEMENTS

Our model of societies and social process draws on a variety of traditions. It is extensively based on the Marxian model but draws also on elite analysis in sociology and political science of Edward Shils and Harold Lasswell; existential phenomenology of Peter Berger; neoevolutionism and the revival of historical materialism of Marvin Harris and a number of his fellow anthropologists; works of J. K. Galbraith, Barrington Moore, Jr. and Herbert Marcuse; and new conceptions of American history by young historians such as Staughton Lynd, Eugene Genovese, Christopher Lasch, James Weinstein, Jesse Lemisch, and others.[3] We are proposing this model not as an explanatory straitjacket, but as a useful paradigm for generating interesting questions and orienting the collection and presentation of data.

Here are our major assumptions:

1. There are three analytic levels of society; a substructural level, *the level of production* (including techniques, material culture and technology, work organization, and relations to the environment), can be distinguished from the middle level, a *social-structural* level (including the relations of production—class relations—and political structure). Third is the superstructural level, the *ideology and value system* level.

The higher the level, the greater the number of alternatives given a specific pattern of the substructure. That is, given a particular system of production, there is only a limited number of class systems compatible with it, a somewhat less restricted but small number of political arrangements in harmony with it, and a considerable flexibility in value and belief systems.

Obviously, these remarks make sense only as statistical statements, that is, as probability statements that hold over time and cross-culturally. In the long run, for most societies, a specific system of production will be associated with only a limited number of social structural and ideological configurations. Our assumption is not to be taken as an absolute article of faith, allowing no exception. However, the exceptional society will tend to arise infrequently and it will be beset by internal problems: where a compatibility between substructure and superstructure or between different levels of the superstructure is completely lacking, the society will manifest contradictions. Severe individual stress, alienation and anomie, concern about ritual pollution and fear of witchcraft, ritual, and assorted whimsicalities of the belief system represent efforts by contradiction-ridden societies to come to terms with the disharmonies of their structure. In the long run, such societies prove to be structurally unstable. Nevertheless, it should be emphasized that not only are such incompatibilities not impossible, but that the relationship of substructure to superstructure is one of high correlation only, not of logical necessity. For additional material on this subject, see Marvin Harris, *The Rise of Anthropological Theory*.[4]

Two brief examples illustrate our general model. One is provided by the analysis of post-classical (early medieval) circum-Mediterranean societies. These are societies of scarcity. They are based on sheepherding and plow agriculture carried on in a rather arid setting and certain features are common to all: they are characterized by sharp class disparities, tiny literate elites, and large rural masses; their institutions are male-dominated, patrilineal, and highly developed in regard to the ideology of shame and honor; they are marked by intergroup hostilities derived from the scarcity of the resource base and expressed in some form of "amoral familism" (a double standard whereby kinsmen are included in a circle of trust and cooperation while outsiders are treated as potential enemies and victims); and they profess monotheistic faiths as similar—or as different—as Roman Catholicism, Eastern Orthodoxy, and Islam. Variations within this large culture area can be explained quite effectively by the nature of the environment and the subsistence base.[5]

The United States and Soviet Russia provide another example. The large-scale industrial economy of each of these societies imposes a similar class system on both nations—a system characterized by extremely concentrated political power and control over wealth, an important, subservient, highly rewarded intelligentsia, and widespread welfare measures and redistribution of income. Politically, there is convergence in the growth of state (or quasi-state) bureaucracies, pervasive surveillance, and some outlets for local decision-making. Because of America's liberal history and more effective productive system, Americans enjoy more subtle forms of social control (through advertising, channeling, and repressive desublimation) than Russians do. Finally, while the ideologies pretend to be totally opposite, they serve similar functions and share many elements that—at least in the past—were important correlates of the productive system: an achievement ethic, a myth of classlessness, secularization, and nationalism.

These examples illustrate the general postulate: the nature of the productive system (abundance and scarcity, environmental conditions, technology, and basic productive enterprises) constrains the class system (the relations of production—the distribution of wealth and power). In turn, the class system is reflected in the political system, and both limit the number of possible ideologies. All these levels are linked by a series of probability statements holding over time and cross-culturally.[6]

2. Our second postulate is that the most important elites of a society are those groups that control the relations of production. These elites constitute a ruling class only in a carefully circumscribed sense. Even under the most favorable circumstances, a ruling class depends on the support of political and intellectual (ideology-creating) elites. Generally, the "ruling class" is not directly involved in ruling; it influences certain key decisions rather than participates in all decisions. Many sectors of decision-making will not be affected at all by economic dominants. Second, economic dominants are not a clique and perhaps not even a self-consciously unified group; there can be a fairly high level of conflict within the ruling class. Third, in modern or modernizing societies in which state socialism prevails, the political elite is identical to the ruling class, and although it defines itself in political terms (as a party), it clearly controls the productive system. Fourth, in the neocapitalist states, the political elite may have a considerable degree of autonomy; it is constrained by the relations of production but can threaten or even overwhelm some of the economic dominants (as is true of the Pentagon, which cannot be dismissed as a simple servant of American corporations). Thus, the concept of a ruling class must be understood as a shorthand for "groups holding power as a result of substructural process," rather than as a synonym for "economic dominants." "Power elites" is perhaps a preferable term. Thus, we reject any vulgar Marxist conspiratorial model; our own model is fairly compatible with the work in elite analysis carried out by Lasswell et al. Keep in mind that substructural processes shape sociopolitical and ideological patterns; we do *not* assume that this shaping is self-consciously imposed by a group of individuals.

Obviously, any attempt to analyze the political level as wholly autonomous is unrealistic. The autonomy of the political system becomes possible only when men are freed from the realm of necessity (that is, only under substructural conditions which have not yet been attained).

3. Our third postulate is that societies are structured by the existence of a center and a periphery, a perspective based on the work of Edward Shils. Shils defines the center of a society as a realm of both symbols and action, identifiable as the values pursued and affirmed by a diversity of elites and the institutions shaped by the authority of these elites. Neo-Marxists rank these elites, but Shils does not; economic institutions do not necessarily shape political institutions, nor is the intellectual realm a derivative of the sociopolitical sphere. (It is vulgar Marxism to argue that economic elites consciously create the state and the ideology; nevertheless, a Marxist view does have a stronger stand on the question of a hierarchy of elites than does Shils'.) Shils does use the term "ruling class" (but without its connotation of economic origin), remarking that

> the power of the ruling class derives from its incumbency of certain key positions in the central institutional system. Societies vary in the extent to which the ruling class is unitary or relatively segmental. Even where the ruling class is relatively segmental, there is, because of centralized control of appointment to the most crucial of the key positions or because of personal ties or because of overlapping personnel, some sense of affinity which, more or less, unites the different sectors of the *elite*.

> The different sectors of the elite, even in a highly pluralistic society where the elite is relatively segmental in its structure, are never equal. One or two usually predominate, to varying degrees, over the others, even in situations where there is much mutual respect and a genuine sense of affinity. Regardless, however, of whether they are equal or unequal, unitary or segmental, there is usually a fairly large amount of consensus among the elites of the central institutional system. This consensus has its ultimate root in their common feeling for the transcendent order which they believe they embody or for which they think themselves responsible.[7]

Shils identifies three important types of elites—the economic, the political, and the cultural-ecclesiastical. These elites correspond to our three levels of analysis—namely, economic substructure, political structure, and ideological superstructure. Shils outlines his conception of a central value system, a construct that corresponds to the Marxian notion of ideology or hegemony, as follows:

> The centre, or the central zone, is a phenomenon of the realm of values and beliefs. It is the centre of the order of symbols, of values and beliefs, which govern the society. It is the centre because it is the ultimate and irreducible; and it is felt to be such by many who cannot give explicit articulation to its irreducibility. The central zone partakes of the nature of the sacred. In this sense, every society has an "official" religion, even when that society or its exponents and interpreters, conceive of it, more or less correctly, as a secular, pluralistic, and tolerant society. The principle of the Counter-Reformation: *Cuius regio, ejus religio,* although its rigor has been loosened and its harshness mollified, retains a core of permanent truth.
>
> The centre is also a phenomenon of the realm of action. It is a structure of activities, of roles and persons, within the network of institutions. It is in these roles that the values and beliefs which are central are embodied and propounded.
>
> On the whole, these values are the values embedded in current activity. The ideals which they affirm do not far transcend the reality which is ruled by those who espouse them.[8] The values of the different *élites* are clustered into an approximately consensual pattern.[9]
>
> One of the major elements in any central value system is an affirmative attitude towards established authority. This is present in the central value systems of all societies, however much these might differ from each other in their appreciation of authority. There is something like a "floor," a minimum of appreciation of authority in every society, however liberal that society might be. Even the most libertarian and equalitarian societies that have ever existed possess at least this minimum appreciation of authority. Authority enjoys appreciation because it arouses sentiments of sacredness. Sacredness by its nature is authoritative. Those persons, offices or symbols endowed with it, however indirectly and remotely, are therewith endowed with some measure of authoritativeness.[10]

Shils certainly would not identify himself as a neo-Marxist; nevertheless, there is sufficient overlap between his model of society and the materialist paradigm to suggest that productive cross-referencing and borrowing of terminology is possible. In particular, his emphasis on *central* institutions, values, and elites corresponds to the Marxian concept of an identifiable ruling class and the ideology or ideational hegemony that sustains its power. In both theories, the society is seen as more or less unified by and focused on a dominant set of institutions, decision-makers, and values.

We are now in a position to define specific movements and state some propositions that follow from the preceding paradigm.

A revolutionary movement is one that is aimed at changing the relations of production and the political system; it is directed against the central value system and the central institutions of the society. It uses methods that are not defined as legitimate (or even quasi-legitimate) according to the ideology.

A reform movement is one that is not aimed at changing the relations of production or at displacing the incumbent ruling class. It uses only methods that are fundamentally legitimate (albeit novel or slightly questionable) and, generally, it is aimed at manipulating or cajoling elites.

A coup d'etat is aimed at illegitimate displacement of political incumbents without change in class structure or ideology: personnel changes, but positions and their interrelationships are not altered.

Now we can return to the problems of premovement phenomena and prepolitical and subpolitical movements. Premovement phenomena lack any analysis of the social order; prepolitical movements (the Ghost Dance movement of the American Indians, for example) either analyze the social order in exclusively nonsecular terms or embed an essentially political view of the social order in a nonsecular symbolism that entails nonrational methods of changing the social order. Political movements are at least partially secular and they combine the goal of ideological change with the goal of social structural change even though they may lack recognition of the relation between political structure and class structure. Finally, we can identify class-conscious movements as those that have developed a perspective that includes the relations of production. Notice that our typology cuts across the commonplace and analytically confused division into expressive and instrumental movements. All movements

include both expressive and instrumental elements. Following are examples of each type of phenomenon:

Premovement phenomena. Various types of collective behavior, such as the Labor Day riots of the 1950s; the Hell's Angels, and perhaps social bandits (a borderline example).

✓ *Prepolitical movements.* Cargo cults and the Ghost Dance; the nonconformist British working-class sects.

Political movements. The English revolution of the seventeenth century; the civil rights movement.

Class-conscious movements. The Industrial Workers of the World; the new left.

Temporal relations between these types of movements are very complex: with the general secularization and modernization of societies through internal processes and colonialism, social movements tend to become "disenchanted"—to substitute secular political analyses for magico-religious analyses.

Nevertheless, movements that accept these magico-religious analyses may have assessed the power relationship shrewdly, as was clearly true of Melanesian cargo cults and the Indian Ghost Dance participants. Both groups combined a correct understanding of oppression by whites with magical—and, hence, futile—efforts to expel the oppressors, in one case by preparing for the miraculous arrival of a cargo of guns and goods and in the other case by engaging in pan-Indian ecstatic practices. The shift from prepolitical to political movements is part of the trend toward the worldwide dominance of modern, industrial, urbanized mass (or proletarianized) societies. On a smaller time scale, we may find cycles of these phenomena in which the premovement and prepolitical forms are both the manifestations of unrest during repressive periods and symptoms of coming political outbursts. Thus, the premovement juvenile delinquency and "greaser" subculture of the quiet and repressive 1950s preceded the prepolitical beatniks of the late 1950s which, in turn, preceded the political civil rights movement of the early 1960s and the class-conscious radicalism of the late 1960s. In this context, we may question whether it is useful to speak of postpolitical movements, composed of persons who believe that any collective action to change a modern society is hopeless and that one can only react by withdrawing in despair into drugs, magic, or agrarian communes.[11]

Shortcuts from one level of movement to another are also possible; thus, classes that originally produced only juvenile delinquents yesterday may produce fully class-conscious movements today.

Our typology is, of course, not to be interpreted too rigidly; it merely represents useful cutting points of a spectrum rather than discrete compartments. Borderline and mixed phenomena abound: class-conscious street gangs; radicals whose tactic is transformation of the individual as part of a strategy of changing the whole social order; class movements that are perfectly in harmony with the language of traditional religion (for instance, those of the Catholic worker-priests, those led by Camillo Torres and other revolutionary clergymen in Latin America, and those of the Quaker and Catholic war resisters in the United States).[12]

DETERMINANTS AND EFFECTS OF SOCIAL MOVEMENTS

Although their roots are in the substructure and their attitudinal branches are in the ideological system, social movements are fundamentally a phenomenon of the middle level of our paradigm, the *social-structural* level.

Ultimately, social movements are caused by transformations of the material substructure, but it is more useful to analyze them as reflections of transformations of the relations of production. Because this analysis necessarily leads into a discussion of what relations of production means in terms of class, ethnicity, and gender, we will briefly list the types of effects social movements can have before we discuss the causes.

Effects

1. Because a variety of ideologies can be associated with a single substructure, movements can frequently change the ideology of a society without greatly affecting the substructure or even the social structure. However, this ideological flexibility is limited, and the social movement will tend to fail where it seeks ideological changes that do not correspond to structural transformations. (The Women's Christian Temperance Union after the fiasco and subsequent repeal

of Prohibition is a good case in point; its efforts to impose small-town Protestant morality on an advanced-industrial urbanized heterogeneous nation have been futile.)[13]

2. Social movements are especially likely to change institutions associated with but not central to the class structure—especially working conditions, welfare measures, consumer protection, and income distribution. The more institutional change in these areas threatens power relations and control of property (for example, the relations of production as opposed to a variety of manifestations of the underlying relations), the more it is resisted.

3. Movements may be quite successful in changing peripheral institutions as opposed to central institutions. In every society there are a number of arrangements over which elite control is weak (by choice). Obviously, such arrangements are changed fairly easily in response to social movements. In America, the greater vulnerability of the periphery can be understood in a geographical as well as a social sense. Local and national government decisions about local matters can be affected by social movements in a way that basic economic and foreign policy cannot be; the periphery is one area in which the pluralistic bargaining model is most applicable—that is, in which political decisions can most convincingly be described as the outcome of legitimately exerted pressure by a large number of influential interest groups that are roughly equal.

The broader the goals of a social movement, the more central its focus, and the greater its threat to class structure, the less likely it will be to succeed. Such movements face stronger resistance and must overcome deep-seated ideological beliefs in the minds of its potential supporters. Thus, each movement is faced with an optimizing problem in which large possible gains must be balanced against greater risks of total failure. In this respect, there are great risks in proceeding from an analysis that emphasizes formal political roles to an analysis of *class* that implies attacks not only on political incumbents, but also on the distribution of power throughout the society as well as on controlling elites outside of the formal political system. A movement that confines itself to attacks on political incumbents runs fewer risks than does one that attacks the political system as a whole and/or attacks economic and ideological elites; a movement that focuses on a single issue is more likely to succeed than is a movement that has broad goals, but its success is necessarily limited.

Some important illustrations of solutions to this optimizing problem will be presented in Chapters 7 and 8 in our discussion of the parallel growth of reform and radical movements around the turn of the century. A number of the reform movements won single-issue demands torn from the context of broader reforms that resulted in minute or pro forma changes, while the radical movements sought broad goals and a class-conscious analysis that led to suppression and to widespread ideological rejection.

The optimizing problems of movements can also be analyzed from the perspective of elites. Elites can concede small gains to reform movements and thereby defuse and prevent more threatening radical movements; alternatively, they can refuse to make any concessions and thereby run a greater risk of having to face movements that threaten the class structure. Ultimately, both sides must develop an analysis of their ability to control the available means of violence. Not only can elites make concessions, but they also can create moderate reform movements to defuse issues and channel dissatisfaction. Harold Lasswell has called these techniques of concession and movement creation "resistance by partial incorporation." [14] Herbert Marcuse treats these techniques as an aspect of "repressive tolerance," [15] and others refer to them as "co-optation." (Properly used, co-optation refers to the structural level while Lasswell's and Marcuse's terms refer more to the ideational level of this technique.) The enormous concentration of ownership of the mass media and opportunity for state control have made these techniques of defusion extraordinarily available to modern elites.

We now return from this consideration of effects and goals (that is, intended and anticipated effects) to our discussion of structural causes.

Determinants

Our statement that all social movements can ultimately be traced to structural (and substructural) transformations is too broad to be practical; it will be refined and made concrete in our discussion of specific social movements in America. Three further objections can be made and must be responded to at a theoretical level; the responses will lead us from our materialist-structural model to a phenomenological paradigm.

1. *Ethnicity and Other Ascriptive Factors.* The reader's first objection will probably have been that our analysis has neglected *ethnicity* (as well as gender, geographical location, and other ascriptive factors) and that we have proceeded as though societies are ethnically (sexually, regionally) homogeneous and have only class conflict, not ethnic conflict. There are several responses to that objection. The first is to state that ethnic cleavages are ultimately translated into class and/or political conflict, focused on the distribution of power and wealth. Conversely, ethnic relations are usually also relations of production. It is the reflection of ethnic cleavage in the distribution of power and wealth that makes the goal of cultural pluralism an unrealistic liberal dream under present conditions. Only the rare individual in an industrial society is so prejudiced or fanatic that he is unwilling to tolerate the existence of life styles and value systems other than his own; but when these diverse cultural systems of ethnic groups manifest themselves in competition for scarce resources (local or national power, control of key economic sectors, control over entrance to schools, unions, bureaucratic careers, desirable residential areas, and the like, and ultimately, ruling class positions) tolerance turns to hostility. A number of illustrations help to support this point: Suttles has remarked that Chicago Italian-Americans were tolerant toward blacks—that they did not object to blacks as neighbors or disapprove of their life styles—as long as the black people did not attempt to gain local political power;[16] Columbia University officials were not demonstrably personally bigoted, yet despite their lack of hostile attitudes toward blacks, they acted in "institutionally racist" ways consistently, as blacks were unintentionally victimized and exploited by university policies because Harlem is an economically vulnerable area. The existence of rational calculation of gains and losses in intergroup competition has been well demonstrated by John Dollard. The oppression of blacks is not an irrational prejudice that will wither away in an industrial society but a system of shortrun rationality that will cease to operate *only* when changes in social and political conditions make the costs of oppression to whites exceed the gains in deference, wealth, and sexual access.[17]

Under some conditions, ruling groups may find it useful to create or channel hostility toward ethnic minorities; the number of persons in a society with confused notions of social structure and ill-focused resentments is usually high enough to enable this ploy to work. Isaac Babel, the writer, said that anti-semitism is the socialism of fools. The simplest cases of movements of displaced hostility are the various persecutions of nonelite merchant minorities by the indigenous poor, such as the attacks on Jews throughout European history, on overseas Chinese in southeast Asia, and on Indians in South Africa. Currently in the United States, blacks are being used as scapegoats for inner-city problems. In this instance, the close dependence of ethnic hostility on class structure also can be seen.

Related to the translation of ethnic group *differences* (at the cultural and ideological level) into ethnic group *hostility and competition* (at the political and class-structural level) is the fact that some ethnic group cultures handicap their adherents in operating in the existing social structure—at present, for instance, in the opportunity system defined by the relations of production of the new industrial state. Thus, for example, in addition to being subjected to genocide and deportation practiced upon them by whites in the struggle for scarce resources of land, Indians are burdened by a rural tribal culture (often characterized by reverence for nature, emphasis on collective responsibility, and other non-Western features). Attractive as this culture may be, it consigns them to the bottom of the ladder in political and economic competition. Under the present class structure there is only one route for an Indian (or a black or a female) to power and wealth. If he hopes to achieve even the middle level, he must abandon much of his culture and transform himself ideologically into a white man. The dream of cultural pluralism comes to grief in the reality that there is only *one* economic and political system in the society and that some ethnic groups will, for external and internal reasons, be pushed to the bottom of the system.

Thus, ethnic differences are converted into different positions in the social structure. In particular, over the last two hundred years or so, traditional and tribal peoples virtually everywhere have been proletarianized.

This consideration leads us to a second and perhaps somewhat superficial manner of denying ethnicity the status of an independent dimension in the determination of social movements: ethnicity can be viewed as false consciousness, as an identity, and as a way of organizing experiences that obscures the underlying politicoeconomic structure. But "false consciousness" is only a label for a particular way of giving meaning to some very real experiences, experiences that persist over generations. An examination of these experiences leads us into two further considerations, that of the unique aspects of American history and that of phenomenology. The former will be discussed in detail below; here, it is sufficient to state that in American history, ethnicity is chronologically prior to immersion in the class structure and therefore of tremendous psychological importance. The course of American history has made ethnicity extraordinarily difficult to dismiss as "false consciousness" (while there is much more justification for such a dismissal of European workers' repeatedly asserted nationalism, which seems to be simply the result of irrational ideological indoctrination).

But beyond considering the unique aspects of American history, we must turn to a third way of approaching ethnicity and that is phenomenologically, as an important culturally transmitted way of creating cognitive order out of varied and confusing experiences. In the American context, often, it has been simpler to understand one's experience from an ethnic analysis than from a materialist analysis, even though as we have argued, the materialist analysis subsumes the ethnic one. (That a materialist analysis has been deliberately obscured by ideological indoctrination is only one factor among many.) We must therefore present a framework for discussing experience.

That ascriptive categories are also class categories is perhaps most clearly demonstrated by the case of sex, which makes clear that in the United States women have *no* controlling roles in the relations of production; the subtleties of the other ascriptive identities (religion, ethnicity, region) are entirely lacking in the case of sexual identity—women *are* a class, in a much simpler and homogeneous way than are ethnic groups. Therefore, our case for treating all ascriptive categories as special cases of the relations of production is strengthened; for historical reasons, class and ascriptive categories are no longer independent dimensions of the social structure.

2. *Status Politics*. A second objection of the reader will also lead us to the phenomenology of social movement participation: he will question whether there is any clear relationship between class exploitation and the emergence of social movements. He will point to

movements initiated by the relatively gratified and even by disgruntled elite members; he will ask why the most oppressed are so often acquiescent. Finally, he will propose that we reexamine the concept of *status politics*, the politics of groups defined by life styles rather than by class position. To this, we reply that status politics (and the related phenomena listed above) have been described by a variety of writers in the late '50s who wished to disassociate themselves from a neo-Marxist class-oriented analysis. On closer inspection, status politics proves to be class politics coupled with inappropriate ideologies (to be "false consciousness"). Its adherents tend to fall into one of four groups:

1. The upwardly mobile whose upward mobility has confirmed the American ideology of limitless opportunity and has brought its beneficiaries closer to the ruling groups;
2. The "doomed and dying" classes, economically, a very precarious entrepreneurial bourgeoisie that sees itself caught between the ruling class and a proletariat and relentlessly forced into the latter. This group has been very astutely described by Martin Trow in his study of supporters of Joe McCarthy in a small Vermont town;[18]
3. A new salaried middle class, essential to the state and corporate bureaucracies but without autonomous power. In large part, it overlaps the upwardly mobile class;
4. A working class that is still largely confused in its analysis of the social structure.

These groups have often engaged in the right-wing movements that first led to speculation about status politics: the Know-Nothings, the more intolerant reaches of the Womens' Christian Temperance Union, the vigilantism of the Palmer era, Father Coughlin's supporters, McCarthyism, the John Birch Society, and the Wallace campaign. But these groups have also been involved in quasi-left wing causes: Huey Long's Share the Wealth movement, and in the case of the new middle class, the civil rights and anti-war movements of the 1960s. The class bases of *all* these efforts are clear; nevertheless, our analysis must be directed toward explaining why these groups sometimes refuse to accept a class analysis of their discontents and why they sometimes behave in ways inappropriate to their class and even in bizarre ways. Relabeling "class" as "status" is not an answer;

rather, what is needed is a careful examination of the conditions under which structural position and substructural processes are perceived as "class problems" by an individual and those conditions under which this perception is altered or expressed without the language of class consciousness.

3. *The Role of the Individual.* We have arrived at our hypothetical critic's third objection: that we have not devoted sufficient attention to the individual. In particular, an individual must go through at least two steps before he engages in the collective action we have identified as a social movement: he must come to accept (or develop) a certain perspective of the society (including a definition of his own identity) and he must go beyond the attitudinal level to engage in some collective action. For some individuals these two steps occur simultaneously; others may find their whole lifetime intervenes between the first step and the second step. For still others, the order may be reversed; the social bandit guns down the lawman in a desperate effort to save his own skin or to avenge the family honor; only much later does he perceive himself as robbing from the rich to give to the poor or as otherwise challenging the existing social structure and ideology.[19]

As with the question of ethnicity and the problem of the politics of false consciousness, the issue of individual motivation forces us to reexamine the structural paradigm in terms of phenomenology, as an exercise in comprehending the individual's construction of reality.

THE PHENOMENOLOGY OF COLLECTIVE ACTION

An examination of our macrosociological objective framework has forced us to turn also to the other pole of sociological analysis: the subjective world of the individual. An understanding of the individual's experience provides the linkages between the prevailing conditions and the collective action that we have called a movement. Our complete model is, then, more or less as follows:

A base of objective conditions, rooted in the reality of satisfying material needs but generating social and ideological structures beyond the material concerns, is experienced by the individual in a variety of ways. Depending on the structuring of this experience, the individual may or may not engage in overt behavior associated with a movement. The conditions of the base not only shape the nature of *individual* experience but also influence the likelihood that the individual will be exposed to certain shared modes of interpreting experience; that is, to certain social constructions of reality.

The techniques for analyzing these different levels of reality must be varied and flexible. As social scientists, it is our contention that the initial input level—the "objective conditions"—and the output with which we are here concerned—the overt behavior and expressed attitudes that constitute the social movement—can be approached objectively, perhaps almost positivistically. Some of the key variables of these levels—system of production, class relations, political system, and overt behavior—can be operationally defined, observed, and recorded, although not always will they be converted into quantitative measures. Studies of income and prestige distribution, industrial and political decision-making, voting behavior, industrialization, and formal organization can provide the relevant data. Categories can be firmly established. Furthermore, they are unquestionably our own. (Anthropologists refer to such an analysis as an *etic* one, that is, one that is patterned after the "objective" externally imposed categories of phonetics.) Contrasted to this analysis is the analysis of the structuring of experience, the linkage between the two objective levels of base and movement behavior. Parts of this linkage can also be mapped carefully by an outside observer: the physiology of cognitive processes; the linguistic categories that constrain experience for all members of a given language community; the patterns of interaction and the modes of disseminating ideologies and counterideologies that determine exposure to a particular construction of reality; the charting of typical life histories and careers. Nevertheless, the observer can recapture part of this area only insofar as he immerses himself in the same world of meaning that the actors themselves share, only by reexperiencing in some way the experiences he is trying to comprehend. (Anthropologists refer to this effort to understand in terms of the categories of actors in the system, as *emics*, in reference to the meaning-oriented perspective of phonemics.) Even so, perhaps much of this realm of experience must remain unique, totally individual, and unrecapturable, only to be vicariously glimpsed in the reading of life histories and works of art. That all this unique experiencing is *in the aggregate* predictable from, and thus explainable by, the base of objective conditions makes our task of tracing the linkages between objective conditions and social movements only easier *in theory*.

There are two crucial moments in this elusive intermediate level (between the objective conditions and the collective action) that are of special concern to the student of social movements: one is the point at which the individual frees himself from the prevailing ideology and the second is the point at which he acts as a member of a social movement. The two points may or may not be distinct in time and they may occur in reverse order to their listing here; the first moment—of cognitive liberation—may be only partially realized, as is the case with many reform movement adherents. Using this terminology, we can characterize a variety of movements:

1. Partial cognitive liberation with ensuing action: the reform movement.

2. Full cognitive liberation with ensuing action: the radical movement.

3. Initially disjoint cognitive orders with ensuing action, that is, no initial acceptance of the prevailing order: the anticolonial or subcultural movement (such as the Ghost Dance movement or socialist and anarchist movements imported into America during the late nineteenth century by European immigrants).

4. Cognitive liberation with little or no ensuing action: an "inner resistance," typically assumed by those groups with a predilection to inactivity or by those for whom all action would be futile, and possibly suicidal (for example, slaves in the South).

It is tempting but difficult to make predictive statements linking these two levels of the structuring of experience; thus, one might argue almost on definitional grounds that full cognitive liberation comes only when the individual acts or (by contraposition of the preceding statement) that when the individual fails to act, sooner or later, he comes to be mentally as well as physically submissive to the existing order. One could claim that cognitive liberation can develop in the course of action itself, as in the case of social bandits who develop a belief system counter to the prevailing one in the course of their more or less accidentally commenced careers of crime. The data on American social movements will confirm some of these conjectures under certain conditions; but the two moments of which we are speaking should not simply be lumped together by definition.

Liberation from the prevailing cognitive order (the ideology of the society) need not mean a "correct" analysis of the society, in terms of our model of societies. Goals, tactics, and general constructions of reality propagated by movements may be far more bizarre and inappropriate to realizing concrete individual goals than is the ideology; one need only glance at the flying saucer cults for proof of this claim. However, there may be benefits to the individual regardless of a movement's ludicrousness as a vehicle for change of the collectivity, for the participant may gain a sense of purpose and solidarity; movement activity can reduce confusion, loneliness, and a sense of futility even when there is little or no likelihood of more tangible rewards, and it can contribute to the individual's sense of growth and worth. Movements of communal experimentation that have periodically appeared in America are especially good examples of movements that create little structural change but are satisfying to their members.

In closing this train of thought, let us note that a class-conscious movement is one that shares the author's cognitive order, at least to a degree; in this case, the categories for analyzing the social order as social scientists are also the categories of the members of movements—etics coincides with emics.

Three major perspectives have been brought to bear on this general area of inquiry (the structuring of experience). First is the analysis of groups and other social structures that define situations for individuals; thus, for instance, some research has been done on primary group affiliation and movement activities. Consideration has also been given to the work settings and other kinds of environments in which constructions of reality conducive to joining a movement are generated; the examination of how structural conditions produce movement-creating or movement-sustaining primary groups is a major way of linking "objective conditions" to subjective responses.

A psychological explanation of recruitment to movements is a second major approach to the structuring of experience. All too often, such an orientation has been *substituted for,* instead of *added to* an analysis of the existing social structure; and all too often, psychology has been used to ridicule and debunk social movements. But the researcher who is aware of the limitations, incompleteness, and political uses of psychological perspectives may find them productive as one among several explanatory devices. Psychoanalytic concepts have been widely used in explaining motivation for participation in social movements, especially movements that include a conflict of generations. Altered states of consciousness—"consciousness" in a psychological sense—as doors to new states of *sociopolitical* consciousness is a new avenue that has been only partially explored. Such an analysis would focus on the ways in which individual repatterning of reality through experiences of conversion, enlightenment, mystic ecstasy, or perceptual distortion provide a basis for collective reassessment of the social order. Altered states of consciousness and forceful movement leadership are by no means incompatible personal characteristics. This fact is demonstrated by early Christian leaders, Luther, Ignatius Loyola, and Theresa of Avila, and by Wovoka and other shamanistic leaders of anti-white millenarian movements. In the last decade, radical political action and the use of psychedelic drugs appeared at the same time (although they are not necessarily causally related), again suggesting links between the weakening of conventional perceptual categories and the weakening of political legitimacy.

A third perspective on changes in individual experiences, associated with the last mentioned possibility, is the examination of cognitive structures and the patterning of meaning in everyday life. Developments in cognitive psychology, structuralist anthropology, and ethnomethodology are only beginning to be applied to collective action and social structural change; frequently, these approaches have had a static, idealist, and hyper-abstract quality that made them singularly inappropriate for contributing to an understanding of the effects of the material substructure, the actions of men and the unfolding of history. Possibly, they can grow in directions that will make them more productive than their intellectually barren past suggests.

MOVEMENT TRANSFORMATIONS

The final task of our analytic introduction is to define a variety of possible outcomes of movements; this terminology will aid us in our examination of the fate of American social movements.[20] Movements undergo transformations in response to both external pressures and internal processes, which in turn are often triggered by environmental conditions. Most of these transformations are vicissitudes of the movement *organizations*, the formal structures that tend to be the acting components of the movement. Therefore, in each case, we must determine the effect of the transformation on the larger movement; even when the transformation produces the end of movement action, still we must explain the fate of the attitudes—the individual structuring of experience that impelled individuals into the movement and was, in turn, created and spread by the movement.

The first transformation that we can specify is associated with the appearance of a social movement: the *formalization* of a movement—its embodiment in one or more movement organizations. Some movements, especially those oriented toward life style change with an implicit, rather than an explicit political content, are never formalized into movement organizations but exist as individual or informal group behavior. Thus, Bohemian movements and defiance of Prohibition and marijuana laws are examples of largely unformalized movements. Formalization is a complex process that is dependent on both characteristics of the individuals in the movement and its environment.

A second important process, in this case externally imposed, is *suppression*, which we may define as the destruction of movement organizations and the bringing of sanctions against unorganized individual behavior.

The key question raised by an examination of suppression concerns the disposition of the energy of the movement. If suppression is accompanied by *co-optation* (a structural process of placing movement personnel into elite-sponsored positions) and *resistance by partial incorporation* (a cultural process of incorporating portions of movement belief systems into the prevailing ideology), suppression may prove to be successful; the movement produces only minor changes in the society and the relations of production even if there is some change of personnel—for example, some recruitment of movement members into politically important roles. Suppression without accompanying co-optation tends to decrease the size of the movement and to radicalize it; its view of the world becomes increasingly hostile to the prevailing view, its tactics more desperate and more secretive, and its members fewer and more committed as full-time professionals. Extreme suppression may make even such a secretive "hard core" movement impossible to sustain.

A movement may undergo *goal displacement*, a process in which the goals of organizational maintenance override the initial goals of social change. Often goal displacement is accompanied by *oligarchization*, in which an originally democratically structured movement organization separates into a decision-making elite and a disaffected and unheard rank and file; the movement elite consolidates its power by gaining specialized skills and controlling the flow of communication within the movement. Once entrenched, the movement elite is extraordinarily hard to dislodge and tends to *conservatize* the movement, for it owes its sinecure to the inoffensiveness (and consequent longevity) of the movement. A conservative movement—one that does not attack the ideology or social structure in vigorous and/or fundamental ways—is more likely to be a continuing source of funds and decision-making roles for its leaders than is a nonconservative movement; decision-making is, however, increasingly confined to organizational maintenance decisions—for example, funding and internal structure. Note how superficially there can be structural similarities in a *radicalizing* movement and a *conservatizing* movement—in both, rank and file numbers diminish, leaders become more professional, and decision-making *may* be centralized. The conservatized movement often is finally transformed into the *institutionalized* movement, which is structurally and ideologically thoroughly incorporated into the status quo, that is, it supports the existing class relationships and political system. Some movements (such as Christian Science or the YMCA) are institutionalized near the periphery of the society, while others (for instance, the American labor movement) become part of the very center of society. Finally, *routinization of charisma* may be related to conservatization, goal displacement, oligarchization, and institutionalization; the success and internal structure of the movement are no longer dependent on the extraordinary qualities of a leader but on the ordinary societal ways of distributing power—the extraordinary charismatic leader is usually a threat to existing structure and ideology by his very existence (even when he preaches no revolution), and thus a movement that has lost such leadership is more able to accommodate to the prevailing situation.

Different from the varieties of accommodationist transformations, is the movement *becalmed*. It too may undergo goal displacement and/or oligarchization but its key feature is that it has lost its class support base. It speaks for a constituency that no longer exists. Its membership dwindles to a small steady number and it may vegetate without dying for decades.

All movement organizations are prone to *factionalization,* an inherent problem of movements since while there is only one status quo, there is a variety of alternatives to it and of methods of attaining the alternatives; each alternative potentially could be associated with a separate movement organization. Furthermore, the individual circumstances of joining a movement encourage factionalization; once an individual is liberated from the prevailing system of beliefs and values, he is likely to repeat his rejection of a proffered cognitive and normative order. His initial rejection of the prevailing ideology sets a precedent for ideational rebellion. Structurally and pragmatically, this tendency means that the movement participant is likely to take part in hair-splitting and factionalism. Finally, the intangible nature of the rewards a movement provides for its members encourages factionalism, while the more indivisible concrete material rewards of status quo institutions act as incentives to loyal service.

Movement organizations may also *coalesce or incorporate* smaller rivals within a broad movement.

Finally, an interesting case of movement transformation is presented by *goal realization.* It is important to distinguish two totally different subcases; one is the situation discussed above, in which the movement has undergone goal displacement, partial incorporation and conservatization, and the realized goals are fairly modest modifications of the status quo. Movements that have attained such modest success may die entirely; discontent in their membership base awaits a new more radical movement to reawaken it—the nineteenth century women's movement, shrunk down into the women's suffrage movement and in coma until Women's Lib in the 1960s, is an excellent example of this apparent realization of trivialized goals. This moderate type of success may merely set the stage for a later attempt to redefine the situation more radically. Sometimes goal realization may be followed by constituency loss and becalment, as in the case of Prohibition and the Women's Christian Temperance Union; the victory was won when the issues were already dead and the class situation altered.

A very different case of goal realization occurs when a movement achieves profound structural change. Because of the way in which political change is constrained by the productive system, profound change of any kind is quite rare. The observer of revolutions will wish to know to what extent the *nature* of relations of production has been changed, as opposed to mere change in incumbents of class positions. He will also ask about the nature of ideological change and the extent of continuity in political and legal forms. Considerable amounts of the old ideology and legal-political forms may be incorporated into a new ideology. At a more descriptive level, even revolutionary change may not penetrate into the countryside or into other socially peripheral areas of the society. It is difficult to decide at what point the analysis of a revolutionary movement must give way to the analysis of a new status quo, complete with its own class system and ideology. The problem becomes especially difficult when the revolutionary movement has been dedicated to abolishing class and to propagating a permanent revolution. Even if the researcher refuses to take the rhetoric seriously, he must look for efforts at changing the social structure that continue for years or even decades beyond the initial upheaval. It is only in the terminology of the state—the political system and its accompanying ideology of legitimacy—that one can speak of a definite shift from the illegitimate prerevolutionary movement to the legitimate new post-revolutionary elite; in terms of class structure (as well as nonpolitical components of ideology, family structure, and a number of other aspects of society), revolution is a much longer, less sharply focused process.

NOTES

[1] Max Weber, *The Theory of Social and Economic Organization* (Glencoe, Ill.: The Free Press, 1947), p. 154.

[2] *Ibid.*, p. 152.

[3] Edward Shils, *Selected Essays* (Chicago: Center for Social Organization Studies, University of Chicago, 1970); Harold Lasswell and A. Kaplan, *Power and Society* (New Haven, Conn.: Yale University Press, 1950); Harold Lasswell, *Politics* (New York: Meridian World, 1958); Harold Lasswell and D. Lerner, *World Revolutionary Elites* (Boston: MIT Press, 1966); Peter Ber-

ger and T. Luckmann, *The Social Construction of Reality* (Garden City, N.Y.: Doubleday, 1967); Marvin Harris, *The Rise of Anthropological Theory* (New York: Crowell, 1968); John Kenneth Galbraith, *The New Industrial State* (Boston: Houghton Mifflin, 1967); Herbert Marcuse, *One Dimensional Man* (Boston: Beacon Press, 1964); Herbert Marcuse, *Eros and Civilization* (Boston: Beacon Press, 1955); Herbert Marcuse, *Essay on Liberation* (Boston: Beacon Press, 1969); Staughton Lynd, *The Intellectual Origins of American Radicalism* (New York: Random House, 1969); Eugene Genovese, *The Political Economy of Slavery* (New York: Random House, 1965); Eugene Genovese, *The World the Slaveholders Made* (New York: Random House, 1969); Barrington Moore, Jr., *The Social Origins of Dictatorship and Democracy* (Boston: Beacon Press, 1966); Christopher Lasch, *The New Radicalism in America 1889–1963* (New York: Random House, 1965); Christopher Lasch, *The Agony of the American Left* (New York: Random House, 1969); James Weinstein, *The Decline of Socialism in America* (New York: Random House, 1967); Jesse Lemisch, "The American Revolution Seen from the Bottom Up," in Barton J. Bernstein, *Towards a New Past* (New York: Random House, 1968).

[4] Harris, *op. cit.*

[5] Jane Schneider, "Of Vigilance and Virgins: Honor, Shame and Access to Resources in Mediterranean Societies," *Ethnology* 10, no. 1 (January 1971): 1–24.

[6] Harris, *op. cit.*

[7] Shils, *op. cit.*, pp. 9 and 10.

[8] *Footnote in original*: "This set of values corresponds to what the late Karl Mannheim called 'ideologies,' i.e., values and beliefs, which are congruent with or embodied in current reality ('*seinskongruent*'). I do not wish to use the term 'ideology' to describe these value orientations. One of the most important reasons is that in the past few decades the term 'ideology' has been used to refer to intensely espoused value-orientations which are extremely *seinstranszendent*, which transcend current reality by a wide margin, which are explicit, articulated and hostile to the existing order. (For example, Bolshevist doctrine, National Socialist doctrine, Fascist doctrine, etc.) Mannheim called these 'utopias.' Mannheim's distinction was fundamental and I accept it, our divergent nomenclature notwithstanding."

[9] *Footnote in original:* "The degree of consensuality differs among societies and times. There are societies in which the predominant *elite* demands a complete consensus with its own more specific values and beliefs. Such is the case in modern totalitarian societies. Absolutist regimes in past epochs, which were rather indifferent about whether the mass of the population was party to a consensus, were quite insistent on consensus among the *elites* of their society."

[10] Shils, *op. cit.*, pp. 1 and 3.

[11] Theodore Roszak, *The Making of a Counter-Culture* (Garden City, N.Y.: Anchor-Doubleday, 1969).

[12] Our definition of social movement contained a distinction between

goals and methods; this distinction has frequently been used as the basis for a typology of social movements, not always productively. For we believe that there is unity between goals and tactics and that the more radical the movement—the more it insists on an analysis of the totality of the social order—the more illegitimate its methods must become. For methods and goals are linked in the same ways that substructure, social structure and ideology are, as we shall attempt to demonstrate in our substantive chapters. In the short run, of course, the correlation between goals and tactics is only imperfect, but even so, these two variables do not lend themselves to the construction of a typology, because the short-run linkages between goals and tactics are constrained by the environment in which the movement must operate. The factor of environment is so complicated and yet so fundamental that a careful consideration of its impact on tactics would produce a body of theory rather than a usable typology.

[13] Joseph Gusfield, *Symbolic Crusade* (Urbana: University of Illinois Press, 1969).

[14] Harold Lasswell, *World Politics and Personal Insecurity* (New York: McGraw-Hill, 1935).

[15] Herbert Marcuse, "Repressive Tolerance," in Robert Wolff, Barrington Moore, Jr., and Herbert Marcuse, *A Critique of Pure Tolerance* (Boston: Beacon Press, 1969).

[16] Gerald D. Suttles, *The Social Order of the Slum* (Chicago: University of Chicago Press, 1968).

[17] John Dollard, *Caste and Class in a Southern Town* (New York: Harper, 1939).

[18] Martin Trow, "Small Businessmen, Political Tolerance and Support for McCarthy," *American Journal of Sociology* 64 (1958): 270–81.

[19] Eric Hobsbawm, *Primitive Rebels* (New York: Norton, 1965).

[20] Mayer Zald and Roberta Ash, "Social Movement Organizations: Growth, Decay and Change," *Social Forces* 44 (March 1966): 327–40.

2

A Descriptive Introduction

All analyses of social change are constrained by two facts, each of which forces the presentation of data into a chronological and descriptive framework: first is the ultimate *uniqueness* of all historical phenomena; second is the passage of *time* during any period of social change. In this chapter, we will accommodate to the pressures of uniqueness and temporality to the extent of discussing the American setting to which our general theoretical framework must be applied. Our two major foci are certain unique features of American society and a description of the major historical substructural trends that limited the possible nature and scope of American social movements.

THE UNIQUE ASPECTS OF AMERICAN SOCIETY

The characteristics of American society that we are about to discuss are not exceptions or counterexamples to our paradigm, but rather special conditions of the American case that require separate consideration.

First and perhaps most obvious, American society is physically isolated from European society. All of its other special characteristics *derive* from or are related to its location in the Northern portions of the New World: the existence of a frontier; the opportunities for immigration, and the consequent multiplicity of ethnic groups; its quasi-colonial record of black slavery and Indian genocide; the marginality and provincialism of its intellectuals; and the innovations in its legal and constitutional forms. As we will see, these characteristics have contributed to an obscuring and softening of the class basis of American society. As a result, class seemed less important in America than in Europe. Class conflicts were defused by the frontier (and when this frontier ceased to exist, by the myth of its existence); class conflicts were transformed into and obscured by ethnic hostility. Class conflicts lacked intellectual vigor, and they were dissipated by the extraordinary resistance of the political system to third-party movements.

America as an Offshoot of British Society

Each special circumstance of American society emerges from the fairly simple geographical fact of physical separation of the New and Old World but is complex in its nature and consequences. All are interrelated.

The sixteenth century through the nineteenth century was a period of Western expansion during which Europe established a worldwide hegemony—economic, political, and ideological. This process of expansion, colonization, and ideological dominance took a variety of forms: primarily economic exploitation with or without political rule, as in Africa or China; the development of syncretic cultures as in Meso-America; and the creation of settler states, established chiefly in the temperate zones and based on genocide of the tribal "natives." The British colonies of North America (like those of Australia) belong in the last category. Thus, North America (exclusive of the French-Canadian areas) became an extension of seventeenth and eighteenth century British society, mirroring its ideologies and inheriting substantial portions of its class structure. The aristocracy (a waning class in Britain, also), workers in the royal court (civil servants, ideologues, and courtiers, for example), and the rural poor in Britain are classes that were not transplanted to the New World.

There was a corresponding absence of the belief systems of these classes—the ideologies of a waning feudalism, of a royalist hegemony, and of rural traditionalism. Rather, America inherited Britain's urban merchants and artisans as well as a significant number of the gentry class that was transforming a feudal agrarian economy into one of commercial farming, livestock raising, and incipient industrialization both at home and abroad. With these classes, came an ideology of Lockeian liberalism suited to the establishment of the political rights of a bourgeoisie; this liberalism saw men as rational and independent and supported a state with parliamentary political forms and a laissez-faire stance toward economic and private matters (the sphere that Marx called the civil society).

Thus, the geographical and historical circumstances of the beginnings of American culture permitted it to become a fossilized fragment of eighteenth century British culture, in which institutional and ideational innovations of the eighteenth century could be developed and elaborated in isolation from the sociopolitical changes that later transformed European societies.[1] The process of fragmentation and fossilization is itself a product of substructural and stratification changes in British society. The movement of settlers across the Atlantic has many characteristics of a social movement, especially in the case of the religious dissidents who came to New England and Pennsylvania; thus, although a large component of change was involved in the founding and splitting off of the American colonies, much of the history of these colonies can be examined in terms of the sociopolitical circumstances of British society. In some respects, fragmentation and fossilization produced features that were unique but could be explained in terms of the parent society's structure.

The geographical isolation of America and its initial liberal bourgeois ideology has had further important consequences: the continued hegemony of liberalism;[2] the embodiment of liberalism in a constitution that limited political development of social movements; the isolation of American intellectuals from European intellectual and political currents; the existence of the "safety valve" of the frontier; and the immigration of large numbers of diverse ethnic groups. These developments occurred at different levels of the social system and at different points in time.

First, America was a profoundly bourgeois (and petty-bourgeois) society from the start. The groups associated with feudalism and monarchical absolutism failed to leave Britain in large numbers and were, in any case, not as strong in Britain as in Continental Europe. One consequence of the nature of initial immigration was that while America was beset by conflicts, including extraordinarily violent ones, these conflicts were fought out within a liberal political and ideological system. Many of the conflicts *were* class conflicts, but, generally, the language of class struggle was absent or unclearly developed. American liberalism duplicated *within* itself a number of the conflicts that were fought out by far more class-conscious groups in Europe. In many respects, classes in the early decades of American history were substrata of the bourgeoisie, both objectively and subjectively. Thus, the Federalists, the Jeffersonians, and the participants in Shays' Rebellion were in some sense liberals ideologically; they perceived themselves as subspecies of the bourgeoisie, and should be perceived as such by the observer. Even in situations in which shared bourgeois liberal interests became purely a fiction, the conflicting class groups refrained from stripping away the fiction; thus, Calhoun and other southerners still used liberal rhetoric to defend themselves, as did large sections of proletarian labor movements. Fitzhugh—among the southerners—and the IWW and Marxists—among the proletarians—stand out as isolated examples of attempts to challenge liberal hegemony. These remarks must *not* be taken to mean that America has existed in a state of harmonious consensus; that there has been no violent conflict; that nonbourgeois classes (such as propertyless urban and rural workers) cannot be identified; that there has been no conflict within the bourgeoisie of debtor against creditor and small entrepreneur against monopoly capitalist; or that a liberal consensus produces the best of all possible sociopolitical worlds. Our statements simply mean that virtually no class or subclass in American society, no matter how desperate or violent its struggle, has seriously suggested an alternative organization of society.

In part, this dearth of ideological alternatives is attributable to the underdevelopment of the American intelligentsia. Again, the geographical and class circumstances of America's founding contribute to a provincialism and lack of consciousness among American intellectuals. In Europe, the relationship of intellectuals to ruling groups has been problematical since the late Middle Ages. Intellectuals repeatedly have struggled against their status as the co-opted ideologues for the ruling class as well as accepted this status. From the twelfth century (with the founding of the universities and the Inquisition as devices to capture a free-floating stratum of autonomous intellectuals) through the Reformation and its aftermath of religious wars, this struggle was phrased chiefly in religious terms.[3] After secularization and the Enlightenment, it was transformed into an explicitly class and political rebellion. But in America, this struggle is not merely forgotten; initially, it was meaningless. The American revolutionary bourgeoisie *is* the intellectual stratum: class position, political activity, and intellectual production are fused in the same persons. During the Revolution and for several years thereafter, intellectuals and ruling classes overlapped to a great degree in background and personnel, and it is hard to identify an alienated or dissenting intelligentsia. When intellectuals and bourgeois rulers parted ways, intellectuals responded by objecting to the Mexican War and slavery; much of this discontent, however, took the form of individual alienation and utopian experimentation. Even when once again it took a political form (in the Progressive Movement), it retained a fairly narrow regional, ethnic, and class base (Northern, WASP, bourgeois). With the expansion of its class and ethnic base in the 1930s, the American intelligentsia showed some restlessness, but as the expansion was very rapidly co-opted, intellectuals seemed content to become ideologues for the advanced industrial state, to be generally submissive, and to remain unaware or unimpressed by their capacity to dismantle the prevailing ideology. Even self-identification as an intellectual was weak, and often it was superseded by a technological or technocratic self-image. These impulses of withdrawal into private life style experimentation and academic gentility on the one hand and technological subservience to business or government employers on the other, have led to misunderstanding and rejection of European sociopolitical thought and to a lack of productive cooperation between intellectual radicals and working-class radicals. (The absence of outstanding American scientists and artists before the 1930s is an interesting, though not directly relevant, side effect of American intellectual marginality.) Whether the New Left heralds a significant break with the absence of political rebellion among American intellectuals remains to be seen.[4]

The nature of the Constitution and the legal forms that constrain political activity have been major consequences of the fragmenting process. In addition, they have been important in molding and contributing to the course of American social movements. The difficulty of establishing a third party is an unintentional consequence of the legal underpinnings of the American political system. As a result, the options available to political social movements are limited. First, a movement can operate as an intra-party interest group that either works within the framework of the two major parties (and, hence, without the scope of public debate on party and media-defined issues) or devotes its efforts to testing the legal system (again, outside the mass base). Second, it can struggle as a third party. Third, it can develop a parasitic but exploitative relationship to a government bureaucracy. Finally, it can operate outside legitimate channels by developing para-military tactics or nonviolent resistance.

Examples of these strategies are the antiwar faction within the Democratic Party in the late 1960s and early 1970s (operating as an intra-party interest group); the court and administrative proceedings for legal equality for women currently instituted by the National Organization of Women (working as an interest group through the courts); the defunct Peace and Freedom Party of the 1968 election (acting as a third party); antipoverty agencies, programs, and civil service positions established as part of the war on poverty during the 1960s (acting in relationship with the state); black capitalism rhetoric (pursuing economic goals); and the Weathermen and the religious war resistance (operating outside of legitimate channels). Under these conditions and with these strategies available, some movements have become violent and wholly extralegal. Nevertheless, the net effect has been to defuse and narrow movement goals and to remove from the public those issues that are not directly at stake in elections. In a multiparty system, voters are offered markedly different choices; that they have not been confronted with such choices has been heralded as a victory for American consensus and a means of preventing serious conflict. Obviously, this limitation also has impeded the political system's capacity as a source of fundamental change. In this respect, the system has made liberal values *more* difficult to realize (the liberal believes that only the political arena is the meaningful and autonomous public sphere of action). Coupled with the lack of politically involved intellectuals, the two-party system has strengthened substructural trends (especially mass media oligopoly) toward lowering the level of political debate in America.[5]

So far, we have chiefly discussed the superstructural aspects of American fragmentation and liberal fossilization, that is, the reflection of these processes in the creation of ideology and in constitutional-legal forms. We have already indicated that the sources of fragmentation and fossilization lie in the class situation that America inherited from Britain as well as in its geographical location. In this inheritance lies freedom from feudalism and monarchism, both in terms of class structure and in the absence of a truly conservative ("ancien regime") ideology. We can now turn briefly to factors that sustained the liberal hegemony long after the substructural situation and class relationships changed. Here, we will discuss three major factors: the frontier, slavery, and immigration.

The Frontier

In reviving the frontier thesis, so often attacked and discredited, the effects of the existence of the frontier and the level of the social system in which they operated must be specified. First of all, we must emphasize that frontier, as we use the term here, refers primarily to Appalachia, the Ohio Valley, the Midwest, and the West Coast—not to the areas of Puritan and Mormon settlement or the plantation and ranch economies of the South and the Southwest. We are not proposing that frontier settlements were laboratories for participatory democracy; frontier towns promoted democracy by providing access to public office and local decision-making for a stratum of small entrepreneurs, a petty-bourgeoisie of commercial farmers, local merchants, independent artisans, and small speculators. More or less excluded from decision-making were farm laborers and tenant farmers who constituted more than half the agricultural population in some parts of the Midwest.[6] As we shall see later, the strata that *did* hold power lost control over key decisions throughout the last half of the nineteenth century. Nevertheless, the experience of relatively easy access to public office (outside of the eastern seaboard and a small number of inland cities) strengthened respect for political liberalism. A strongly local and decentralized political structure probably has strengthened parliamentary democracy also in Britain; even while quasi-monopolies make key decisions in the economic system, localities enjoy a vigorous political life, but they are becoming economically dependent on the national government. By contrast, the strongly centralized French *political* system (in large part inherited from the ancien regime) has sensitized the provinces to the *cultural* and *economic* dominance of the capital.[7] In the United States, the vigor of local political life was strengthened even further by its openness to the petty-bourgeoisie (often because no other class groups were present in the community) and the possibility of geographic mobility. The impact of this entrepreneurial stratum will be discussed in more detail in chapters on social movements between the Revolution and the Civil War, particularly the "Jacksonian Revolution." In short, the experience of participation in a local liberal political system was sufficiently vivid and widespread to sustain the ideology of participatory democracy long after no important decisions were made at that level and the unimportant decisions were completely controlled by a small local elite. Repeatedly, researchers have found that the myth of small town democracy, an important part of liberal hegemony, was sustained as late as the 1920s and even the 1950s.[8]

Geographic mobility—the opportunity to leave it if you don't love it—is an aspect of the frontier closely associated with the generally discredited safety valve hypothesis (that the frontier attracted dissatisfied urban workers, thus reducing labor turmoil and proletarian radicalism). By the late nineteenth century, few urban workers actually could leave the factories; many were far too impoverished to be able to move their families. Generally, farmers and immigrants, not urban workers, migrated to frontier farms.[9] Opportunity—and such opportunity became a myth only by the turn of the century—did have an impact on rural populations (farmers preserved their beliefs even after migration to the cities) and the urban petty-bourgeoisie. These groups helped create the belief in unlimited opportunity for the industrious and the individualistically competitive. (Perhaps the lack of a feudal past—a situation in which each man's destiny was fixed regardless of his efforts—contributed to the myth that the race was open to all and would be won by the swift more than frontier experiences did.) As the geographic frontier disappeared, the myth of the frontier was increasingly reworked as a prototype for upward social mobility; the striving restless individual turned to a search for wealth and status rather than to the rigors of pioneering.

As the frontier became a symbol of upward mobility, it became subtly altered. The original frontiersman was hostile to established authority and, in a sense, fled from it (especially in the case of the oldest frontier area, the Eastern hills settled by the indentured servants and the poor of the southern seaboard). The new social mobility frontier was won by persons of working-class and petty-bourgeois background who demonstrated excellence within established norms and obedience to established authority. This new version of the frontier was related not only to the disappearance of the real frontier, but also to the loss of power of the petty-bourgeoisie. The frontier myth supported liberalism by a rationale for urban working conditions (since workers could, in theory, flee to the frontier), for stigmatizing the poor as lacking initiative, and for glorifying a restless individualism.

Slavery

Slavery is another issue that gave rise to the formation of many social movements. It was the source of abolitionism, southern separatism, northern nationalism, and black movements. As early as the American Revolution, radicalism among whites was diminished in a number of ways, because *blacks* were the underclass. This made possible the neglect during the Revolution of what Hannah Arendt calls "the social question": the revolutionary bourgeoisie could shut their ears and eyes to the plight of the oppressed whereas in France, political liberalism had to take into account—and almost foundered on—the problem of integrating the very poor into the body politic (that is, the liberal bourgeoisie had to convince themselves and the poor that political freedom rather than socioeconomic equality was the revolutionary goal). In America, blacks, the most exploited minority, were not only socioeconomically exploited, but also politically excluded. This twofold oppression was made possible by their relatively small numbers; unlike the Paris mob or the French peasantry, they could not force their way into notice of the public, that is, of bourgeois liberals. Slavery was not an issue of the revolution. Arendt has summarized the political consequences of the white population's blindness to black slavery.

> Since then, the passion of compassion has haunted and driven the best men of all revolutions, and the only revo-

lution in which compassion played no role in the motivation of the actors was the American Revolution. If it were not for the presence of Negro slavery on the American scene, one would be tempted to explain this striking aspect exclusively by American prosperity, by Jefferson's "lovely equality," or by the fact that America was indeed, in William Penn's words, "a good poor Man's country." As it is, we are tempted to ask ourselves if the goodness of the poor white man's country did not depend to a considerable degree upon black labor and black misery. . . . From this we can only conclude that the institution of slavery carries an obscurity even blacker than the obscurity of poverty; the slave, not the poor man, was "wholly overlooked." [10]

At a less ideological level, black slavery diminished class-conscious radicalism because propertyless whites did not systematically cooperate with blacks. Together these two groups were a sizable proportion of the urban population and of the rural southern population. Repeatedly, accounts of colonial riots and disturbances mention blacks as an important element of the mob. Nevertheless, drastic differences between the position of the poor white (even the impressed sailor or the indentured servant) and the enslaved black, augmented by Anglo-Saxon traditions of racism, hopelessly precluded the possibility of any combined mass movement of the oppressed. Indeed, aside from irrational prejudice, these two groups did perhaps have opposed interests. In most countries, primitive capital accumulation—the process of freeing financial resources for use in industrializing—has involved exploitation and dispossession of a peasantry whether by gentry turned commercial farmer and wool producers in Britain, by a land-owning modernizing aristocracy (in Germany, the Prussian Junkers and in Japan, feudal lords), or by a revolutionary party (in Stalinist Russia).[11] In the United States, a large share of capital was pried from the process of exporting southern raw materials (that is, ultimately, from the labor of black slaves). Thus, the burden of financing industrialization was shifted from white farmers to black slaves. Only by the Civil War did this situation begin to change. As a white urban proletariat developed, whites with small land holdings found themselves in increasing debt and a black tenant class that really did share most of the problems of rural, propertyless southern whites appeared. Indeed, in this later period we *do* find radical agrarian movements that include both races, but in the earlier period, plantation slave labor brought a variety of indirect benefits to farmers throughout the nation. As blacks disappeared from northern urban areas, any hope of forming radical movements with the white urban ppor became unrealistic; indeed the end of black slavery in the urban North was partially attributable to a desire to eliminate from the already rowdy urban situation any element as potentially explosive as the black slave element.[12] With the exception of a few years during the late nineteenth century and again, during the 1960s, racial hostility and a difference in interests of whites and blacks have been a major dampening factor in the history of American radicalism.

Immigration

A third important factor in the history of American social movements has been mass immigration from Europe. Later, we will discuss its effect more thoroughly. Here we will confine ourselves to three remarks. First, immigration itself became an important issue for social movements, a number of which formed specifically around sentiments of nativist hostility (for instance, the anti-Irish Know Nothings of the nineteenth century) and an even larger number of which were built around opposition to the immigrants' life style (the temperance movement, for example). In this respect, the issue of cultural diversity raised by immigration offered an excellent vehicle for the discontent of a petty-bourgeoisie. Small town WASP entrepreneurs allowed the cultural threat of ethnic diversity to obscure the fact that their way of life was threatened more by substructural trends toward oligopoly capitalism and urbanization than by ethnic diversity. Even among intellectuals (who, at the end of the nineteenth century, continued to share the WASP culture of the small town petty-bourgeoisie), genteel hostility at foreigners was linked with outrage at the urban politics that the immigrant poor made possible and with anger at the economic interests that exploited the immigrants. This fusing of cultural, political, and economic issues and the consequent easy transformation of class politics into status politics is a recurrent theme in American social movement history.[13] The cultural threat of ethnic diversity obscured the far greater substructural threat to small town WASP entrepreneurs. American workers also felt threatened by immigration and converted the hostility that resulted from their own exploitation into hostility toward foreign laborers. Second, ethnic diversity had an important effect on social movements among the immigrants as well as on their reluctant hosts. Each European immigrant group conceived of itself as having separate interests, just as black and white Americans did. In part, the sequencing of immigration and the funneling of newer arrivals into the least desirable urban jobs really did produce class (or, at least, substratum) differences between the groups. Earlier immigrants had better access to national political and economic elite positions and more opportunity for starting businesses than did later immigrants, who were forced either to be content with manual labor or to shape new and sometimes illegitimate institutions (the rackets, for instance) as their vehicle to upward mobility. Organizing the interethnic groups was hampered by barriers of language and custom. Two kinds of movements were relatively successful: those representing one ethnic group exclusively and those promising to draw all foreign groups into a more solid American identity and American social structural position.[14] The reinforcement of belief in opportunities and, consequently, in the realism and justness of liberalism was the third consequence of immigration that was important for movements. Some authors go so far as to suggest that immigration was a selection process in which the most restless, individualistic, and rootless (as well as the most ruthless) freed themselves from community and family ties to seek their fortune in the New World: that is, that Americans are predisposed in a very fundamental, perhaps even hereditary way, to believe in a competitive anomic liberalism.[15] Where others have hailed this self-selection as the source of the enterprise and initiative of Americans, these authors have condemned it as the basis of American competitive loneliness. Only in America is the belief that individualism and collectivism are necessarily in conflict so widely held. We need not even postulate such self-selection. Immigrants found themselves catapulted from feudal traditional poverty into an urban liberal setting where they were often just as poor but—at least in theory—able to become fabulously wealthy. The roads were not really paved with gold, but everyone's wagon could be hitched to a star. Because American immigrants never had developed an anti-feudal ideology or organized a collective struggle against an *ancien regime*, they were lacking in attitudes and skills that could be used in struggles against capitalism or the development of radical antiliberal ideologies. (The German immigration after 1848 and, to some degree, the East European Jewish immigration are exceptions.) The very experience of emigration and immigration confirmed the American liberal ideology.

SUBSTRUCTURAL TRENDS IN AMERICA

The ideological and structural idiosyncracies of America discussed in the preceding section contributed to a continuing hegemony of liberalism as an ideology long after substructural trends completely altered the original distribution of power and wealth. These trends toward modern oligopolistic industrial capitalism were well under way by mid-nineteenth century: during the period between the Civil War and World War I, industrial ownership and organization took on modern forms. An important political component, cooperation between the federal government and the large corporations, was added during the New Deal period and greatly extended after World War II. Finally, the last two decades have seen further changes in technology—above all, in the technology of ideology (that is, the mass media). These trends can be summarized as the bases of the New Industrial State, but the date of onset and their sequencing require further comment.

    The earliest aspects of the transformation of America are early industrialization and commercial farming. Both aspects are traceable in the North and West to the Jacksonian period and are clearly associated with the socio-political changes of that era. (Insofar as the South had a plantation economy, it was in some sense involved in "commercial farming" at a much earlier time; nevertheless, it deserves to be analyzed separately for numerous reasons—the institution of slavery, its plantation system, its distinct class structure, and its peculiar paternalistic version of liberal ideology.) By early industrialization we mean manufacturing based on steam and water power, the extensive use of iron in building and machinery, the use of canals, waterways, and railroads in transportation; and the shift from cottage industries and craft workshops to a factory system—in short, the very changes that had taken place in Britain as much as a half-century earlier. Associated with these substructural changes are changes in class relationships: the beginnings of the transformation of an urban lower class into factory laborers; the appearance of a class of manufacturers quite distinct from the commercial elite of the revolutionary period; the dissociation of traditional intellectual, familial, and churchly status from economic and political power—namely, the decisive appearance of an entrepreneurial bourgeoisie,[16] a shift of political power away from the seaboard, and the appearance in the "Northwest" (the Midwest) of propertyless farm laborers and tenant farmers as well as a small town petty-bourgeoisie.

The Civil War ended this heyday of liberalism, the period of entrepreneurial experimentation by the common man. However measured, the trend toward industrialization continued, but as the technology became more sophisticated, enterprises became larger-scaled and a tendency toward oligopoly appeared. Certainly, not all types of enterprise were thus affected, but monopoly capitalism did become a possibility in railroads, utilities, and extractive industries. Urbanization proceeded rapidly. Immigrants and poorer rural people came to the cities and joined an urban proletariat, and rural entrepreneurs (farmers and the small town self-employed) experienced great difficulties that frequently drove them into the ranks of a salaried urban labor force.[17] The period between the Civil War and World War I was rife with social movements stemming from these sources of deprivation and anxiety—agrarian revolt, proletarian radicalism, and bourgeois progressivism. The period between the Revolution and the Civil War saw the extension of liberalism in several directions: vertically, in the social structure in the extension of the franchise, the spoils system, the "revolt of the common man," and the sweeping away of vestiges of traditional status; and geographically, westward in American expansion at the expense of Indians and Mexicans and, in the "last bourgeois revolution," southward, in the conquest and subjugation of the South in the Civil War. The period between the Civil War and World War I was a period of redefinition of liberalism, as an emerging class of monopoly capitalists succeeded in maintaining both their domination and the continued prevalence of a liberal ideology in the face of class dissatisfaction caused by the disappearance of the previously objectively present conditions for liberalism. Continued liberal hegemony was attained by a twofold mechanism—income dispersion that created a substantial body of materially comfortable "middle Americans" and the interlocking of the state and the economy by the appearance of regulatory agencies, large-scale government contracting, interchange of personnel, and federal responsibility for economic growth.[18] In the New Deal and post-World War II eras, both of these developments were continued, especially the trend toward political centralization and the blurring of boundaries between a private economic sector and a public political sector. Some liberals term the result, "the New Industrial State," some radicals call it the hegemony of the power elite over a mass society, and Marxian radicals term it the most advanced form of monopoly capitalism. Obviously, these differences in terminology reflect differences in attitudes and interpretations. The "New Industrial State" is a Soviet and Chinese as well as a Western phenomenon, while "monopoly capitalism" is not. The New Industrial State has virtually no use for the impoverished populations within and outside of its boundaries, whose raw materials and labor it once exploited but now can reproduce more cheaply by its technology and who cannot provide a profitable market for its products;[19] monopoly capitalism, however, continues to need and exploit Third World peoples. Finally the New Industrial State's intelligentsia is indistinguishable from a ruling class, but monopoly capitalism's ideologues could revolt against their subservience. The radical non-Marxian position is essentially intermediate on all these issues. Nevertheless, despite the differences in interpretation, there is also a great amount—a preponderant amount, perhaps—of convergence.

All social movements of much of the twentieth century have been shaped and constrained by this emergent behemoth. Its power has come to seem so great that even where liberal ideology has failed (or never penetrated), as among black and Latin ethnic groups, social movements must take the form of alternatingly supplicating the New Industrial State (by cooperating with its antipoverty agencies, job training programs, and other income dispersing apparatus) and harassing it in a co-optable fashion. The liberal hegemony finally has lost most of its liberalism; the myth of free competition for opportunities is giving way to income dispersion mechanisms; efforts at political integration of dissatisfied groups on certain negotiable issues; the ideology of consumerism and a high standard of living; the emergence of a youth culture "frontier" in which experimentation with sex, drugs, and life style channels the repressed instincts into politically harmless outlets (the condition of somatic gratification and servitude that Marcuse has called "repressive desublimation"); and the state's appearance of invulnerability.

The student of social movements should not, however, be content to accept this new hegemony. He must ask himself whether there are substructural transformations occurring that will decrease the state's invulnerability and will make possible social movements that can completely change the existing relations of production, the present political state, and the prevailing ideology. We will explore this question in Chapter 9. Our more immediate task is to discuss the patterns that American social movements have taken in the past.

NOTES

[1] The reader may well recognize the thesis of Louis Hartz, *The Liberal Tradition in America* (New York: Harcourt, Brace & World, 1955), in the preceding remarks. We concur with Hartz' analysis of the underlying (Lockeian) liberal consensus in America. Our only objection is that Hartz is excessively idealist in that he fails to discuss the class basis of both the origin of the Lockeian ideas and their vicissitudes in the nineteenth and early twentieth centuries. He fails to proceed from the idea of a liberal consensus to the concept of an ideology, that is, a belief system that is universally shared but not universally beneficent. Unlike the historians of consensus, Hartz has no illusions about the inequities and *potential* conflict in American society, masked though they may be by the liberal ideology, but he seems unwilling to specify concretely the classes or groups that generate and benefit from the ideology.

[2] I became familiar with the concept of hegemony through the work of Eugene Genovese—in particular, his essay on Antonio Gramsci. [Eugene Genovese, "On Antonio Gramsci," in James Weinstein and David Eakins, eds., *For a New America* (New York: Random House, 1970).] Genovese is one in a sequence of commentators on Gramsci who has been excited by this concept and has found it useful in analyzing American society; there is, incidentally, a considerable convergence of Genovese's remarks and Marcuse's views on new forms of social control, as outlined in Herbert Marcuse, *One Dimensional Man* (New York: Beacon Press, 1964). Genovese's ideas seem well worth a lengthy quotation: "Gramsci's notion of hegemony is perhaps his most important contribution to Marxian political theory and forms a necessary counterpart to Lenin's development of the Marxian theory of the state. Gramsci's notion has been summarized by Gwynn Williams: '[Hegem-

ony is] an order in which a certain way of life and thought is dominant, in which one concept of reality is diffused throughout society in all its institutional and private manifestations, informing with its spirit all taste, morality, customs, religious and political principles, and all social relations, particularly in their intellectual and moral connotations' [Gwynn Williams, as quoted by John M. Cammett, *Antonio Gramsci and the Origins of Italian Communism* (Stanford, Calif.: Stanford University Press, 1967), p. 204]. Hegemony, therefore, is achieved by consent, not force, through the civil and ostensibly private institutions of society. . . . Cammett observes further, 'In its general sense, hegemony refers to the spontaneous loyalty that any dominant social group obtains from the masses by virtue of its social and intellectual prestige and its supposedly superior function in the world of production.'

"It follows that hegemony depends on much more than consciousness of economic interests on the part of the ruling class and unconsciousness of such interests on the part of the submerged classes. The success of a ruling class in establishing its hegemony depends entirely on its ability to convince the lower classes that its interests are those of society at large—that it defends the common sensibility and stands for a natural and proper social order. It is nonsense to think that an economic depression or devastating war could alone revolutionize consciousness. For the masses to be able to attribute their particular woes to the social system they must be more broadly convinced that the interests of the ruling class are at variance with those of society in general and of their own class in particular. To bring the masses to such a point we need to face the fact that such an identification between bourgeois and general interests exists and has existed, with the exception of the antebellum South, throughout American history. . . . If all we had to contend with was the force of political society, as so many of our ultra-leftists as well as dogmatic revisionists like to believe, our prospects would now be much brighter. If, as is the case, we have to contend with a pervasive world view that identifies exploitation and social injustice as minor concomitants of the defense of a proper order, of religious and moral truth and of elementary decency in human relationships, then we had better begin doing our homework in philosophy, sociology, political theory and even theology. It is the totality of the bourgeois world view—the enormous complex of prejudices, assumptions, half-thought-out notions and no small number of profound ideas—that infects the victims of bourgeois rule, and it is the totality of an alternative world view that alone can challenge it for supremacy." (Genovese, *op. cit.*, pp. 300–2.)

[3] Friedrich Heer, *The Intellectual History of Europe* (Garden City, N.Y.: Doubleday, 1968), p. 202.

[4] Christopher Lasch, *The Agony of the American Left* (New York: Vintage, 1966), Chapter 1.

[5] Maurice Duverger, *Political Parties* (London: Methuen, 1964).

[6] Richard Hofstadter and Seymour Martin Lipset, eds., *Turner and the Sociology of the Frontier* (New York: Basic Books, 1968); and Paul W. Gates,

"Frontier Estate Builders and Farm Laborers," in Hofstadter and Lipset, *op. cit.*, pp. 100–19.

[7] Brian Chapman, *Introduction to French Local Government* (London: Allen and Unwin, 1953), Chapters 1–4.

[8] Arthur J. Vidich and Joseph Bensman, *Small Town in Mass Society* (Princeton, N.J.: Princeton University Press, 1958).

[9] Hofstadter and Lipset, *op. cit.*, pp. 172–86.

[10] Hannah Arendt, *On Revolution* (New York: Viking Press, 1965), pp. 65–66.

[11] Barrington Moore, Jr., *The Social Origins of Dictatorship and Democracy* (Boston: Beacon Press, 1966).

[12] Herbert Aptheker, *American Negro Slave Revolts* (New York: International Publishers, 1969), p. 18.

[13] Richard Hofstadter, *The Age of Reform* (New York: Random House, 1955).

[14] Oscar Handlin, *The Uprooted* (New York: Atlantic Monthly Press, 1951).

[15] Philip Slater, *The Pursuit of Loneliness* (Boston: Beacon Press, 1970).

[16] Robert Dahl, *Who Governs?* (New Haven, Conn.: Yale University Press, 1961), Book I.

[17] Charles Beard and Mary Beard, *A Basic History of the United States* (Philadelphia: Blakiston, 1944), pp. 287–426.

[18] Gabriel Kolko, *The Triumph of Conservatism* (New York: Free Press, 1963).

[19] Paul Baran and Paul Sweezey, *Monopoly Capital* (New York: Modern Reader Paperbacks, 1966); John Kenneth Galbraith, *The New Industrial State* (Boston: Houghton Mifflin, 1967); and C. Wright Mills, *The Power Elite* (New York: Oxford University Press, 1957).

3

The Colonial Era and the First American Revolution

From the religious settlements in Massachusetts, Rhode Island, and Pennsylvania to the Revolution itself, the first century and a half of American history is one of refusal to compromise, unnegotiable demands, and resistance—including violent resistance—to those in power. The history of the Colonial era begins with social movements of Pilgrims, Puritans, the followers of Anne Hutchinson and Roger Williams, and the Quakers and culminates with a mass movement—superbly organized, but a mass movement, nonetheless—that overarched the diverse interests of the settlers and joined them in coalition against their common oppressor. Two-thirds of the population participated in this movement, the American Revolution. The entire span between the founding of the first colonies and the surrender of Burgoyne is an exciting period for the student of social movements. These years were a time of remarkable clear-sightedness and awareness of interests and understanding of the social and political order.

This does not mean that I hail the Colonial Era as a Golden Age. Quite the contrary. It was an exceedingly brutal period marked by the pervasive oppression of the poor, the slave, and the female, but perhaps precisely because of this brutality, casual cruelty, and constant recourse to physical force to protect the existing distribution of wealth and power, the oppressed and neglected were generally aware of their oppression and acted against it to the best of their ability, judging their betters with that clarity of mind that Thomas Paine described and immortalized as common sense.

Three phenomena will be of special importance in our analysis of social movements: the secularization of movements, part of the general secularization of Western society in the late seventeenth and the eighteenth centuries; the high degree of understanding of issues and class interests—that is, the high degree of agreement between *our* analysis of colonial movements and the analysis of the participants themselves; and the organization of the revolutionary movement, a masterpiece of radicalization, coalition-formation, and the creation of dual institutions that could effectively sap the power of British Colonial institutions. But before we turn to these three special problems, a brief delimitation of the period—a discussion of its social structure and description of its major movements—is necessary.

AN OVERVIEW OF THE COLONIAL PERIOD: 1607–1781

A Delimitation of the Period

The colonial period is delimited by the founding of Jamestown, the first viable English Colony in North America, and the ending of the Revolutionary War. During this period, the 1670s marked a turning point. After this decade, colonial social structure began to shift, and with the exception of the Great Awakening, social movements were largely secular.

Broadly speaking, this period is not only America's colonial era, but also her preindustrial era.

The Social Structure of Colonial America

The colonists themselves seem to have perceived three classes, referred to as the "better sort," the "middling sort," and the "meaner sort." Of course, they were quite aware that such a simple division did great violence to the variety of occupations and types of property ownership represented in the colonies.

Colonial society was primarily rural. On the eve of the revolution, the population of all cities having more than 8,000 inhabitants was less than 10 percent of the total population of the colonies and only 5 percent lived in the five major cities—Boston, Newport, Manhattan, Philadelphia, and Charleston.[1] This fact is important not only for our understanding of the class structure but also for our analysis of the origins of pre-Revolutionary social movements and the organization of the Revolution.

At the top of colonial society—in wealth, power, and prestige—were the landed wealthy whose estates were chiefly along the Coast and in the Hudson Valley. In the South, their fortunes were based on rice, indigo, and, above all, the tobacco of the Virginia Tidewater region; in the North, they were founded on cattle in Rhode Island and wheat and more diversified crops in the Hudson Valley. There were major differences between these areas because in the North (although Rhode Island is a partial exception), the estates were worked chiefly by tenants and in the South, by indentured servants and, by mid-eighteenth century, primarily by slaves. All of the wealthy proprietors shared certain characteristics regardless of the internal structure of their holdings: they were entrepreneurs producing cash crops, not a feudal nobility or slave-owning subsistence farmers (such as the South African Dutch settlers who were more or less their contemporaries). They were a political as well as an economic elite; in both eastern Virginia and the Hudson Valley, their political power was unassailable.

A second component of the colonial elite was a wealthy urban mercantile class. The wealth and power of this class were based on commerce. Its relationship to the landed gentry was complicated; in part, the merchants preferred to transform themselves into landlords (for example, those in Newport); in part, the urban elite was merely the urban branch of the rural elite. The urban elite also included the British (managers, officers, and appointed officials). It is not productive to argue whether the interests of the landed and the urban elite coincided during the colonial period; insofar as both perceived themselves as a ruling class and intermarried, there was no great conflict between holders of "realty" and holders of "personalty." Theoretically, both strata of the ruling class were open to anyone who could amass sufficient wealth; practically, this occurrence was rare—especially in the lowland Virginia Tidewater area by mid-eighteenth century. In the colonial period, we can see seeds of the trend that is so characteristic of American society in the nineteenth century: formal ascriptive barriers to wealth and power became fewer, yet power and wealth also became more concentrated.

In urban areas, below the ruling class were a variety of groups constituting the middling sort: professionals (chiefly lawyers and clergymen) who often had a marginal status within the elite; lesser merchants; and even the most elevated rank of the "mechanics"—shopowners and master craftsmen. Members of these generally prudent, thrifty, hard-working and public spirited strata participated in political affairs as militia officers and officials. As we shall see, they contributed relatively little to colonial social movements until the 1760s and the Revolution itself.

Quite to the contrary, their rural counterpart, the freeholders and middling farmers, were the most vociferous and best organized dissidents from the 1660s until the Revolution itself. They were the largest population group, especially numerous in New England and Pennsylvania and farther south in the back country, west of the large estates. Away from the cities and the plantations, this group involved itself in political decisions (although these decisions often made little impression beyond the local level).

The strata below this level tended to be classified as the "meaner sort." At the top of their ranks were artisans and journeymen ("mechanics" who were not prosperous and self-employed) whose voting status was often uncertain and who were frequently disfranchised. Below them were poor laborers who, in turn, shaded off into hawkers, prostitutes, and the destitute. Also near the bottom in power and income were sailors and dock workers perennially subject to legal and illegal pressing, that is, forcible conscription into the British Navy. By the 1770s, the poor and the very poor—the propertyless urban workers—comprised perhaps about 30 percent of the male population of Boston.[2]

The rural equivalent of the propertyless poor were the tenant farmers, numerous in the Middle Atlantic estate areas (New York and New Jersey), and the indentured servants. Indentured servitude was only a temporary status, usually one lasting four, five, or seven years; fully half of all immigrants to the colonies south of New England arrived as indentured servants.[3] Despite the rise of some of their number into the freeholder stratum, their lot was not a happy one; it is estimated that 80 percent "died, became landless workers, or returned to England."[4] In assessing the scope of rural poverty, one must also bear in mind that the small farmers were not at all secure, and under adverse conditions, easily fell into the ranks of landless workers.

At the very bottom of colonial society was the black man. Enslaved Africans or their descendants, virtually all condemned to unending servitude, comprised fully 20 percent of the population. In the North, slaves were usually urban; in the South, they were both urban and rural.

The urban and rural poor, black and white, enslaved, indentured, pressed or free, were not only a large group (perhaps 40 percent of the population) but also an angry and rebellious one.[5] In the rural areas, rarely did they have the resources to organize social movements as farmers did, but in the cities, they were a formidable threat to the property, security, and, ultimately, to the political stability of the elite.

Our description of the social structure closely coincides with the perceptions of the participants in it; it was no longer an age of feudal unity and not yet an age of mass media—packaged ideology. Harsh and inegalitarian as the age was, it was a time of awareness of interest.[6]

A SURVEY OF MAJOR COLONIAL MOVEMENTS

Religious Movements

The first movements in America were religious ones, organized around a Protestant interpretation of the world. This interpretation was the ideological driving force behind British emigration to New England in the 1620s, '30s, and '40s; the movements can really only be understood in terms of the general upheaval of European society in the seventeenth century. In Europe, the Reformation was the most dramatic ideological manifestation of the breakup of feudal Catholic hegemony. Very broadly speaking, in the century and a half after Luther nailed his theses to the door in 1517, counter-Reformation Catholicism became the religion of the monarchical states governed by a court bureaucracy and Protestantism became that of the rising bourgeoisie and the nations ruled by this class. But for a number of reasons, Protestantism continued to fragment into dissenting sects; partly, this fragmentation was attributable to Protestant ideology itself with its inherent strain toward dissension, individualism, and controversy; partly, it was due to the fact that the rise of the bourgeoisie had only begun, and religious conflict had to be the carrier for frustrated political hopes and class demands; finally, fragmentation resulted from the diffusion of Protestant ideology to the social groups below the bourgeoisie, the propertyless poor of urban and rural areas, who used the doctrinal struggles of the sixteenth and seventeenth centuries as an opportunity to carry Christian norms to their logical conclusion in "leveling" and communism. In short, then, Protestant sectarianism acted as a powerful carrier for political and social struggles in Western Europe; religion provided a language, a series of symbols, for conflict over wealth, power, and status.[7]

Protestant sectarian movements were instrumental in the founding of several colonies. Each group created its settlement to flee intolerance in its previous community and to establish its heaven on earth in the wilderness. First were the Pilgrims (Plymouth, 1620) and the Puritans (Massachusetts Bay, 1629). The latter provide the first, and especially interesting, example of the transformations that social movements undergo as they become the new orthodoxy and their leaders become the new elite. Control of the Puritan community by an elite was hastened by the doctrine of rule by "saints"; the saints were the small minority who could satisfactorily demonstrate their conversion and condition of grace, which was the prerequisite for membership in church, status as "freemen" of the colony, and eligibility for voting and office-holding.

The elite in Boston tended to overlap with the successful entrepreneurs and wealthier men of the colony as did the elite in Calvinist Geneva; the oral character of legal proceedings (rather than the exchange of documents) and the prohibition of paid attorneys and advocates strengthened the hand of the elite in the legal sphere. In 1642, Thomas Lechford noted that hired lawyers "are necessary to assist the poor and unlearned in their causes, and that according to the warrant and intendment of holy Writ and of right reason. I have knowne by experience and heard divers have suffered wrong by default of such in New England." [8] The practice of Half Way Covenanting, first proposed in 1662, by which a new class of church membership was created for those who did not have a conversion experience but were descended from those who did, also maintained the closed and oligarchical character of the Boston elite. On the other hand, pressures within the colony led to some curbing of the powers of the magistrates, and, in 1641, a Body of Liberties that was closely modeled on English law and was to be added to in subsequent years was published; thus, the colony was provided with a penal code and a set of rights, and some of the earlier abuses of power were curtailed.

In summary, as Massachusetts Bay became secularized, the unity of the ecclesiastical, commercial, and political elite diminished; social movement fervor declined, the patterns of life became routinized and less sacred, and the overall atmosphere became less rigid. The lasting impact of Puritanism as a social movement in America includes a strong moralistic spirit, expressed in the legal system; emphasis on the judiciary as a source of social control and normative order; and the emergence of an urban commercial elite (as opposed to a feudal aristocracy), oligarchical in relation to the community as a whole, but democratic within its own ranks.[9]

The Puritans provided a rigid fixed point of orthodoxy in opposition to which other movements could test themselves and new movements arise. Three of these movements are of special interest: the Quaker movement that was transplanted to the New World and the movements of Roger Williams and Anne Hutchinson. These groups must also be understood as products of the religious controversy and sectarianism of seventeenth century Protestantism; they represent somewhat more radical tendencies than do the Puritans (although by no means as radical as the Levellers and Gerald Winstanley's Diggers).

Let us turn first to the Quakers, who have been a source of dissent and resistance to elites and prevailing norms throughout American history.

Quakerism was founded by George Fox, an Englishman whose theological views were distinctly different from the gloomy misanthropic doctrines then current in Protestantism; where many sects emphasized original sin, Fox stressed that "every man was enlightened by the Divine Light of Christ." As corollaries of this tenet, the Quakers valued equality, pacifism, the refusal to take oaths, the extension of religious freedom to all, the utmost informality in dress and speech, and opposition to the development of a body of esoteric doctrine within the Society of Friends. These levelling tendencies and implicit resistance to the state, although not carried as far as the expropriations attempted by the radical sects, earned them persecution in England. In the colonies, the Friends challenged the intolerance of Massachusetts Bay throughout the 1650s and were subjected to the full brutality of the Puritans' penal system—repeated whippings with a rope, mutilation, and hanging—in an effort to silence their preaching to both whites and Indians. Nevertheless, like the Puritans, eventually they found themselves rulers of a colony rather than radical martyrs; in 1682, they founded Pennsylvania, established its Great Law, and set about the business of transforming a social movement into a new social order. In some respects, their history paralleled that of the Puritans; they prospered and became the economic and political elite of the colony. Within the Quaker ranks, there was some dissension between the more radical and democratic "country party" and the more conservative city merchants. But the most serious problems faced by the Quakers arose from their efforts to maintain their principles and act as a ruling class, being both prosperous and in control of the colonial assembly. The most important issues were the issue of taking and (as public officials) administering oaths, the supposed need for capital punishment (with which the Great Law of 1682 had virtually done away) as an effective means of social control, pacifism and neutrality in the face of English demands for militias and military expenditures (in the War of the Spanish Succession, the War of the Austrian Succession, and the French and Indian Wars), and above all, the issue of the treatment of Indians. As Quaker elites found that they could not effectively rule a growing and heterogeneous colony without compromising their principles, they withdrew from political rule. Like the Puritans, their social movement could not survive the realities of ruling a diverse people in a hostile environment, but their choice in the face of this dilemma was different: the Puritans maintained their economic and political power at the price of secularization and ideological fragmentation, while the Quakers relinquished their political dominance in favor of preserving their values. In part, this choice was determined by the fact that because Puritan institutions were initially inegalitarian, they were incompatible with the class society that developed in the colonies, while Quaker institutions were quite unsuited in their democratic levelling to the rule and organization of large units inhabited by diverse classes. The end result, in the short run, was not strikingly different; in both Pennsylvania and Massachusetts, secularization set in, the political elite split off from the theologians and the descendants of the original theocratic elite maintained economic control. Nevertheless, the voluntary self-conscious withdrawal of the Quaker elite from political institutions had consequences for both the Quaker community and the society as a whole that were quite different from the consequences of the more gradual processes that took place in Massachusetts. The gradual transformation of Puritan society allowed Puritanism to work its way into the core of American institutions. The sharp break chosen by the Quakers had as its consequence that Quakerism has maintained a distinct identity and its impact on America has been felt essentially as an external force—a stern voice of conscience. The Society of Friends, despite its brief sojourn as an elite of an ongoing social order, has maintained most of the characteristics of a social movement.[10]

Roger Williams' founding of Rhode Island was an explicit challenge and contrast to the social order of grim Puritan Boston. Because Williams, like the Quakers, spoke in a fusion of political and religious language, the political issues seem extraordinarily contemporary despite their religious phraseology. The participants themselves avowed that the conflict between Williams and the Puritan elite concerned institutional forms more than doctrine. Starting with the proposition that "God had made of one blood" all mankind, Williams demanded the embodiment of this tenet in the following political structures: equal treatment of all human beings, necessarily implying the end of the forcible taking of Indians' lands; the complete separation of church and state, and complete freedom of conscience and worship—a blow against the ideology that supported Boston's oligarchy; the end of oath-taking; the vesting of all power in the people (that is, their right to establish any form of government and to dismantle it); and the extension of political power to all citizens, not merely to the "saints." After their banishment from Boston, Williams and his followers (first numbering only sixty) succeeded in obtaining a Charter for Rhode Island. In 1647, they established a colony in which slavery and servitude were absent (although slavery was later introduced) and a humane penal code dictated the abolition of imprisonment for debt, complete freedom of conscience, yearly elections participated in by all males, safeguards for the religious rights of women, and the provision that land could be obtained from Indians only by honest purchase.[11]

While the Puritan elite could stay in power only by relinquishing the more extreme aspects of its ideology, and the Quakers could sustain their ideology only by relinquishing power (a rather exceptional case), in Rhode Island, the early establishment of a modern liberal ideology and political structure was quite compatible with the subsequent growth of an economic elite. Under Williams, Rhode Island came close to attaining the liberal ideals that figured so prominently in later American political thought. The belief system of Roger Williams and his followers was closer in content and spirit to the programs of the imminent Enlightenment than were the Puritan and Quaker ideologies. Its religious tenets opened the door to secularization. The political principles associated with it allowed a more routinized and differentiated democracy than did the thorough-going egalitarianism and anti-authoritarianism of the Quakers.

In this context, Anne Hutchinson, the religious dissident and Rhode Island exile should be mentioned. Although she was far less innovative in political structure than was her fellow-exile, Roger Williams, Hutchinson is remarkable as an example of how the interplay of social milieu and life experiences produces radicalism. In her case, it is difficult to find the sources of her proud resistance to the Boston elite in any kind of class or (narrowly speaking) political dissatisfaction. Rather, her antinomian, individualistic—almost anarchic—emphasis on an inner light seems to have emerged from her childhood as a minister's daughter, her experience of altered states of consciousness (possibly, in conjunction with her pregnancies) and her status as a woman in a male-dominated society. Unable to achieve the elite position that would have been open to a man of her wealth, social standing, and religious fervor, she formed discussion groups that the elite perceived as both structurally and doctrinally threatening and that led to her banishment as a heretic. Hutchinson is best understood as illustrating two important aspects of seventeenth century sectarianism: the fragmenting antinomianism inherent in all ideologies of grace, which splits and resplits sects and emerges precisely in the most orthodox settings (a peculiar forerunner of the factionalism of modern revolutionary movements) and the remarkable role of women as leaders of Protestant sects—as "extremists"—precisely because the existing religious and political institutions left no opening for their talents.[12]

Finally, we may turn to the Boston and Salem witch trials of the late 1680s and early 1690s as a special sort of social movement. We will not review here the details of this sequence of incidents. Rather, we will present a brief analysis of these incidents. Essentially, all witch hunts (whether of witches, of Trotskyites, or of Communists) are essentially movements that are created by an elite. The apparatus of the witch hunt always involves the existing political and legal institutions. In this respect, witch hunts differ from lynchings or pogroms that usually are also initiated by elites but can appear in popular antielite movements. Witch hunts are carried out through the courts and are covered by the media (or their functional equivalents in premodern societies) in an effort to arouse popular hostility against the "witches." A chief goal of witch hunts is the confession of the witch. This bolsters the ideology, the cognitive system, that supports the elite. An unrepentant witch, like a defiant witness before the House Un-American Activities Committee, threatens the ideology in one of two ways—either she denies the existence of important categories of the ideology ("there are no witches, Trotskyites or subversives") or she proudly reverses the evaluation that the elite would like to propagate. Often, witch hunts are initiated in an effort to strengthen the ideology when an elite feels ideologically (and, hence, politically) insecure and threatened. Precisely for this reason, witch hunts became widespread *after* the middle ages, during the emergence of secularization and the Enlightenment in Europe;[13] the colonial witch hunts occurred as the religious ideology of Massachusetts weakened. The year of the Salem witch hunts (1692) followed the year that a new charter enfranchising *property owners* rather than church members and guaranteeing religious freedom for all Protestants was granted the Colony.[14] What lay behind the effort by the religious wing of the oligarchy to reassert its control over the colony was its separation from, and loss of power to, an economic elite that accepted secularization and an emergent liberalism. The witch hunts were a final attempt to phrase the affairs of the colony in terms of a nonsecular cognitive system. Although created by an elite—or an ex-elite—the witch hunts included movement-related phenomena such as "Conversion" experiences, in which individuals fully committed themselves to a witch-infested cognitive order, and a general excitement and deroutinization of behavior. We must, of course, recognize that witch hunts draw on local animosities and individual pathologies such as the hysteria of ignored or oppressed women, adolescents, and servants. But an analysis that focuses only on this microsociological level of personal troubles would fail to indicate how these troubles are linked to the larger structure in three ways: first, the animosities and hysteria are partly consequences of community and family structures; second, the ideology of the society provides the witchcraft framework for conceptualizing and expressing personal troubles; third, the witch hunt-created fear that evil is abroad in the land strengthens elites who sustain their power with a magicoreligious ideology—the self-fulfilling prophecy that only those who are trained to spot the devil's work can protect the society inhibits more secular efforts to resolve community conflicts and weakens secular elites.[15] Ultimately, the witch hunts were extinguished by a combination of the lack of support for them among the emergent secular merchant elite, by a countermovement of brave petitioners against the proceedings, by the growing disgust of the juries, and, finally, by a counterconversion among the informers who collectively confessed to having lied. Most of the victims of the witch hunts were poor; imprisoned, tortured, and hung, they bear witness that an elite armed with courts, media of opinion, investigating committees, and ever-present malicious and/or weak-willed informers can all too easily institute terror against a people that is beginning to scoff at its ideology and resist its power. (In Stalinist Russia, the purge trials were instituted not by a doomed elite, but by a new one eager to consolidate its power.)

A discussion of American colonial religious movements would not be complete without mention of the Great Awakening, that wave of religious fervor that swept the colonies in the 1720s, '30s, and '40s. It demonstrates that religious problems were still vivid and intense for many Americans and that they could even still act as a vehicle for social conflicts; but that by and large, religious issues no longer concerned the political elite.

Although it was exciting to individuals, the Great Awakening cannot be said to have had a great impact on the sociopolitical history of early America. In form, it was a return to religion for many individuals, an involvement in religious activities for the hitherto ecclesiastically neglected back country population and an expressive outlet through evangelical preaching and "glory shouting." It is associated with a series of ministers: Theodore Frelinghuysen (New Jersey: Dutch Reformed Church, 1725); William Tennent and sons (Middle Colonies: Presbyterian, 1730s); Jonathan Edwards (Massachusetts: evangelical Congregationalist, 1730s); Samuel Davies (South: Baptists and Presbyterians, 1740s); and, most magnetic of all, George Whitefield, the English revivalist whose glory-shouting tours were enjoyed throughout the colonies.[16] The activities of these men and their lesser emulators often split church organizations, usually along class lines. The lower classes within a congregation wholeheartedly welcomed the religious revival and constituted themselves as "New Lights" (in the Congregational Church) or the "New Side" (among Virginia Presbyterians), while the "better sort" genteelly turned away from the unseemly uninhibited enthusiasts. These intrachurch class antagonisms became one more issue around which class conflict could develop. Thus, the Great Awakening indirectly may have contributed to the more explicitly political and economic disturbances of the 1740s through the 1760s, which we shall discuss below. Apart from any long-run cognitive reassessment of the social order, its direct political effects were few. At the level of individual experience, however, the Great Awakening must have provided a wonderful release from a dreary round of toil, usually only alleviated by hard drinking. If sophisticated Bostonians could be aroused by the preaching of James Davenport to the point where they shook and shouted "more like a Company of Bacchanalians after a mad Frolick, than sober Christians," [17] these conversion experiences must have been a source of marvelous pleasure in the back country.

Religious enthusiasm is a paradoxical phenomenon. It reduces politicized movement action and at the same time encourages it. On the one hand, it provides an imaginary individual escape from a situation that can be altered only by collective sociopolitical action and, in so doing strengthens the existing class system. On the other hand, it frees individuals from the existing cognitive order and from the norms of proper conventional behavior, thus undermining the normative and ideological status quo. A single religious movement may exhibit both the accommodating and radicalizing tendencies at once.

Resistance of the Indians as a Social Movement

A good many historians have been inclined to treat Indians as though they were simply a natural barrier to American expansion. A discussion of Indian resistance to white expansion not only has inherent interest and a humanistic and political value, but also contributes insights into specific aspects of American institutions and ideology. Indian wars shaped the American military in a variety of ways. Most important of these ways was in creating a style of unlimited warfare for punitive ends supported by an ideology of protecting civilized morality.[18] Second, frontier political attitudes and institutions were shaped by the ever-present threat of Indian attack, as we shall see shortly. Third, Indians became an important part of American ideology, a symbol of the frontier and of instinctual freedom, but also of white Americans' oppression of other races. During the colonial period, Indian resistance did not constitute a social movement as we have defined social movements, because Indians were outside the social order they fought; strictly speaking, actions by Indians became social movements only by the end of the nineteenth century when Indians were incorporated within American society as defeated and expropriated survivors. But the boundary between wars of opposition to the establishment of colonial rule and wars of national liberation *from* colonial rule is difficult to draw; in some sense, Indian social movements against American society began in 1675, when Metacom ("King Philip") organized a coalition of New England Indians, attacked fifty-two and destroyed twelve of the ninety existing English towns, and met defeat and death primarily because of the treachery of some of his followers.

The futile resistance of the Indians, like the heroism of the Quakers, should be a theme of a history of American social movements—a theme to which we will return in more detail below.

Agrarian and Predominantly Agrarian Revolts

A series of disturbances among farmers and tenants presents a much more clear-cut example of class conflict than does seventeenth century religious dissension. In religious movements, structural cleavages are only dimly perceived by the participants; such movements may have economic and class foundations, but their adherents cannot be said to have economic motives or clear conceptions of class interests. Class interests became the central issue for the agrarian rebels. Several waves of these revolts tended to coincide with general depressions (usually following one of England's frequent wars) or local economic setbacks. The first of these waves began as early as 1652 and continued into the early 1690s; most of the incidents occurred in the Southern and Middle Atlantic colonies. These outbreaks took many forms, ranging from demonstrations and collective refusals to cooperate with laws or regulations to the seizure of towns and the armed capture of colonial assemblies. Farmers (and in some cases, tenants) were the chief participants in these acts of revolt. They formed the bulk of the free population and were the chief victims of taxation schemes, credit policies, legal arrangements, rising prices, and refusal of the authorities to protect settlers against the Indians. The outcome of these movements included incorporation of their demands into the colonial political system, execution of their leaders, and widespread amnesty for their followers. Violent in their tactics and radical in their analyses of colonial society, these movements succeeded only in some political reforms; fundamental problems of the frontier farmer could not be solved by these means and remained in some sense a chronic source of discontent in America until the late nineteenth century when the American social and economic structure was transformed.

A tabular presentation of the late seventeenth century revolts is presented in Table 3.1. This type of presentation might be more useful to the reader than a detailed description of each movement would be.[19] These three sequences of movements—the extended revolts against the colonial government in Maryland, South Carolina, and North Carolina, Bacon's Rebellion, and Leisler's Revolt—share a number of characteristics:

1. The interplay of economic and political causes, both types

Table 1

	Action	Perceived causes	Outcome
Anti-Proprietary Revolts, 1652, Maryland	Armed opposition to the governor's use of force in seizing control of the assembly	1. Increasing concentration of land ownership; 2. Economic depression; 3. Proprietor's lack of support for the Protectorate in England; governor's effort to reassume control of the assembly; and general hostility to the Proprietor.	Temporary local control of Maryland, ending in 1661.
Anti-Proprietary Revolts, 1676, Maryland	Meeting of 60 persons to present demands.	Opposition to taxation and franchise policies; refusal to swear loyalty to the Catholic proprietor.	Immediate: execution of two leaders. Long range: minor changes in taxation and suffrage

Comment: None of these movements had profound effects on colonial economic arrangements much less on the class structure itself; impact greatest on the political system.

Table 1 (cont.)

Action	Perceived causes	Outcome
Anti-Proprietary Revolts, 1681–89, Maryland	Continuation of previous demands	Immediate: suppression. Long range: moderate success. End of the Proprietor's political power; Maryland becomes a royal colony with governor, council, assembly.
Anti-Proprietary Revolts, 1676–79, North Carolina (Albemarle)	Resistance to quit-rent and tobacco tax payment.	Immediate: recall of the Proprietor's agent; release of imprisoned leaders.
Anti-Proprietary Revolts, 1685–91, South Carolina	Similar.	

Comment: None of these movements had profound effects on colonial economic arrangements much less on the class structure itself; impact greatest on the political system.

Table 1 (cont.)

	Action	Perceived causes	Outcome
Bacon's Rebellion, 1676–77, Virginia	Bacon leads unauthorized expedition against Indians, 1675–76. Battle between Baconians and governor's forces, 1676; Baconians control colony. Unsuccessful plans to expand rebellion to Maryland and Carolina.	1. Local and general economic setbacks; Anglo-Dutch Wars; 1667 hurricane; 1672–73 cattle epidemic; prohibitive tobacco shipping tax, 1673. 2. Colonial and county tax systems (armed tax revolt in 1674), which favored large landowners. 3. Governor's control of the House of Burgesses, and 1670 disenfranchisement of non-landowners. 4. Governor's refusal to act against Indians, for fear of disrupting the fur trade.	Immediate: with 1100 British troops, governor regains control in 1677; 37 Baconians executed. English investigating commission effects recall of governor. Long range: all free men, including blacks (till 1723) gain suffrage. Council powers curtailed; county government democratized; popular control of taxation; amnesties.

Comment: Bacon's Rebellion was potentially a revolutionary movement against British rule as well as against the local oligarchy. But like the other movements of this period, resulted in reform rather than radical change.

Table 1 (cont.)

	Action	Perceived causes	Outcome
Leisler's Revolt, 1689–91, New York	Mutiny in the militia; control of most of New York; dissolution of some landed and commercial monopolies, and political tax reforms.	1. Support and emulation of the "Glorious Revolution" in England; 2. Opposition to New York landlords and merchants.	Immediate: English military intervention; execution of Leisler; most reforms undone. Long range: New York Assembly, instituted during revolt, is kept.

Comment: 1. Leisler's Revolt was much less agrarian than the others; the Coalition included smaller merchants, storekeepers and various types of "mechanics". 2. Note effort to establish and maintain unity with the rebel government in Maryland—a forerunner of revolutionary inter-colonial communication and organization.

being quite clearly perceived by participants, who had grievances against the economic elite and the colonial political system.

2. The translation of the underlying class antagonisms into demands for both political and economic reforms.

3. A strong support base among smaller landowners and, in the case of Leisler's Revolt in more urbanized New York, among an urban petty-bourgeois and working class as well.

4. Efforts at intercolonial cooperation and communication, generally unsuccessful, but forerunners of both American nationalism (at the ideological level) and intercolonial revolutionary organization (at the structural level).

5. Tactics of armed resistance to the British and mutinies against the British within the militias—as Bacon's opponent, Governor Berkeley, lamented: "How miserable that man is that Governes a People when six pacts of seaven at least are Poore, Endebted, Discontented, and Armed." [20]

6. Efforts to institute both economic and political changes, some quite radical but most ultimately reversed or diluted to minor reform measures.

7. An ideology of hostility not only to local oligarchs, but also toward British institutions and the British king; as Anthony Arnold, Bacon's comrade, told the royal judges shortly before his execution, "Kings have no rights but what they got by conquest and the sword, and he who can by force of the sword deprive them thereof has as good and just a title to them as the King himself. If the King should deny to do me right I would think no more of it to sheath my sword in his heart or bowels than of my mortal enemies." [21]

A second wave of more narrowly agrarian class movements swept the colonies in the 1740s and 1750s. The most violent and spectacular outbreak occurred among the poorer rural people of New Jersey in 1745 and continued intermittently until 1755. In the northern and eastern parts of the colony, farmers and tenants were oppressed by quit-rents (rents paid in lieu of labor service) and fraudulent land seizure, against which they had little political or legal redress. They retaliated by defying court orders, attacking sheriffs' sales, squatting on landlords' property, and freeing the imprisoned. Despite a mutiny in 1740, the revolts were eventually suppressed. The rebels gained few benefits other than the abolition of quit-rents.

Class conflict took a less violent form in New England where agrarian debtors (as well as less prosperous urban groups) supported a land bank, that is, a mechanism for the expansion of credit through the use of land as a basis for currency issue in Massachusetts in 1741. Farmers controlled the assembly and held out against the governor and the merchant oligarchy, who opposed the scheme. These farmers went so far as to march on Boston when they felt threatened. Nevertheless their cause lost, as Parliament intervened to support the urban oligarchy by outlawing the land bank (by an extension of the Bubble Act of 1720, designed to curb speculation). Another act of Parliament was required in 1751 to end similar measures instituted by agrarian debtors in Rhode Island. This second wave of hostilities in New Jersey and New England almost merges in time with a third wave, triggered by the depression following the end of the French and Indian War (the Seven Years War) in 1763.

Three outbreaks are particularly important. First was the Paxton Boys' revolt in Pennsylvania in 1764, which culminated in an abortive march on Philadelphia to demand more equitable representation of the western counties, lower prices, tax reform, debt relief, equitable administration of justice, and protection from Indians. Some concessions were made. The Regulator movement in North Carolina (1768–71) was on a larger scale and used tactics similar to those of the New Jersey rebels: interference with the operation of the courts (which were perceived as hopelessly biased in favor of the wealthy), attacks on jails to release prisoners, armed resistance to evictions and tax collection, and assaults on the houses and offices of officials. The Regulators were not suppressed until 1771, when their army of over 2,000 men was defeated at Alamance, N.C. by a special militia led by well-to-do officers; seven of the Regulators were executed and the rest fled westward or accepted amnesty. Equally uncompromising was the suppression of the third major agrarian movement of this period—the 1766 uprising of Hudson Valley tenants. Agrarian disturbances over the tenancy system in the Hudson Valley and the political and legal system that supported it had begun as early as 1711; in 1766, discontent over the operation of the courts turned into armed combat that had to be suppressed by British troops but did not result in any executions.

These movements are important for several reasons. First, they are evidence of the extent of class hostilities; they are the spectacular peaks of an iceberg whose submerged portions are nonviolent conflict in courts and assemblies and private dissatisfaction. This pervasive agrarian discontent was a necessary condition for the organization of militias and local revolutionary groups (Sons of Liberty, committees of correspondence and public safety, and others) that made the American revolution possible. Second, violent class conflict created an atmosphere in which armed challenges to authority were part of the everyday experience of many Americans. Again, the sense that British rulers and the American elite were vulnerable was a prerequisite for revolutionary mass action. Third, the movements are interesting and important because they show an extraordinarily clear understanding of class interests and of the ways in which political and legal institutions support the ruling class. As William Prendergast, the leader of New York tenants, said, "tenant farmers could not be defended in a court of Law because they were poor; therefore they were determined to do themselves justice; poor men were always oppressed by the rich." [22] The American Revolutionaries' demands for political liberty could be formulated only in an atmosphere in which existing institutions were so unsentimentally stripped of their ideological pretensions. Finally, these movements are important as forerunners of later American agrarian movements.

Uprisings of the Poor

The large-scale well organized and ideologically sophisticated movements of freeholders and tenants stand in sharp contrast to the actions of the very poor—black slaves, indentured servants, and the urban proletariat. These groups were by no means content with their lot, but lacked the social and geographic independence that was an important resource of the farmers. The pressures of servitude and of urban street life were too immediate to permit articulation of demands and organization of a radical movement; furthermore, the urban poor and white servitors were less numerically powerful than were farmers. Although blacks were numerous in the southern colonies by the beginning of the eighteenth century, they were isolated in a white society that was entirely hostile to them. Under these circumstances, the revolts of the most oppressed groups took the form of killing or assaulting isolated individuals of the more fortunate classes, looting, and futile efforts to escape into the wilderness. Social movements of the very poor tend to take the form of crimes. As a result, technically, they fall outside the field of social movement analysis. On the one hand, they lack arms and access to the means of communication and organs of opinion by which they can both secretly and publicly create a mass movement. On the other hand, threatened elites find it expedient to dismiss violence against the rich as criminal (that is, individualistic and inarticulate) and refuse to acknowledge violence as a primitive form of class-conscious action. The ideological fusion of crime and radicalism (and expression of the radicalism of the poor in crime because of a lack of resources) is still prevalent.

While keeping sight of this general observation, nevertheless, we can find a rather large number of "incidents"—revolts, troubles, murders of whites, attempts to escape, and so forth—among blacks in colonial America. This period was far more productive of slave revolts than were later decades. Perhaps this is so because large numbers of slaves were still African-born, cherished memories of freedom, and were not socialized to submission. As we use the term here, insurrection is an incident in which at least ten participants are involved; freedom is an avowed aim; and contemporaries label the incident a plot, uprising, or insurrection. Using this strict definition, Aptheker lists over fifty incidents in the period between 1663 (when blacks and white servants in Gloucester, Virginia, conspired to rebel) and the end of the revolutionary war (in which blacks tended to support the British).[23] During the early part of this period, there was cooperation between black, white, and Indian servants. Some blacks succeeded in establishing "maroon" settlements and others escaped to freedom in the Spanish city of St. Augustine; most of these rebels were caught and brutally punished. Even the largest of the revolts involved fewer than a hundred persons; in other words, neither maroon colonies nor revolts reached the scale of either the colonial farmers' movements on the one hand or of the black kingdoms of Brazil on the other.

The mass actions of the urban poor were fewer in number than were slave revolts but they were even more threatening to the colonial elites. Like the uprisings of farmers and slaves, such incidents became especially numerous during periods of economic stagnation. Thus, the 1740s and the postwar depression era in the 1760s were particularly stormy periods. High prices, scarce money, and unemployment (particularly among troops returned from the French and Indian War) were precipitating factors, but the single most frequent cause was British impressment of sailors. Major press riots—participated in chiefly by seamen, dockworkers, blacks and youths—occurred in varied forms in Boston in 1745, 1747 and 1768, in Newport in 1765, and in Manhattan in 1764; there were numerous smaller incidents along the seaboard from Maine to Virginia.[24] In the 1760s, actions of the urban poor were increasingly directed toward issues facing a broader spectrum of colonial classes. Thus they fall beyond the scope of this discussion. Nevertheless, one cannot draw the conclusion that the urban proletariat was not politicized or aware of its interests in the earlier period; rather, it lacked the resources necessary to give effective political form to its efforts to obtain redress from poverty and exploitation.

The American Revolution

So far, we have devoted attention to movements and disturbances involving two classes, farmers and the poor. The American Revolution can be understood as a coalition between these two groups and three others—the urban bourgeoisie (primarily concentrated in the North), the urban petty-bourgeoisie and "middling" mechanics, and the large landowners in the South. The urban bourgeoisie and petty-bourgeoisie supported the movement for independence for a relatively simple and straightforward reason: to satisfy English merchants and West Indian planters, England had passed a series of measures that threatened to bankrupt and destroy colonial entrepreneurs. In the case of urban merchants, class interests and purely economic motives coincided. Support of the landed wealthy for independence is more difficult to explain. In part, the gentry, too, suffered from British economic policies—from British monopolization of all Western land speculation (1774), from passage of the Currency Act of 1764, and from enumeration (prohibitive taxation) of tobacco and British manipulation of the tobacco market. Nevertheless, their economic reasons were strongly fused with political and ideological ones, and they played a preeminent role in formulating the ideas of the American Revolution. Each of these strata—small farmers, urban poor, urban bourgeoisie, and the petty-bourgeoisie and landowners—had a key part in the Revolution.

The urban groups were especially important in precipitating open hostilities. As we have seen, the urban poor had been restive and militant for several decades. They were strongly opposed to the British, but the issues that aroused them—chiefly, pressing—had relatively little appeal to more prosperous townsmen. Only when the wealthier townsmen as well felt themselves oppressed did urban disturbances become more widespread; only then were the diverse class grievances united by the ideology of political freedom and independence from Britain. Britain began to oppress the colonial bourgeoisie for two major reasons; her own merchants and West Indian planters demanded the suppression of their colonial competitors, and the Seven Years War (the French and Indian War terminated in 1763) had left Britain in need of revenues. Consequently, Parliament passed a series of measures designed to raise revenue, destroy colonial trade (and smuggling), and protect the British West Indians from the Yankee sugar trade with the French, Dutch, Spanish, and Danes in the Caribbean. A list of the most important of these policies would include: the Molasses Act of 1733 (outlawing sugar, molasses, and rum trade between the colonies and non-British countries—an act that proved to be unenforceable); the Currency Act of 1764 (outlawing legal-tender paper money in the colonies); the Stamp Act of 1764 ("enumerating" a wide variety of colonial and non-British goods in order to force colonial dependence on British manufacturers and merchants and imposing duties on legal and commercial transactions); the Townshend Act of 1770 (imposing duties on paper, paint, and glass); and, finally, the Tea Act of 1773 (by which the East India Company could directly dump its surplus stock in the Colonies, thereby saving it from collapse but ruining colonial importers). Each of these measures was an economic blow to the colonial bourgeoisie and, as such, each indirectly harmed smaller entrepreneurs and the propertyless urban strata that suffered from economic stagnation.[25] Some of the acts—above all, the Stamp Act—directly affected individuals of all classes by the imposition of duties on newspapers, legal documents, and commercial papers. This act enraged the populace. A theory of mob manipulation by conspiring revolutionaries is quite unnecessary; indignation at British economic oppression of the colonies was widespread, genuine, and based on a clear understanding of the importance of a thriving colonial economy for all strata. The combined outrage with which the bourgeoisie, petty-bourgeoisie, and propertyless city dwellers reacted to the Stamp Act produced rioting in Boston, Charleston, Manhattan, and Newport. The events in Boston were particularly interesting; masses of men were fired up by the press, by secret caucus meetings, and by public town meetings, and hung the Crown's stamp agent in effigy. After a fortnight of intermittent rioting, the crowd looted Lieutenant Governor Hutchinson's house as well as the homes of other notable loyalists. Most important, the Boston mob became highly politicized. Two powerful rival gangs who traditionally had broken each others' heads in a Pope's Day riot on November 5 of each year pledged their unity. Thereafter, riots in Boston were disciplined, organized, and explicitly political; as a loyalist noted, Boston rioters acted "from principle and under countenance." The militants were arranged in a class system: At the bottom were servants, blacks, and sailors under the command of the Master Mason's carpenters; above them, and deployed for more subtle action, were the merchants' mob and the Sons of Liberty, known as the "Mohawks"; at the top was a special corps of one hundred and fifty men, "trained as regular as a military corps," that had been established specifically for this purpose.[26] This politicization of street gangs (and the subsequent transfer of attacks from each other to the elite) is parallel to the politicization of youth gangs in the 1960s (for example, the Young Lords, the Appalachian Young Patriots, the Blackstone Rangers). In both cases, groups at or near the bottom of the class structure had expressed their discontent in rowdy and criminal activity. As the society became more politicized, and discontented classes that were wealthier and more powerful sought allies among the very poor. Furthermore, the poor themselves began to reinterpret their condition as the result of structural patterns. Gang and criminal activity increasingly was directed against the elite and became increasingly self-conscious, legitimated by a revolutionary conceptual framework, and rational in its acquisition and use of resources. This politicization of gangs and the "criminal element" is not simply the result of manipulation by revolutionary leaders; rather, it is caused by the general politicization of society in a period of crisis and change and is conveyed by informal personal contacts as well as by the media and identifiable leaders. The evidence from eighteenth century Boston and 1960s America as well as from the urban wings of revolutionary movements in Algeria, Cuba, and elsewhere suggest that the very poor and the deroutinized working class are potentially radical and that crime is the poor man's revolution only as long as resources and beliefs for a more purposive struggle are lacking.[27]

The Stamp Act riots in Charleston are also of interest because they demonstrate the lack of unity between dissatisfied blacks and whites; they began merrily enough with nine days of rioting, but as soon as the blacks joined in the disturbances, the whites became afraid of a slave insurrection, immediately stopped their own action, and thereafter kept the city quiet and well disciplined. Fear of black liberation outweighed the desire to protest British oppression.[28]

Concurrent with the politicization and organization of urban rioting came widespread organization of the Sons of Liberty. Building their revolutionary structure around existing sociable and mutual-aid associations of mechanics (artisans) and small tradesmen, the Sons of Liberty became the most important nucleus of resistance to the British in the colonies. Despite their opposition to British policies, the wealthier merchants were disgusted by mob activities, but, often, they felt compelled to join local chapters of the Sons of Liberty. These associations and others like them were not at all averse to forcing the hesitant to comply with their demands for defiance of the Stamp Act. Furthermore, particularly in rural areas, the Sons of Liberty formed paramilitary groups with explicitly anti-Parliamentary (although not as yet, anti-crown) stances, ready to declare that they would not be "enslav'd by any power of earth without opposing force to force." At a more conservative level, the Stamp Act led to the establishment of an intercolonial congress of protest, moderate in tone but an important forerunner of intercolonial political structure.

By the time the Stamp Act was repealed in 1766, probably, it was already too late for the British to reverse the colonial movement for independence. Too much of the structure of a revolutionary movement had been established. Thus, by the late 1760s, the coalition of an aroused merchant class, a well-organized and politically sophisticated stratum of artisans and petty-bourgeois, a politicized urban poor, and a militarily ready group of farmers was well underway. Three other ingredients were necessary: the punitive acts of Britain in her attempt to suppress resistance, the ideological contributions of the radicals, and the involvement of the Virginia landowners.

In the years between 1766 and 1774, the British attempted some concessions, but their commitment to British domestic economic interests and their reactions to colonial unruliness forced them into more repressive measures. We have here an excellent example of how structural conflict (manifested by Parliamentary support of British interests) develops within a context of chance incidents and situational factors. The connection between class interest and the Townshend Act, the repeal of the tea tax, and the closing of the West is fairly clear; that conflict of some kind was imminent could be predicted from these events. What could not be predicted is the precise form that acts of resistance and suppression would take. Thus, the Boston Massacre of 1770, in which British troops opened fire on a crowd of brick-throwing hecklers and killed five of them, is an important but unpredictable incident in the chronology of the revolution. (How reminiscent of Kent State and Jackson State is this incident in circumstances and in the refusal of official investigating bodies to treat the killings as a criminal act.) After the "ominously quiet" years of 1771 and '72,[29] the Boston Tea Party of 1773 and the ensuing strictly punitive Intolerable Acts (barring entry of commodities other than food until receipt of payment for the tea, voiding of the Massachusetts Charter, removing all trials of British soldiers from the colony, and quartering troops) constituted the opening of hostilities. At this point, we must turn from an analysis of class interests to an analysis of revolutionary organization and propaganda. Only these elements are sufficient to explain petitioning, the calling of Congress, the clashes at Lexington and Concord, the Declaration of Independence, and the war itself.

We have described the beginnings of revolutionary organization in the 1760s. The key aspect of this organization was the creation of political structures that could generate resistance to the British and act as an alternative source of power to the British officials. In short, a variety of committees formed a dual government opposed to and competing with the Tory-controlled government that existed in the years immediately preceding the revolution. This dual political structure had a vital military branch in the Minutemen and other local militias. In an age when the means of social control were simple, a secret police force nonexistent, and local isolation and autonomy great, it was relatively simple to organize the units of the counterstructure. Even before the Boston Tea Party, many committees of correspondence had appeared (300 in Massachusetts alone). These committees were established by a combination of local democracy in town meetings (often in the face of threats of violence from Tory landowners) and a certain amount of manipulation (as in Boston, where the committee was elected by a radical rump at a town meeting that had earlier twice voted it down).[30] The most powerful and innovative figures in this structure succeeded in forming a Continental Congress (elected by Whig majorities in the colonial legislatures), a central organ that eventually formalized the breach with England and assumed control of the revolutionary war. All of these dual structures began as quasi-legal bodies that gave some consideration to the moderates' proposals that action be limited to petitioning Parliament.

These vacillating units were transformed into fully revolutionary bodies by the actions of the British themselves (such as the British raid on an arms cache at Concord), and by ideological statements that gave coherent form and the legitimacy of the written word to revolutionary sentiments. Most famous and widely read of these statements is Tom Paine's *Common Sense*, published in 1776. Other, less radical, statements served the cause of American independence by emphasizing the unity of the colonials and deemphasizing contradictory class interests, thereby strengthening the coalition of class groups. For the time being, "radical" could come to mean "desiring separation from England." The levelling social radicalism of the propertyless classes was set aside—postponed forever, as it turned out—in favor of a nationalist radicalism and a sociopolitical liberalism.

Let us summarize the most important aspects of the American Revolution as a social movement. The single most significant perspective for analyzing this movement—the most powerful explanatory approach—is the realization that a wide spectrum of classes in the forties, fifties, and sixties of eighteenth century Colonial America were dissatisfied with the social, political, and economic situation. Generally, these class demands were potentially mutually incompatible, but for a short time they shared one element—dissatisfaction with British policies, ranging from pressing and antidebtor fiscal arrangements to restrictions on colonial trade and land speculation. A widespread feeling existed that *British* actions must be curbed (or, if necessary, altogether ended) before any *American* class interests could be attained. Because the British were singularly inept at playing off American classes against each other, they were confronted by a unified society. The proportion of Loyalists and Loyalist sympathizers—estimated at about one-third of the population—was too low and not organized well enough to resist the revolutionaries;

Loyalists drew support from not only the top of the social structure (Tory landowners and professionals), but also, to some degree, from the very bottom (black slaves and Hudson Valley tenants) whose rebellious spirit led them to strike out against their local oppressors rather than the more distant British, when the time came for open hostilities.[31]

The second key feature of the American Revolution was the superb organization of a dual structure of political power. The clubs, associations, militias, and other bodies of this dual structure were present in every locale. They were willing to use force to curb Loyalist action and sentiment and were prepared to step into the power vacuum left by the collapse of British authority. The specifically military units formed an important component of the Revolutionary Army. The nomenclature of the American Revolution is perhaps foreign to us: the Sons of Liberty, Committees of Correspondence, and Minutemen become far more recognizable to us as "revolutionary collectives." These units tended to perform a twofold function; they were units that took into their hands the representation of the colonies to the British either by petitioning or demonstrating (in the two or three years preceding the outbreak of armed action) or by paramilitary action (in the decisive months of 1775 and 1776); second, they created a new distribution of power *within* American communities by persuasion and by more coercive measures. Those who joined the revolutionary committees ran the risk of British punishment in the areas still held by the British; but in the liberated areas, they became the wielders of political power. Although important decisions were made by leaders (some of whom—like Sam Adams—can almost be described as professional revolutionaries), in particular by the Continental Congress, in an area as decentralized and rural as colonial America revolutionary organization was of necessity decentralized and to a large extent under local democratic control.

Finally (and probably *least* important), at the ideological level, the stream of revolutionary propaganda in the form of books, pamphlets and what we now call "the underground media," proposed a fundamental change in the cognitive order of American society, from an identity as British subjects to one as independent American citizens. The emphasis was on political transformation. An emphasis on economic and social upheaval would have been divisive in the somewhat precarious class situation. The language of political transformation was sometimes even conservative, emphasizing British *abuses of legitimate authority* rather than questioning the legitimacy of the political institutions; in its impact, however, even such conservative literature led to the politically radical end of independence. In our terminology, the American Revolution was a manifestly *political* movement whose underlying class discontent was subordinated to the goal of political unity in the national cause. The propaganda was ultimately important, although not decisive, in creating new cognitive patterns for individuals. Many persons must have acted for or against the Revolution with little conscious reflection; their whole life experience left them little choice. But many others did ponder the issues and argue about them with their friends; for them, the formulation of issues in the media provided a patterning of their own thoughts and led them into action. Working on an ever-present basis of class discontent, ideological statements defined the situation as one of crisis and choice. Where the revolutionary committees already existed, they were a very immediate interpersonal structural source of new definitions of the situation; but ideological formulations may have been of special importance to the men who first formed these committees, men who had to risk punishment and abuse to create a local alternate system of political power.

All these elements must be present in any successful revolution: underlying class discontent, which includes a more or less realistic political appraisal of the existing distribution of power and wealth; an organization with military capabilities (whether in the form of paramilitary or guerrilla units or in the form of subversion of the existing armed forces), and collectives operating locally;[32] and an ideology that bridges class issues—or can transform the interests of one class into *universal* rights—and redefines situations—particularly for persons outside or only marginally within the scope of the power of the local collectives. Finally, the American Revolution, like other successful revolutions, benefited from the ineptness of the elite. But vacillating, suppressive, and stupid rule is neither a necessary nor a sufficient condition for revolution. Where there is a clear conception of real class problems and an effective organization, revolution is inevitable; it can be forestalled only if co-optation and concessions remove class issues (without changing the underlying relations of production) prior to the creation of revolutionary dual political and military structure.

CONCLUSIONS

As we have already noted, the colonial period in America coincides with an extraordinarily exciting period in Western history. Three interrelated phenomena can be observed especially clearly in America, although they also appear in more obscure or partial form in Europe; in America, laboratory-like conditions of isolation prevail so the emergence of these patterns is beautifully clear. First, religious interpretations of the social order give way to secular ones based on class and politics; the religious symbolism is stripped away in the Enlightenment and the perceptions of the participants coincide with our own. Second, the colonial period in America is one of almost universal understanding of the social structure; only in order to accomplish the crowning achievement of this cognitive clearsightedness—the American Revolution—are the very ideological concepts introduced that in the future will be used to obfuscate rather than to clarify sociopolitical thought—nationalism and political liberalism. Initially radical concepts and key issues in the revolution, nationalism and liberalism, were to have a frequently (though not exclusively) conservatizing effect as ideological obstacles to further action and as ideational protectors of the bourgeois social order that emerged in varying forms throughout the western world. And third, the colonial period in America is especially significant because it provides us with the first example of a modern revolution, complete with all the necessary apparatus of translation of class interests into universal interests (in this case, nationalism and natural rights) and a revolutionary political and military organization.

NOTES

[1] Carl Bridenbaugh, *Cities in Revolt* (New York: Capricorn Books, 1964), pp. 5 and 216–17.
[2] Jesse Lemisch, "The American Revolution Seen from the Bottom Up," in Barton J. Bernstein, *Towards a New Past* (New York: Random House, 1968), p. 8.
[3] Clinton Rossiter, *The Seedtime of the Republic* (New York: Harcourt, Brace & World, 1953).

[4] Lemisch, *op. cit.*, p. 8.
[5] *Ibid.*, p. 7.
[6] Rossiter, *op. cit.*
[7] A. G. Dickens, *Reformation and Society* (London: Thames and Hudson, 1966).
[8] Quoted in Daniel Boorstin, *The Americans: The Colonial Experience* (New York: Random House, 1958), p. 26.
[9] *Ibid.*
[10] *Ibid.*
[11] Herbert Aptheker, *The Colonial Era* (New York: International Publishers, 1966).
[12] Emery Battis, *Saints and Sectarians* (Chapel Hill: University of North Carolina Press, 1962).
[13] H. R. Trevor-Roper, "The European Witchcraze of the Sixteenth and Seventeenth Centuries," in *The Crisis of the Seventeenth Century* (New York: Harper & Row, 1968).
[14] Aptheker, *op. cit.*
[15] Marion Starkey, *The Devil in Massachusetts* (Garden City, N.Y.: Anchor-Doubleday, 1969).
[16] Rossiter, *op. cit.*
[17] John C. Miller, *Sam Adams* (Stanford, Calif.: Stanford University Press, 1936), p. 7.
[18] Morris Janowitz, *The Professional Soldier* (New York: Free Press of Glencoe, 1960).
[19] This material is based on the following sources: Witcomb Washburn, *The Governor and the Rebel: A History of Bacon's Rebellion in Virginia* (Chapel Hill: University of North Carolina Press, 1967); Rossiter, *op. cit.*; and Aptheker, *op. cit.*
[20] Boorstin, *op. cit.*, p. 355.
[21] Aptheker, *op. cit.*, p. 67.
[22] Quoted in Aptheker, *op. cit.*
[23] Herbert Aptheker, *Negro Slave Revolts in the United States* (New York: International Publishers, 1969), Chapter VIII.
[24] Jesse Lemisch, "The Radicalism of the Inarticulate: Merchant Seamen in the Politics of Revolutionary America," in Alfred Young, ed., *Dissent* (DeKalb: Northern Illinois University Press, 1969).
[25] Louis Hacker, *The Triumph of American Capitalism* (New York: Simon & Schuster, 1940), pp. 145–70.
[26] Miller, *op. cit.*, pp. 69–70.
[27] Eric Wolf, *Peasant Wars of the Twentieth Century* (New York: Harper & Row, 1969), pp. 267 and 271.
[28] Bridenbaugh, *op. cit.*, p. 313.
[29] Carl Becker, *The Spirit of '76* (Washington, D.C.: Brookings, 1962).
[30] Miller, *op. cit.*
[31] Staughton Lynd, "The Tenant Uprising at Livingstone Manor, 1777," in *Class Conflict, Slavery and the U.S. Constitution* (Indianapolis: Bobbs-Merrill, 1967).

[32] No revolution has been carried out purely by a centralized capital city based organization. Such a transfer of power might occur in a *coup d'etat*, but even in this case, some kind of transfer of power (if only in the sense of obedience to the new elite) must occur throughout the society.

4

From Perfection to Progress: 1781–1850

THE INTERREGNUM: LEGITIMACY AND CENTRALIZATION

The seventy years following the Revolution—roughly, the lifespan of a long-lived man—must necessarily seem anticlimactic; permanent revolution is like an unending orgasm—probably not attainable, by definition. We have seen how rapidly the pure dreams of Quakers and Puritans had to come to terms with the realities of establishing an actual social structure in a hostile environment. This same problem of everyday reality, devoid of ideological romance and revolutionary suspension of ordinary time, must be faced by all revolutionaries and students of revolutions. In any case, the leaders of the American Revolution were exceptionally uninterested in the question of permanent revolution; having defined their goals as independence and a limited degree of political democracy, they were eager for both ideological and explicitly class interest reasons to halt any structural upheaval as soon as possible. Although a large number of "leveling" incidents occurred as part of the revolution, especially in the expropriation of Tory landowners, it seems reasonable to state that substantial portions of the class structure remained unchanged. To ask whether the American Revolution was really a revolution, an upheaval in social structure, is to ask whether the glass is half full or half empty. In its political and legal consequences, it was indeed radical. In terms of social structure it was radical in that it unquestionably swept away a substantial portion of the elite; estates of Tory landowners were confiscated and sold, often to former tenants, and Loyalist merchants, lawyers and clergymen were forced to flee. Thus, the composition of the elite was altered and, in the process, upward mobility from tenancy to freehold was created.[2] It failed to be radical in that, if anything, problems of small farmers were exacerbated rather than solved, the condition of the urban propertyless class remained unchanged (and was to deteriorate in the next few decades), and slaves continued to be slaves.

The period between the end of the war and the ratification of the Constitution is interesting to the student of social movements because it furnishes an example of two important phenomena—the cost of revolution and the problem of legitimacy. The violence associated with revolution—especially the violence of the wars that have followed each major revolution—tends to diminish the egalitarian, participatorily democratic and psychologically liberating aspects of the revolution. On the one hand, revolution creates a solidarity and sense of control among the revolutionary groups, but, on the other hand, it weakens these groups because the accompanying war is fought on their territory, disrupts their usual productive activity (an especially serious problem for small-scale or subsistence farmers), and generates pressures toward centralization and hierarchy. These costs of revolutionary warfare are evident in the American case (although less acute than in the case of France or Russia). Probably, the severe depression and unemployment that followed the Revolutionary War were factors in explaining the support for the centralization (and consequent loss of local control) embodied in the Constitution.

The new confederation had to face not only economic problems, but also the problem of institutional legitimacy. Individuals hoped for a restoration of order—a political solution to the state of anomie in which they felt immersed, but the habits of rebelliousness and ready opposition to authority, such valuable assets in making the revolution, were hard to give up. Economic problems and rebellious habits came together in the major movement of the period, Daniel Shays's Rebellion in Massachusetts in the fall and winter of 1786–87. Massachusetts (along with New York) had acquired one of the least democratic constitutions; its House of Representatives, a body of propertied men, voted 86 to 19 against the issuance of paper money, a perennial demand of debtors. Following the lead of Worcester, fifty towns of Hampshire County sought legal redress by demanding paper money (and, thus, relief from foreclosures and taxes), but the protest turned into an armed uprising. It was led by the bankrupt Captain Shays and followed the pattern of earlier revolts—interference with the courts, opening of the jails, and attacks on creditors. The rebels were eventually suppressed by the "regulars," who were paid by funds the state solicited from the wealthy.

In this setting, there was widespread support for Hamilton's call for revision of the Articles of Confederation at a Constitutional Convention. Here, a rather conservative body—that is, a group that was heavily weighted by men of property and from which were absent those among the wealthy who were ideologically radical (Jefferson, Henry and the like)—created a new structure of political and legal legitimacy. The calling of the convention and its creation of a constitution (both at the ideological level of the *Federalist* and similar writing and at the structural level in the appearance of a Federalist party) have many of the aspects of a social movement.

We have now set the stage politically for a major substructural transformation, the coming of the Industrial Revolution to America.

SUBSTRUCTURAL TRANSFORMATION

In Europe, the substructural transformation of incipient modernity was a major factor in the colonization of America; this substructural transformation was the one in which traditional agriculture was replaced by commercial farming (including the enclosure system), feudal nobility became a stratum of innovative gentry, a mercantile commercial capitalism flourished, colonial expansion occurred, especially into tropical and subtropical plantation areas, and the beginnings of industrial capitalism appeared. The American substructural transformation with which we are concerned here was, above all, an increase in the rate and scope of this last development—industrial capitalism.

The political independence that the colonies had won from Great Britain removed a major political impediment from incipient industrialization—namely, Parliamentary suppression of American development in order to protect British interests. A less formidable domestic obstacle to industrialization was erected by the Jeffersonians. It is useful to think of the Jeffersonians as a coalition of farmers (who were capitalist entrepreneurs only in a very small way, and certainly not industrialists) and slaveholders (who were capitalist entrepreneurs only in a very peculiar way—more of this later). Much of the struggle between this group and the groups associated with industrialization did not take the form of a movement in a strict sense of the word.[3] Some movement characteristics are to be found in the Democratic Societies, a network of clubs that sprang up in 1793 around the ideological issue of support for the French Revolution and were the structural vehicle of Jeffersonian opposition. Insofar as the clubs were not suppressed by the Federalists' Alien and Sedition Acts, they came to form an important part of the emerging party system. A more violent and less legitimate incident of this movement was the Whiskey Rebellion against the excise tax on stills, in Pennsylvania in 1794, in which the tax was resisted and the collectors' offices burned. But this whole episode of conflict between Jeffersonians and Federalists is above all an important piece of evidence in favor of our proposition that movements that resist substructural trends are doomed to failure. When the smoke of ideological and political battle cleared in 1800, it became evident that the Jeffersonians had won the White House and lost their hopes. They were able to democratize the political forms established by the Federalists; they permitted the Alien and Sedition Acts to lapse and pardoned their victims, swept away ceremonies and titles, ameliorated criminal and debtor laws, and began the process of revoking property qualifications for voting. But they did not stop business affluence and industrialization, accepted both protective tariffs and the national bank, and even hastened the process of centralized decision making in the Louisiana Purchase. Not only is the case interesting as support for the thesis that movements do not effectively halt major changes in the productive system, but it is curious also in that the more radical ideology here was advanced by the materially conservative faction while the Federalist industrialists, innovators in production, maintained an aristocratic front. This strange situation in which each group's ideology was at cross-purposes with its commitments to economic institutions can be explained in a number of ways. To some extent, the Federalists were attempting to revive the language of feudal corporatism to legitimate the class interests of a mercantile bourgeoisie—an effort at reality construction that was doomed to failure in a new society in which the majority of citizens had supported a war for liberalism and fancied themselves entrepreneurs of one sort or another. Furthermore, the economic growth and shift to industrialization that the Federalists sought were benefits that were not reaped by the mercantile class that supported the Federalists; this class mistakenly hailed a program of industrial growth as consonant with its own interests, when in fact industrial development undercut its political and social hold on northeastern cities. In carrying on a class conflict with the rhetoric of democracy vs. aristocracy and with a model of class interests based on conflict of realty versus personalty, both sides obscured for themselves the rise of an entrepreneurial industrial bourgeoisie, which would prove more powerful economically and politically than either of the parties in the official political arena. The subsequent shift in party nomenclature, programs and sources of support suggest efforts to bring political structure into closer alignment to class realities. The whole incident supports the proposition that, generally, American ideological struggles have taken place within a liberal frame of discourse. Despite the aristocratic rhetoric of the Federalists and the radical rhetoric of the Jeffersonians, both camps drew upon, and contributed to, a fundamentally bourgeois and petty-bourgeois property-owner's view of the social order. Despite the half-hearted and futile experimentation of the Federalists with the language of British monarchical aristocracy, the ideologies of feudal-corporate conservatism and proletarian-communalistic leveling were both absent from the conflict.[4]

The substance of the industrializing substructural transformation included the manufacture of finished products (as opposed to earlier crafts production), the introduction of a factory system (as opposed to earlier workshop organization), the appearance of production for mass markets (instead of custom production), the investment of capital in commercial ventures, the creation of a network of canals and (by the end of our period) railways, the invention of the cotton gin (which committed the South to the commercial production of cotton and to the maintenance and expansion of slavery), the acceleration of all types of commercial agriculture (and the consequent stagnation of subsistence farming in New England and Appalachia), the westward expansion into the Northwest territory and beyond, and rapid population growth and urban growth.[5] Consequences of these changes for the relations of production are immediate: the emergence of an urban industrial proletariat, the declining importance of the subsistence farmer, the expansion of slavery, and the emergence of a southern "slavocracy," the transfer of political and economic power in Northern cities from the mercantile elite to an industrial bourgeoisie—these are some of the major changes in the class system.[6] These changes must be understood as the background of the major types of social movements in the period.

We will be concerned primarily with three types of movements; very briefly with the nascent organization of urban workingmen, with widespread utopian experimentation and with the paradoxical phenomenon known as Jacksonian democracy.

WORKINGMEN'S MOVEMENTS

We begin our discussion of social movements in the years between 1800 and 1850, with a brief consideration of the movements of poorer urban people who begin the era as mechanics and end it (their ranks swollen with immigrants) as proletarians. Their organizations are expressions of class discontent simpler than the more complex and heterogeneous phenomena of Jacksonian democracy and utopian experimentation. Furthermore, they are relatively quiet and insulated from other classes during this period, in contrast to the much more militant radicalism of their European contemporaries that culminated in the broadbased revolutions of 1848.

Two aspects of the variety of workers' movements are particularly important. First, these organizations faced backward towards the mechanics' associations of the revolutionary period. There was a certain amount of historical continuity between the revolutionary workingmen's clubs and the workingmen's parties and factions within parties of the Jacksonian period; perhaps Tammany Hall is the most famous of these old, more or less institutionalized, urban political clubs. Furthermore, the composition of workingmen's movements was still substantially a preindustrial one. The members were often artisans or "mechanics" working in relatively small establishments. Nevertheless, a second feature of the workingmen's associations is a clear forerunner of the shape that movement organization was to take in America; in goals and tactics, the associations were moderate and reformist. They experimented with two major strategies of American movements: organization to make economic demands on employers and organization to gain power within the party system, both as separate parties and as factions within the Republican (later Democrat) party. They did not organize as a mass movement of opposition to the entire class and political structure of the society. Thus, they accepted the employer-employee relationship (although they tried to ameliorate it) and the growth of political parties within the liberal framework. A brief chronology follows:[7]

1827   A carpenters' strike that occurs in Philadelphia for a ten-hour day is unsuccessful but leads to formation of a Philadelphia-wide organization, the Mechanics Union of Trade Associations.

1828–34   Rise of sixty-one workingmen's parties and sixty-eight labor newspapers.

1829   Six thousand workers meet to protest lengthening of work hours from ten to eleven and create a new party. The work hour protest is successful; one candidate is elected to the State Assembly from New York City; several more are elected upstate.

1830   Unionists in New York and elsewhere march in support of the French Revolution of 1830.

1830   In Philadelphia and elsewhere, workingmen's parties operate as a faction of Democrats. By 1831, these groups have really ceased to be a political movement. The demise of workers' parties is hastened by the end of the 1828–31 depression.

1833–34   Successful strikes for wages and shorter hours occur throughout the Northeast.

1835   Workingmen form radical factions within the Democratic Party, especially the "Locofocos." Massive demonstrations are

held to support strikers and to gain the acquittal of twenty-five union tailors convicted of conspiracy.
1836   Equal Rights Party is formed as a radical challenge to the Democrats in the Northeast.
1837–40   A great depression creates fierce competition for jobs and widespread hardships, which weaken and destroy the unions.
1840   Dorr uprising in which a radical dual convention drafts a "Peoples Constitution" takes place in Rhode Island; although martial law is declared and Dorr is sentenced to life imprisonment, Rhode Island does grant free suffrage and drops its property qualification.

The gains of these interrelated movements were twofold. First, they swept away the remnants of suffrage restrictions and made American workers a major force within the political system. No elections could be won without some appeal to propertyless (and petty-bourgeois) urbanites in the Northeast. The political participation of the worker in the United States was in marked contrast to his lengthy exclusion from politics in much of Western Europe and all of Eastern Europe. Political liberalism—the opportunity to participate in elections and political parties—was realized for virtually all white males in America.

Second, these movements attained some social and economic reforms. As reform movements, they acted by petitioning and pressuring those in power rather than by seizing the decision-making apparatus themselves. In this manner, they gained higher wages, shorter hours, the end of imprisonment for debt, the abolition of the militia system, and free public schools. They were influential in the movement against the national bank, but were unsuccessful in their opposition to the legal decisions that established the basis of corporations. Like the Jeffersonians, they won when they fought for formal political participation and lost when they opposed the institutional structure of industrial capitalism. But they did succeed in winning the first of a long series of decisions that ameliorated and softened the harshness of employer-employee relationships by more equitable income distribution, better working conditions and the opening of paths of individual upward mobility (in the school system, above all).

UTOPIAN EXPERIMENTS

The utopian experiments were as nonviolent and superficially legitimate as the workingmen's associations. In their class basis, they were very heterogeneous; they were a multiclass withdrawal from early industrial capitalism rather than a class-based movement against it. In their value system, if not their tactics, they were very hostile to it. In these respects, the Utopians of the first half of the nineteenth century provided some striking parallels to the communalists of present-day America.

Three major streams feed into the spurt of communal experimentation that resulted in the establishment of several hundred communities. One was a religious current with its sources still in the whirlpool of early Protestantism: in this general movement we can include the Shakers, Harmony, Amana, various Anabaptist groups, and the Mormons. These communities were often quite rigid, antiliberal and antiindividualistic in structure and value system. Frequently, they imposed various types of abstinence on their members—abstention from alcohol, meat or tobacco, celibacy, or prolonged sexual abstinence, and plain dress. They were held together by ritual, and by various mechanisms of psychological surrender of new members to the groups; special supernatural powers were ascribed to the leadership; the daily round was strictly scheduled, as illustrated by the following instructions to Shakers: [At the first trump (bell)] . . . put your right foot out of bed first. Place your right knee where your foot first touched the floor in kneeling to pray. Do not speak, but if absolutely necessary whisper to the room leader.[8]

Intellectuals were a second element in utopian experimentation. With the linked rise of industrial capitalism and political egalitarianism, intellectuals had been dislodged from their association with the mercantile New England elite; and as the South expanded westward and developed into a cotton-growing region, the landowning radical intellectuals of the revolutionary era were swamped by the rather superficially cultured Southern planter. Thus, the Jacksonian period was one of withdrawal of intellectuals from politics; some of their energy was channeled into utopian experimentation. Best known of these rather individualistic intellectual communities was Brook Farm, where seventy participants (more or less) limited work to ten hours a day, supported all the children, the old, and the sick, created a very influential school, enjoyed a constant stream of intellectual visitors, and numbered among its members leading New England intellectuals. About thirty-five of these intellectual communities (including Brook Farm in its last two years) were based on the principles of the French Utopian planner, Fourier. Interesting tenets governed Bronson Alcott's Fruitlands (a food faddism based on the avoidance of all animal substances and root crops and the eschewal of manure because its use in farming would "force nature"), Oneida (promiscuity and prolonged intercourse without male orgasm), and Modern Times (individualist anarchism and labor exchange based on production time). With isolated exceptions—Oneida for one—these communes did not last long. Some succumbed to the hostility of the environment, their founders' lack of agricultural experience, and natural disasters (especially fires); others ended in quarrels or peaceably disintegrated. The very features that made them attractive—intellectual liveliness, eccentricity, individualism, hostility toward monotony and drudgery—made them vulnerable and hastened their end. Religious communities were generally more long-lived precisely because they were disciplined and rigid.[9] Nevertheless, only the inveterate positivist would write off the intellectual communes as failures. Most were short-lived and as a movement, they completely failed to transform American industrial capitalism into a technologically sophisticated, rurally based cooperative social order, but for the individual, they provided experiences of cooperation and experimentation and an opportunity to develop an alternative to contemporary conditions. I contend that a similar judgment will be made of the communal experiments of the 1960s and 70s. Alone, they cannot transform society; they are too few, too limited to middle-class intellectuals, and ultimately too dependent on the amused tolerance of conventional society. Even as single units, few will survive, yet they are important as tiny laboratories in which men can dream about alternatives and pick and choose the most humane elements from advanced technology and primitive culture.

A third element in communal experimentation was the effort to combine the intellectuals' utopias with more solidly working class-based socialist and cooperative ventures. Robert Owen and his son, Robert Dale Owen, are leading figures in these ventures. Most were also unsuccessful in concrete terms (although perhaps enormously exhilarating and enjoyable for individuals). Best known of these experiments is the socialist community at New Harmony, Indiana. It had 800 members and rose and fell in the 1820s. A more modest and less physically isolated effort in creating communities of laborers was the establishment of cooperatives in the 1840s and '50s by iron molders in Cincinnati, foundrymen in Pittsburgh, nail cutters in Wheeling, seamstresses in Boston, Philadelphia and Providence, and consumers throughout the Midwest. But all of these failed by the Civl War. The lack of any government support (in the form of low-cost loans, for instance) was certainly a factor, but equally important, perhaps, was the ideology of upward mobility and individualism; as we have seen, even the advances of the labor associations were not in the area of cooperative solidarity as much as in the increase of well-being and opportunity. Nevertheless all of these religious and secular communities are important as providing the only alternatives to liberal capitalism in the first half of the nineteenth century.

THE BROADER CONTEXT: SOCIAL MOVEMENTS AND JACKSONIAN DEMOCRACY

Our description of movements of the first half of the nineteenth century left out at least three other interesting movements: the women's movement that officially began at the Seneca Falls convention of 1848 and can best be understood as a component of the general drive for political participation; the movements of resistance among Indians; and the movements among Anglo settlers in Texas (1836) and California (1846) whose demands for independence from Mexico precipitated the sequence of events that led to American seizure of these areas. The Indian and settler movements can best be understood as aspects of the "Manifest Destiny" movement, a broad ideological expression of Western settlers' desire for more land and national strength.

All of these diverse movements must be placed in the larger context of American society between 1800 and 1850. It was a relatively quiet period for social movements. The violence, class consciousness, and experimentation with dual political structures that characterized the colonial period had passed. Abolitionism and labor organization were beginning, but were not major movements during most of the earlier part of the period under consideration. Although the movements of this era were not particularly spectacular, it was an important period for social change in America for two reasons. First, as we have already seen, the substructural changes that created the conditions for later movements occurred. Second, some of the basic strategies of American movements were first established in this period as a concomitant of political democratization; thus, movements adopted reform tactics, became pressure groups within the major parties or third parties that were *in effect* pressure groups directed against one of the major parties, brought economic pressure to bear against employers, and withdrew into utopian experimentation. The strategies of violence and dual political structures of the colonial era disappeared and were replaced by more reformist tactics of campaigning, party politics, and strikes; radicalism was expressed in communal withdrawal, where it was stripped of its class base. Parallel to these tactical changes were changes in ideology; to some degree, the language of class consciousness remained, but it had to be accommodated to action *within* the legitimate political structures. Demands were oriented toward better working and living conditions and more opportunities rather than toward violent overthrow of the elites. Liberalism meant political inclusion and a program of state support for entrepreneurs and those who hoped to become entrepreneurs. With mass entry into politics came a genteel withdrawal of intellectuals from politics (and into individual protest and communal experimentation), which paralleled the gradual relinquishing of political and even economic power by the Northeastern mercantile elite to a new elite of industrial entrepreneurs.[10]

In retrospect, radicals deplored these changes in tactics (from class warfare and dual government to party politics and strikes) and in ideology (for liberal political and economic demands wiped out even the vestiges of "leveling" rhetoric). They saw these changes as bulwarks of class oppression and cognitive manipulation. But from the point of view of individual participants in the situation, these tactics of moderation, this respect for political legitimacy, and this belief in individual mobility all made sense. What objectively, collectively, and historically led to capitalist hegemony could indeed rationally be welcomed and furthered by each individual. In the words of Harriet Martineau, an astute British traveler who visited the United States in 1834, "As a mere matter of convenience, it is shorter and easier to obtain property by enterprise and labour in the United States, than by pulling down the wealthy."[11]

From our discussion of social movements in early nineteenth century America, we have gained some insight into the "Jacksonian paradox" as a whole. Its paradoxical elements become clearer once we make the distinction between structure and ideology, and the distinction between political structure and class structure. When these distinctions are made, we are no longer puzzled by the coexistence of the struggling farmer's support for Jackson and Jackson's support for the new industrial capitalist. All of them—farmers, industrialists, and Jackson himself—pictured themselves as entrepreneurs and what they expected was state support for economic opportunities. Such support would necessarily bring industrial capitalists into occasional conflict with mercantile capitalists, in which case the Jacksonian administrations generally interceded on the side of the former.[12] Jacksonian support aided the petty-bourgeoisie hopefuls in their fight against the established bourgeoisie and extended aid to some of the weakened and diminishing classes, especially the Eastern subsistence farmer. Jacksonian victory was made possible by, and in turn accelerated, these tendencies in politics as well as in economics: widespread participation—often in superficial ways; a spoils system of competition rather than ascribed elite control; and as necessary corollaries, the disappearance of the mechanisms of public balloting, property qualifications, and appointments that had sustained the mercantile elite. In many respects, the Jacksonian period is a forecast of the Progressive Era and the New Deal (and, to some extent, of the Kennedy administration). Movements during these eras took a reformist course. They had major impacts on political structures, but, often unintentionally, their overall outcome was to use the state to bolster and support certain substructural tendencies. In the Jacksonian period, the substructural shift was one from mercantile to industrial capitalism; in the Progressive era, it was a step towards monopoly capital; and in the New Deal, toward the fusion of the state and the private sector. Yet each of these reformist movements also included elements of income redistribution, protection of the public from a variety of abuses, a sense of greater participation in government, and even a somewhat radical rhetoric. (This reflection may remind the reader of our discussion of the Jeffersonian period where essentially Federalist programs of support for industrial capitalism were carried out in an atmosphere of reform and political democracy). Thus, we are introduced to a central phenomenon in American movement history—movements with the following characteristics:

1. Reformist tactics;
2. An impact on the political system in the form of extension of participation;
3. Co-optability (inherent in reformist tactics), adherence to liberal ideology and political legitimacy; and
4. Partially unanticipated acceleration of substructural potentials by creating favorable political conditions.

The causes of the onset of this pattern in the early nineteenth century are the exhaustion of the revolutionary impulse in war and depression, the establishment of a political and legal system that unintentionally generated a two-party system, the withdrawal of intellectuals from politics (narrowly defined), and the prevalence of a liberal entrepreneurial ideology (which in this period still strongly corresponded to individual experience).

NOTES

[1] Based on Crevecoeur's description of post-Revolutionary America as a society that began in a state of perfection.

[2] Staughton Lynd, "The Tenant Uprising at Livingstone Manor, 1777," in *Class Conflict, Slavery and the U.S. Constitution* (Indianapolis: Bobbs-Merrill, 1967).

[3] Arrayed against the Jeffersonians were not only the federalist industrialists, but, to a large extent, also their employee, the urban northern "mechanic," an incipient proletarian who had supported the Constitution and was viewed with disfavor by supporters of yeoman farmers and of slavery. See Staughton Lynd, *Anti-Federalism in Dutchess County* (New York: Loyola Press, 1962).

[4] Louis Hartz, *The Liberal Tradition in America* (New York: Harcourt, Brace & World, 1955).

[5] Charles Beard and Mary Beard, *A Basic History of the United States* (Philadelphia: Blakiston, 1944), Chapter XIII.

[6] Based on Beard and Beard, *op. cit.*, Chapters XIII and XIV; and Robert Dahl, *Who Governs?* (New Haven, Conn.: Yale University Press, 1961), Book I.

[7] Based on Sidney Lens, *Radicalism in America* (New York: Crowell, 1966), Chapters V and VI.

[8] Rosabeth Moss Kanter, "Commitment and Social Organization," *American Sociological Review* 33, no. 4 (August 1968): 515.

[9] *Ibid.*

[10] Lens, *op. cit.*, pp. 72–73; and Dahl, *op. cit.*

[11] Harriet Martineau, *Society in America* (New York: AMS Press, 1837), Vol. I, p. 23.

[12] Two important Jacksonian decisions will support this contention. One is the decision by the Jackson-appointed Supreme Court majority to permit the building of a new bridge over the Charles River despite the objections of the investors in the toll bridge which had hitherto enjoyed a monopoly. "Taney's majority decision was a plea for the public interest, for technological progress and fresh enterprise." [Richard Hofstadter, *The American Political Tradition and the Men Who Made It* (New York: Knopf, 1948), p. 60.]

More famous is Jackson's veto of the National bank recharter. Let Jackson and Hofstadter speak for themselves:

"The social indictment of the bank was inclusive: it was a monopoly, a grant of exclusive privilege; the whole American people were excluded from competition in the sale of the privilege, and the government thus received less than it was worth; a fourth of the bank's stock was held by foreigners, the rest by 'a few hundred of our citizens, chiefly of the richest class'; it was a menace to the country's liberty and independence. At the end the President launched into a forthright statement of the social philosophy of the Jacksonian movement:

" 'It is to be regretted that the rich and powerful too often bend the acts of government to their selfish purposes. Distinctions in society will always exist under every just government. Equality of talents, of education, or of wealth cannot be produced by human institutions. In the full enjoyment of the gifts of Heaven and the fruits of superior industry, economy, and virtue, every man is equally entitled to protection by law; but when the laws undertake to add to these natural and just advantages artificial distinctions, to grant titles, gratuities, and exclusive privileges, to make the rich richer and the potent more powerful, the humble members of society—the farmers, mechanics, and laborers—who have neither the time nor the means of securing like favors to themselves, have a right to complain of the injustice of their Government. There are no necessary evils in government. Its evils exist only in its abuses. If it would confine itself to equal protection, and, as Heaven does its rains, shower its favors alike on the high and the low, the rich and the poor, it would be an unqualified blessing.'

"Certainly this is not the philosophy of a radical leveling movement that proposes to uproot property or to reconstruct society along drastically different lines. It proceeds upon no Utopian premises—full equality is impossible, 'distinctions will always exist,' and reward should rightly go to 'superior industry, economy, and virtue.' What is demanded is only the classic bourgeois ideal, equality before the law, the restriction of government to equal protection of its citizens. This is the philosophy of a rising middle class; its aim is not to throttle but to liberate business, to open every possible pathway for the creative enterprise of the people. Although the Jacksonian leaders were more aggressive than the Jeffersonians in their crusades against monopoly and 'the paper system,' it is evident that the core of their philosophy was the same: both aimed to take the grip of government-granted privileges off the natural economic order." [*Ibid.*, pp. 88–89.]

5

The Second American Revolution?

INTRODUCTION

I will begin this chapter with a brief summary of my understanding of the Civil War.[1]

First, the North and the West, combined, and the South were two distinct social systems, different in productive systems, class structure, and ideology although unified under the federal government. The North was a bourgeois capitalist society with a liberal ideology, an industrial entrepreneurial class, and free urban workers; the West was more agrarian, but shared the liberal ethos and the fundamental institution of free labor. On the other hand, the South was an altogether different society. Its central productive system was commercial agriculture, especially the cultivation of cotton. Although it had a large number of subsistence farmers, these farmers were economically marginal to southern enterprise and, as we shall see, politically and ideologically accommodating to the slaveholders. The central relation of production was slavery. Less than a quarter of the South's 1.6 million white families (in 1860) owned the four million slaves and only one in ten farmers had twenty or more slaves. These facts can be reworded: one out of every two persons in the South was either a slave or a member of a slaveholding family.[2] Not only economically (as the source of the exportable surplus and as the labor force on the most valuable farms), but also in terms of individual experience, slavery was a dominant feature of southern life.

Second, the southern social order was a slavocracy. A slavocracy is a social system in which the central class relationship is that of master and slave and the main economic incentives are fear of violence on the part of the slave and profit on the part of the Master. Thus, in no sense is a slavocracy "feudal," for the master-slave relationship is essentially one of property ownership, not of control over serfs as a corporate group of human beings. Furthermore, profit is an important aim in a slaveocracy but not in feudal society. Finally, all known (post-classical) instances of slavocracies also have been based on racial differences between master and slave.

Third, substructural differences between northern capitalism and southern slavocracy were *not* a necessary cause of the war. There was no logical necessity to open hostility between the two social orders, no inevitability of conflict. Quite to the contrary; the experience of European colonialism shows that an industrial and liberal metropolitan country is not only compatible with but actually dependent on a mild "slavocracy" in its colonies (indentured servitude or involuntary labor taxes by a dark skinned population). Of course, one may counter that metropolitan industry and colonial raw material production are in harmony only because they do not exist within the same territory. In the case of South Africa, industrial capitalism and "pigmentocracy" (using essentially unfree black labor) are completely fused.[3] In this sense, it is perhaps even erroneous to think of southern slavocracy as a non-feudal pre-bourgeois society. The destruction of this particular slavocracy by a bourgeois democracy does not support the conclusion that the destruction of slavocracy was an inevitable or even the probable outcome of such contact. Slavocracy is not pre-bourgeois in the sense that it is frequently destroyed by a bourgeois society or in the sense that it is a predecessor of bourgeois societies in a given territory. The two orders can exist contemporaneously with relatively slight conflict and considerable mutual dependence. In colonial expansion, bourgeois societies may even generate slaveocracies and, in this way, be chronologically and causally prior to them. Globally, true slavocracies have disappeared and the colonial quasi-slavocracies (such as in Angola, for example) have diminished in number. In a historical and statistical sense, they are indeed a more archaic form than bourgeois societies are. In the particular circumstances of nineteenth century America, in *this* historical situation, the two social orders did engage in mortal combat; the outcome of war is a possible, but not necessary, result of the contact of capitalism and slavocracy.[4]

Fourth, the clash occurred because each social order generated an ideology (and social movements, in a broad sense) that forced showdowns in the political sphere. The war resulted from failures in political mechanisms of compromise and accommodation. Specifically, southern fears that Republicans would use the federal machinery against slavery led to the immediate cause of the war—secession.

Earlier we remarked that ideology tends to be an epiphenomenon of social (class and political) structure. Nevertheless, in the case under consideration, two distinct class situations generate conflicting ideologies; these have a divisive and ultimately shattering impact on the unitary political system. Here, then, is a special situation in which belief systems affect the political structure. We are hardly justified in calling these belief systems "ideologies" (except in a very loose sense) because the competition between them weakens their power as prevailing cognitive ordering devices. (Marx believed that this cognitive competition also prevails in a society on the eve of revolution, at that instant when a revolutionary belief system already exists and is just beginning to claim the universality that has heretofore been asserted only for the ideas of the ruling class.) Certainly, neither the belief system of the North or the South is the basis of hegemony for the whole American society on the eve of the Civil War; by definition, no hegemony exists when classes and/or substructurally distinct regions are in declared conflict with one another.

Fifth, we are concerned here with three ideologies; an especially militant bourgeois liberalism that can be identified with the Radical Republicans and appeared relatively late in the ante-bellum period (later than the other two belief systems) and provided the ideological thrust that makes the Civil War the "last bourgeois revolution" or the "Second American Revolution;"[5] the second ideology under consideration is that of the South; and the third is that of abolitionism. Each of these can in some sense be identified with a movement. We will now examine these ideologies and their movements in detail. To some extent, each of the last two ideologies is based on sources external to Lockeian liberalism; each of the two was adopted by the wider population only in an attenuated liberalized form. But in some sense, it is correct to see the "irrepressible conflict" as arising from two major ideologies of opposition to the liberal consensus.[6] Thus, those who explain the Civil War as a result of moral causes are correct, although the moral causes can only be fully understood in terms of the class sources from which these class-based moral causes developed. These causes developed into a struggle over the political apparatus of the state.

THE ABOLITIONISTS

In examining Abolitionism, we turn once again to the preliberal and presecularized denominational sources of American social movements—in this case, the Quaker movement especially. The Quakers provided a hard core of abolitionist thought and action. Their ranks were swelled by members of other faiths—Baptists (William Lloyd Garrison), Unitarians (Channing), Calvinists (Wendell Phillips), and Methodists (Orange Scott), to name only a few. The important point is that the Quakers provided historical continuity between post-Reformation radicalism in the seventeenth century and abolitionism as a social movement (which can be dated to the 1820s or early 1830s). Second, the religious sources of abolitionism provide the movement with extra-liberal intensity, contempt for political forms, and rhetoric. Naturally, liberals were appalled at the excesses of slavery. They welcomed its end in the North and hoped to see it disappear from the South (as indeed it might have done were it not for the cotton gin and the expansion of cotton production). But they were loath to interfere with the institution of private property in slaves and to violate Constitutional protection of slavery. Furthermore, they vacillated between viewing the black man as a piece of property and as a human being who must be accorded full political rights; not only did this double image lead liberals into contradictory demands for action (as liberals, they were committed both to property and to political equality), but also placed them into cognitive confusion, which was especially exacerbated by the existence of black freedmen and later led into extensive debates over the biological inferiority of blacks.[7]

Thus, in the United States, only an extra-liberal ideology could thoroughly lead men into abolitionism (just as only an extra-liberal ideology could fully justify slavery, as we shall see). This extra-liberal ideology was provided primarily by the remnants of post-Reformation religious radicalism in the Northeast. At the ideological level, some brief quotations will convey the full religious quality, the flavor of chiliasm applied to a this-worldly cause. With the doctrine of inner light (or some slightly secularized version of it), the specious debates over property and the presumed biological inferiority of blacks could simply be swept away; these questions became meaningless once the liberal mode of discourse was replaced by the inner light frame of reference.

Thus, in 1829, Garrison (perhaps the foremost figure of abolitionism) declared: "On a question of shame and honor—liberty and oppression—reasoning is sometimes useless, and worse. I feel the decision in my pulse: if it throws no light upon the brain, it kindles a fire at the heart." He wrote:

> I will be as harsh as truth, and as uncompromising as justice. On this subject, I do not wish to think, or speak, or write, with moderation. No! no! Tell a man, whose house is on fire, to give a moderate alarm; tell him to moderately rescue his wife from the hands of the ravisher; tell the mother to gradually extricate her babe from the fire into which it has fallen; but urge me not to use moderation in a cause like the present! I am in earnest. I will not equivocate—I will not excuse—I will not retreat a single inch—AND I WILL BE HEARD. The apathy of the people is enough to make every statue leap from its pedestal, and to hasten the resurrection of the dead.
>
> . . . How do I bear up under my adversities? I answer—like the oak—like the Alps—unshaken, storm-proof. Opposition, and abuse, and slander, and prejudice, and judicial tyranny, are like oil to the flame of my zeal. I am not dismayed; but bolder and more confident than ever. I say to my persecutors, "I bid you defiance." Let the courts condemn me to fine and imprisonment for denouncing oppression: Am I to be frightened by dungeons and chains? can they humble my spirit? do I not remember that I am an American citizen? and, as a citizen, a freeman, and what is more, a being accountable to God? I will not hold my peace on the subject of African oppression. If need be, who would not die a martyr to such a cause? [8]

Wendell Phillips drew on Calvinist imagery: "No matter if the Charter of emancipation was written in blood and anarchy stalks abroad with giant strides—if God commanded, it was right." [9]

Phillips' association with Abolitionism came as a conversion experience that rescued him from a depression and a lack of the sense of vocation. In 1841, he wrote "None know what it is to live till they redeem life from its seeming monotony by laying it a sacrifice on the altar of some great cause." [10]

Weld, the Western abolitionist, also commented on this aspect: "Great moral reforms are all born of soul-travail. The starting point and power of every great reform must be the reformer's self. He must first set himself apart its sacred devotee, baptised into its spirit, consecrated to its service, feeling its profound necessity, its constraining motives, impelling causes, and all reasons why." [11]

The tradition of the chiliastic apocalypse reached its peak in the life of John Brown, where it was expressed in violence. Emerson described Brown as "that new saint who will make the gallows glorious like the cross." (It must be remembered that Emerson himself belonged to the Transcendentalist intellectual movement that was strongly influenced by the inner light doctrine and rejected Locke's views on psychology.) [12]

Small wonder that liberal historians have detested the Quakers,[13] portrayed the Abolitionists as fanatics, neurotics, and madmen, and castigated their present-day radical heirs as proto-fascists. These are typical "objective" debunking responses to a cognitive order different from one's own, and a way of maintaining an air of value-freeness about slavery.

The radical-Protestant sources of Abolitionism must not, of course, be overestimated. Some abolitionists were quite secular in their beliefs (for instance, Lundy, an early supporter of Garrison) and drew on the Declaration of Independence and Lockeian doctrines. Furthermore, religious rhetoric was widespread throughout the United States and was used by the opponents of abolitionism as well as its adherents.

But the argument of historical continuity and the examination of the social sources of abolitionism again draw us to the conclusion that this movement had roots outside liberal ideology. As early as the Colonial period, Quakers objected to slavery; in 1790, the Society of Friends and the Pennsylvania Society of Promoting the Abolition of

Slavery submitted two petitions against slavery to Congress, the former in religious language, the second in more secular tones. Quakers were among the few who wrote against slavery between 1790 and 1830 in America, had key roles in the British antislavery movement of the period, and engaged in antislavery political action (such as the election of Congressmen). In the late 1820s a more or less secularized Quaker, Benjamin Lundy, was publishing the only antislavery newspaper in the United States.[14]

Beyond the central founding core of Quakers, the abolition movement attracted committed followers from among Baptists and Methodists (whence came its leaders of laboring background, such as Orange Scott and Garrison, as well as Baptist and Methodist clergymen from better-off families) and the New England intellectual community. The relationships between abolitionists, utopian experimenters, and more or less independent New England intellectuals are manifold; certain names—Thoreau, Emerson, Bronson Alcott, John Noyes, William Ellery Channing, James Russell Lowell—appear over and over again in accounts of the movements of the period. The reader can perhaps best capture for himself the spirit of the period by reviewing his knowledge of the interplay between civil rights movements, the Anti-Vietnam War movement, the political radicalism of the late 1960s, and the communal experiments; where contemporary movements include millions, nineteenth century movements were much smaller and more regionally and (to some degree) class confined. One cannot dismiss the abolitionism (or the utopianism) of Northeastern intellectuals as a false consciousness, a "status" movement by an ex-elite that was irascible and confused over its loss of power. The movement presented genuine arguments against and alternatives to the liberal capitalism that it implicitly (and sometimes explicitly) attacked; it did not harp on the futile issue of its past elite status or attempt to bring back a mercantile hegemony. Unlike dispossessed classes that we will discuss later, the class with which we are here concerned was able to develop a belief system that had liberating effects on American political action.

The chiliastic extra-liberal roots of abolitionism had a rather deleterious impact on tactics, however. At the most abstract level, sufficient numbers of abolitionists (above all, the Anti-Slavery Society when Garrison dominated it) were affected by Quaker and Perfectionist doctrines to eschew violence (as pacifists), to eschew political action (because it was confined by the legal forms of the Constitution and by the reality of popular indifference to the slavery issue), and, in general, to engage only in moralizing action. For this wing, Abolitionism was above all a moral crusade carried on in the pulpit and the newspaper and by courageous "bearing of witness" in the hands of mobs and before judges (for resistance to unjust laws was an important element of this approach). Garrison was quite willing to dissolve the Union. Although the Garrisonians aided fugitive slaves and worked for an end to Northern discrimination, their main task was defined by Abby Kelly in 1847 as follows: "Our work is to inculcate these great truths, the right of man to Freedom, the Atrocious sin of Slavery, and the duty of ceasing to give it support, whether in Church or in State." [15] The core movement organizations of this wing were the Anti-Slavery Society and the staff of the *Liberator*, but even these groups were by no means united on tactics and within the broad strategy of extra-legal nonviolent resistence, was to be found a diversity of methods, including boycotts of goods produced by slave labor, pamphleteering, and petitioning. Women, who were barred by law and custom from electoral political action, were especially prominent in this agitational wing.

A second wing of the movement was directed toward political action and constituted itself as the Liberty Party in 1844. Its failure to gain more than 65,000 votes out of the 2.5 million cast that year was discouraging.

The political arena was entered more conservatively by the Free Soil party and by numerous single-issue protests against the extension of slavery in the territories, the Fugitive Slave law, the Dred Scott decision, and so forth.

A third major effort was directed at helping slaves flee to freedom (preferably to Canada); an estimated 2,000 persons per year attained their liberty during the peak years of the Underground Railway, the network of secret way stations and courageous sympathizers. The total number of fugitives who successfully escaped may have been as high as 40,000 or more.[16]

A fourth effort was that of organizing for economic equality among free blacks in the North. Black Abolitionists turned in increasing numbers to the task of building their own institutions—including newspapers and periodicals—and even flirted with emigration. Part of their disillusionment with Garrisonian Abolitionism was expressed in political activity (voting, for one) and in demands for *violent* resistance to the Fugitive Slave law and slavery in general. Some white abolitionists also involved themselves primarily in the problems of the free black man's economic and social exclusion and in the difficulties faced by the newly emancipated slaves in the 1860s (but now we are getting ahead of our story).[17]

The small faction of Abolitionists centered on John Brown were ready to meet the everyday violence of slavery with violence. They engaged in bloody small-scale warfare with the Border Ruffians, para-military units that had been harassing the Free Soilers in Kansas. In 1859, they attacked the Harpers Ferry arsenal in Virginia hoping to touch off slave revolts in the surrounding area and eventually guerrilla warfare throughout the South; hopes for a slave uprising failed to materialize, and John Brown was captured, tried, and hanged.

The diversity of Abolitionist tactics reflected a diversity of goals; some hoped for a forced instant emancipation, some accepted the prospect of gradual change; some were willing to compensate the slaveholders, others were not; some accepted the free black man as an equal, and others desired a long period of tutelage.

Two questions are extraordinarily applicable to both Abolitionism and the radical movements of the present. To what degree did the radicalism of Abolitionism (both the verbal radicalism of the Garrisonians and the violence of John Brown) hurt the Abolitionist cause? And to what degree did the factionalism and diversity of the movement impede its effort?

My own response to these two questions is that both radicalism and diversity were essential to the success of the movement. The movement had roughly the following structure: At its center were groups and organizations of fully committed Abolitionists, pursuing their aim as a calling. Surrounding this core were strong activist Abolitionists who did not see the movement as a full-time effort; among them were frequent attenders at meetings, participants in the operation of the Underground Railway, organizers of boycotts at the local level, key wealthy contributors, and so on. Beyond this level was the outer circle—persons who consumed Abolitionist media, offered occasional support, and accepted the label "Abolitionist." But beyond these truly Abolitionist supporters was a broad penumbra of persons who rejected the label "Abolitionist," did not read Abolitionist papers, did not actively participate in any way yet voted for anti-slavery parties and planks in increasing numbers during the fifties and sixties. It seems likely (but of course impossible to prove) that without the radical agitation of the fully committed Abolitionists, the rest of the northern population would not have become aware of the issues at all, would not have lent any support to the Free Soil and later the Republican party, and would not have had access to a public language for formulating a vague private disapproval of slavery. Once the issue of the inhumanity of slavery (and its lack of obvious economic benefit to the northern farmer or small entrepreneur) was drawn to the nation's attention, growing hostility toward slavery was not difficult to arouse; the great enemy of Abolitionism in the North was not support for slavery, but the general tendency of the public to neglect an issue that had little immediate concrete significance for white northerners and that appealed little to patriotic sentiment.[18] The radicalism of the Garrisonians and even the violence of Brown had their most profound effect in forcing individuals to think about slavery (more explicitly and narrowly, the extension of slavery into the territories) and forcing the major parties to return to an issue that had been more or less plunged into obscurity for thirty or forty years. The activation of the penumbra and the transformation of abolitionism into an election issue were both absolutely essential for the abolitionist cause because until the issue became political (in a narrow sense), the crisis of control of the federal government and the direction of the Union could not occur. Thus, without the *moral* agitation of the abolitionists, the issue of slavery could not become an important election issue for the political parties; and until slavery generated *political* conflict, it could not be ended. That abolitionism could not short-circuit radical moral agitation and simply transform itself into a political body is demonstrated by the failure of such a premature strategy, the Liberty party of 1844. A mild-mannered agitation would also have been self-defeating; drama, oratory, and wrath were important in interesting the wider public in the issue. Anti-slavery speeches had a theatrical impact and were delivered by outstanding speakers (Wendell Phillips and Frederick Douglass were among the best). The techniques of outrageous invective (Daniel Webster was described as a "great mass of dough" by Phillips) and guerrilla theater (Henry Ward Beecher reenacted slave auctions) to attract the media and the public existed long before the Yippies appeared on the scene.[19] For individual abolitionists, radicalism brought beatings, persecution, and even death; but the movement as a whole could not have succeeded without outraging many and thereby drawing the attention of a silent, but eventually sympathetic, public to itself.

Diversity was also necessary. First of all, it provided the movement with a great many roles to offer potential activists and thus attracted fully and partially committed supporters who might not have worked with a movement that had a single tactic and a well-defined goal. Second, as I have argued above, both agitational and political (party) activity were necessary. The analogies to the movement of opposition to the war in Vietnam are left to the reader to construct as an exercise; the similarities are striking, but perhaps the issue itself (a foreign war), the nature of the federal government, and the nature of the media and the public have all changed so much that the lessons learned from Abolitionism cannot be readily transferred to the present.

Was a war in which 600,000 lives were lost necessary to stop the brutality and daily violence of slavery? Had the Abolitionists—many of them Quaker pacifists—no other hope of realizing their goal? To answer this question, we must turn to southern sectionalism as a social movement.

THE SOUTH

If we are to interpret the Civil War as the result of ideological conflict generated by two distinct economic systems and transposed into the political arena, we must turn to southern ideology and the southern secessionist movement.

Southern ideology remained a viewpoint without a movement until Republican capture of the federal machinery threatened to end the expansion and even the existence of the southern way of life.

Southern ideology was generated in its more sophisticated form by southern intellectuals, including a much larger component of university professors than that found in Abolitionism, but at a folk level, this ideology was recreated in the day to day experience of slaveholders.[20] One of the most remarkable aspects of southern ideology was its ready acceptance by prosperous non-slaveholding farmers, by the tiny stratum of southern industrialists, and even by subsistence farmers. Although these southern groups derived hardly more economic benefit from slavery than did the western farmers who opposed it, the southerners accepted the slaveowners' world view; this acceptance should alert us to the power of an ideology to shape the outlook of groups who benefit little from the class structure that the ideology supports. Of course, they obtained some daily gains over blacks in terms of deference and status.

Most southerners experienced no world beyond the one made by the slaveholders; economically, politically, and cognitively they had no choices and therefore demanded none. In this respect, we cannot write of a southern *movement* as we can write of an Abolitionist movement. A brief glance at the South's ideology is useful because without this unity of world view, there would have been no popularly supported movement for secession, an act that from the perspective of the Union was indeed a movement. The central core of southern ideology was as extra-liberal as the central historical core of Quaker (and other Dissenting) Abolitionism. Unlike the latter, it did not grow out of a continuous structure (like the Dissenting Communities of the Northeast, whose roots are in the Reformation); rather, southern ideology had to be created out of thin air, an extraordinarily difficult task for intellectuals who lacked our opportunity of hindsight. Generally, they failed to recognize their world in our terms—as a pigmentocratic slave system based on commercial agriculture and characterized by strong capitalist overtones but, in large part, lacking capitalism's democratic political form. They were additionally burdened by the fact that much of their audience was committed to a liberal humanitarianism and found slavery offensive. One model for their synthetic cognitive construction, therefore, was Athenian democracy, a system in which slave labor enabled a numerically substantial elite to develop participatory democracy. Obviously, the analogy is unsuitable for a wide variety of reasons, and southern intellectuals turned to contemporary European conservative thought. Nineteenth century European conservatism drew on feudalism and used the ascriptive corporate social order of feudalism as its model of the good society; thus, it opposed the alienation, pseudoindividualism, competition, openness, normative "thinness," and cultural leveling of capitalism to the communalness, collectivism, ascriptive rigidity, normative richness, and diversity of status and culture that characterized European feudalism. In an urbanizing and industrializing Europe, this dream was substructurally unrealistic but historically understandable. In America, the feudal model was even less realistic; southern slavery was not feudal and was as historically recent a development as was capitalism. Some feudal elements were present, of course—the patriarchal manor of the large plantation, the ascriptive rigidity of slavery, and the rural setting—but these alone do not constitute feudalism. They were coupled with racism, commercial farming, dependence on Britain (which was almost fully industrialized) as a purchaser of raw materials, and considerable adherence to bourgeois capitalist norms and political forms among the white master race.[21] The effort to create a feudal ideology for the South did generate a shrewd criticism of northern capitalism, but it also produced such bizarre cultural phenomena as the rage for Walter Scott among the more or less leisure class, the staging of tournaments and the adoption of the label "Southron," the imposition of practices of chivalry on southern women, and an excess of sentimental romanticism. These peculiarities existed at a fairly popular level; they coexisted with a folk culture of brutal familiarity toward blacks, everyday economic concerns, evangelical Protestantism, and the simple male pastimes of hunting, drinking and gambling. Nowhere is this incongruous blend better captured than in the chapter in *Huckleberry Finn* in which Huck stays with the Grangerfords, and describes for us their peculiar blend of frontier coarseness, sentimental romanticism, family feuding, and hospitality to a white stranger.

In a Fitzhugh or a Calhoun, these peculiar currents are more articulately presented—in Calhoun, mixed with a basically incongruous economic liberalism, and in Fitzhugh, not without a grotesque side. They do represent a genuine effort to create a new cognitive order for a basically noncapitalist society. They succeeded as popular rallying points (and in terms of social change what more success can one demand of an ideology?) and as critiques of capitalism; but in their own right, they are difficult for the modern American to take seriously. As we shall see, when hard-pressed during the upheaval of Reconstruction, southern ideology boiled down to oppression of the black man.[22]

The movement towards secession is more readily identifiable as a social movement because it had a component of political action. After thirty years of legitimate political struggle for southern advantages, southern political leaders felt defeated by the Republican victory in 1860; it is probably safe to state that the issue that led to the defeat of the Democrats was the extension of slavery to the territories and new states, for this question allowed voters to express their general hostility toward slavery (and toward blacks, an important component in the desire to confine slavery to the South). In the widespread support for secession (for southern Unionists constitute only a short chapter in the history of American dissent), we find it difficult to spot the coalition of class interests that along with a nationalist ideology were so central to the movement for American independence; here, there is no clear recognition of class interests except among the slaveholding elite. There is only a prevailing ideology, a not altogether unrealistic fear of blacks, and a willingness to follow the lead of the economic and political notables. The absence of class consciousness among southern whites can be traced to the fairly realistic dominance of racial identity, to the absence of an urban political culture, to the dominance of one crop and the class that lived off it (thus blotting out conflict among elite strata, which can serve as a powerful stimulant to anti-elite consciousness), and the geographic interlarding of different agricultural strata in much of the south that prevented the fusion of class and regional consciousness that had been so important in the colonial back country.

THE TRAGIC ERA

Here, we will address ourselves to the efforts of the Radical Republicans to engage in the "last capitalist revolution" [23] and the more successful efforts by southern whites of a variety of classes to build a counterrevolutionary movement.

We have seen how two substructurally different regions had distinct belief systems; in the North, Abolitionism competed with the liberal ideology and eventually was able to infuse it with antislavery ideas as abolitionism in turn used liberal thought to attack the South; in the South, straightforward economic motives combined with an extra-liberal southern ideology to create a strong southern sectional spirit. As these ideological conflicts were increasingly expressed in political conflict over concrete issues and specific elections, they were increasingly difficult for the federal machinery to contain. Secession brought about pro-Union feeling in the North and resulted in the Civil War to preserve the Union. With a Union victory, the stage was set for an elite revolution imposed on the South by the Radical Republicans in an effort to translate into structural transformations their dual values of black equality and industrial capitalism.

Such transformations were only partially accomplished. Immediate emancipation and suffrage for blacks was won; and the South was opened to railway interests and to the Pennsylvania iron and steel industry. (The Radical Republicans drew their electoral and financial support from northern workers who supported the Radical program of tariff protection and slow contraction of the war-inflated currency—although caring not at all about black rights—and by manufacturing and railroad interests; they were opposed by low-tariff-endorsing financial and commercial interests).[24] The Radical Republicans were unsuccessful where their goals clashed with liberal values: they failed to expropriate the southern landowners, to distribute the land to the freedman, and thereby simultaneously to depose the ruling class and to transform blacks into a propertied class of subsistence farmers. There were a series of experiments with confiscation, especially along the Atlantic seaboard, but they came to very little. Some of the land was indeed turned over to blacks, but much of it was later reclaimed, and some of it was made available to Yankee land speculators.[25] The liberal value of widespread property ownership clashed with liberal unwillingness to tamper with the prevailing property distribution and to confiscate the land of rebels for longer than one generation. In addition to Congressional opposition on the above grounds, the Radical program met opposition from the many northerners who were sympathetic to white southerners and/or vaguely contemptuous of blacks' capacity for independent farming. Even when military orders in favor of redistribution were made, lower level functionaries (such as the tax commissioners who were sent to the South Carolina Sea Islands) refused to carry them out.[26] Finally, the Radical Republicans' own liberal commitments made them very hesitant to distribute free land, an act that smacked of the paternalism that had sapped the blacks' independence during slavery. With fundamentally little northern support for expropriation and redistribution according to the principle "the soil belongs to the tiller," planters were left as a class that was temporarily impoverished by the war and with monumental debts, but not deprived of its ownership of what was still the South's chief resource. Original owners sometimes were bankrupt and their places were taken by Yankees or by formerly smaller-scale farmers, but as a *class*, landowners remained a central elite in the South. Blacks remained at the very bottom of the class structure—as landless laborers.

In this situation, it was relatively easy for white southerners to regain their *political* power. By the late 1860s and very decisively by the early 1870s, an organizationally strong white movement had developed whose constituent bodies were the Ku Klux Klan, the White Leagues, the Red Shirts, and the Democratic Clubs themselves. This movement used a variety of methods to force whites to vote for the Democrats and to prevent blacks from voting at all (after some experimentation with forcing blacks to support the Democrats): recalcitrants were denied employment and medical care; militia companies were formed to intimidate blacks at the polls and invade Republican meetings; riots, beginning with the Meridian, Mississippi riot of 1871, were a favorite weapon, resulting in the shooting of hundreds of blacks and many white Republicans; and lynchings of individual leaders occurred. There is ample evidence to support the contention that this essentially terrorist movement included all classes of whites, that younger men and boys of the propertied groups were as keen on taking part in its violent actions as were poor whites, that poor whites in turn were quite ready to subordinate to their racial ties any class interests that they shared with blacks, and that the southern newspapers supported the movement. Clearly, some of the "better elements" may have deprecated the use of violence, and many poor whites may have abstained from participation (but did not speak out against the suppression of black people's civil rights until Southern Populism once more opened the door to a black-poor white alliance).[27] Ironically, the effective, broad-based, and terroristic dual organization of the southern counterrevolution was not at all dissimilar to the broad-based coercive dual organization of the American Revolution. As a social movement, the southern counterrevolution was extraordinarily successful; in addition to its organizational strength, it was well timed to coincide with a weakness in Republican electoral strength that forced the Republicans to soft-peddle support for blacks, refuse to protect black rights in the South, and, ultimately, to withdraw federal troops from the South.

Given the nature of American Congressional politics, the Radical Republicans were not responsible for the failure of land reform in the South; political support for land reform was too limited. Both Radical Republicans and more militant friends of blacks also failed to build organizations among the black population that could have withstood the white supremacist movement and secured the lives and civil rights of blacks.

Reconstruction as a revolution remained limited in its transformation of southern social structure; after the success of the southern counterrevolutionary movement, it produced as net gains emancipation, the guarantees of the Fourteenth[28] and Fifteenth Amendments (which were not de facto extended to most southern blacks, however), and the grafting of industrial capitalism onto the pigmentocratic commercial agriculture of the South.

NOTES

[1] Barrington Moore, Jr., *The Social Origins of Dictatorship and Democracy* (Boston: Beacon Press, 1966), Chapter III; Eugene Genovese, *The Political Economy of Slavery* (New York: Random House, 1965); and *The World the Slaveholders Made* (New York: Random House, 1969).

[2] Carl Degler, *Out of Our Past*, rev. ed. (New York: Harper & Row, 1970), p. 163.

[3] Leonard Thompson, "The South African Dilemma," in Louis Hartz, ed., *The Founding of New Societies* (New York: Harcourt, Brace & World, 1964).

[4] The South African case is extraordinarily instructive. Superficially, the Boer War looks like a victory of capitalism over a very primitive (non-profit-seeking) slavocracy; but less than two generations later, an indigenous—rather than metropolitan—capitalism had become merely the productive substructure for a slavocratic system of labor recruitment, social control, and ideology. The forms of bourgeois democracy are turned into grotesque caricatures by their confinement to the ruling race. Equal opportunity—supposedly a cornerstone of a modern industrial society—is entirely subordinated to an effort to bind class to race. In these respects, the results of the Boer War have been reversed. That this bizarre hybrid may come to a bloody end is not to deny that it has already existed for a generation. The fact that it exists refutes any unqualified designations of slaveocracy as prebourgeois or any claims that industrialization wipes out pigmentocracy. See Thompson, *op. cit.*, and Moore, *op. cit.*

[5] Charles Beard and Mary Beard, *A Basic History of the United States* (Philadelphia: Blakiston, 1944); and Moore, *op. cit.*

[6] Louis Hartz, *The Liberal Tradition in America* (New York: Harcourt, Brace & World, 1955), Part IV; and Staughton Lynd, *Intellectual Origins of American Radicalism* (New York: Random House, 1969), Chapter 4.

[7] In contrast, the Latin American feudally derived slaveocracy was quite accustomed to a variety of corporate groups of ascribed status; blacks could therefore either be slaves—but remain human beings, albeit of low status— or free but lacking the rights of the elite; lacking the liberal belief that human institutions should correspond to a supposedly more fundamental natural biological order, Latin Americans could remain quite unimpressed by the question of "natural" rights of all men as well as the question of the "natural" inferiority of blacks. Both manumission and assimilation, therefore, met fewer cognitive (and hence structural) obstacles in the New World fragments of feudalism than in the fragments of liberalism. Hartz, *The Founding of New Societies*, and Genovese, *The World the Slaveholders Made*.

[8] William Lloyd Garrison, quoted in Sylvan S. Tomkins, "The Psychology of Commitment," in Martin Duberman, ed., *The Anti-Slavery Vanguard* (Princeton, N.J.: Princeton University Press, 1965), pp. 288 and 290–91.

[9] Irving H. Bartlett, "The Persistence of Wendell Phillips," in Duberman, *op. cit.*, pp. 102–23.

[10] *Ibid.*

[11] Quoted in Merton L. Dillon, "The Abolitionists as a Dissenting Minority," in Alfred Young, *Dissent* (DeKalb: Northern Illinois University Press, 1969), p. 95.

[12] Sidney Lens, *Radicalism in America* (New York: Crowell, 1966), p. 123.

[13] Daniel Boorstin, *The Americans: The Colonial Experience* (New York: Random House, 1958).

[14] Lynd, *op. cit.*

[15] Larry Gara, "Who Was an Abolitionist?" in Duberman, *op. cit.*, p. 40.

[16] Lens, *op. cit.*, p. 116.

[17] Leon F. Litwack, "The Emancipation of the Negro Abolitionist," in Duberman, *op. cit.*, pp. 137–55.

[18] Gara, *op. cit.*, cites the following complaint of an abolitionist as antislavery sentiment grew: "New anti-slavery friends are becoming as plenty as roses in June. Sometimes when they tell me they have always been antislavery, I smile inwardly, but I do not contradict the assertion; I merely marvel at their power of keeping a secret so long" (p. 49).

[19] Bartlett, *op. cit.*

[20] Hartz, *The Liberal Tradition in America*, pp. 145–200; and Genovese, *The World the Slaveholders Made*, pp. 118–244.

[21] There are more elements of genuine feudalism among the trek boers of South Africa, with their subsistence farming and their unified church (Dutch Reformed); but again, the pigmentocratic element is jarring and what is altogether lacking is the intellectually productive Catholic high culture of the Middle Ages. Thompson, *op. cit.*

[22] Genovese, *The World the Slaveholders Made*.

[23] Moore, *op. cit.*
[24] *Ibid.*, p. 143.
[25] James M. McPherson, "The Ballot and Land for the Freedmen, 1861–1865," in Kenneth Stampp and Leon Litwack, eds., *Reconstruction* (Baton Rouge: Louisiana State University Press, 1969), pp. 132–55.
[26] *Ibid.*, p. 149.
[27] Vernon L. Wharton, "The Revolution of 1875," in Stampp and Litwack, *op. cit.*, p. 481.
[28] The "conspiracy theory" of the Fourteenth Amendment need not be taken too seriously. Its initial purpose was clearly to establish the rights of blacks; that it later came to be used primarily to establish the rights of corporations as "persons" entitled to "due process" was an unintended consequence—one that was perhaps not displeasing to some of the Republicans, but nevertheless not specifically planned.

6

The Era of Unrest: 1865–1900

INTRODUCTION

A few words of introduction to Chapter 6 and to the following chapters are necessary. In this chapter, I will describe a very active period for social movements, especially class movements. None of the conflicts reached the scale of the Revolutionary War or the Civil War, but neither was this period relatively as quiet as were the first decades of the nineteenth century. Violence was commonplace, but compared to the loss of 600,000 lives in the Civil War, quantitatively limited. Neither was it a period during which dual structures were established as in the Revolutionary War and by the South in the Civil War. Radicalism in analysis and violence in tactics did not reach the point of revolutionary organization in the late nineteenth century.

Nevertheless, the late nineteenth century was the last period of widespread movement activity before the closing-in of corporate consensus. Here, we will be concerned with late nineteenth century movements; in Chapters 7 and 8, we will discuss the transformation of movement demands into reform legislation and the consequent containment of most radical movements within the framework of political and ideological legitimacy. Movements falling outside of that framework became increasingly less able to attract members or supporters and by the nineteen-fifties, virtually seemed to have disappeared. We conclude the book with a discussion of the wave of movements in the 1960s and a consideration of the stability of the new industrial state.

SUBSTRUCTURAL CHANGES, 1865–1900

Since the literature on this topic is so voluminous and readily accessible, we will confine ourselves here to the briefest possible summary.[1]

1. Industrialization proceeded at a very rapid pace, especially accelerated by the invention of the internal combustion engine and the electric dynamo.

2. The extension of the railways, aided by federal land grants, accelerated the pace of industrialization by opening markets and raw material sources.

3. The frontier had essentially disappeared by the end of the century in the sense that public lands in the continental United States were vastly diminished, that practically all arable and grazing land in the West had passed into a variety of private hands (including those of individuals benefiting from the Homestead Act of 1862), and that these processes were accompanied by the political transformation of increasingly densely settled territories into states.

4. Immigration to the United States increasingly originated from Italy, Russia, and Austro-Hungary (as opposed to Great Britain, Ireland, Germany, and Scandinavia). Much of this immigration was to cities (coinciding with the closing of the frontier). An even larger component of in-migration to cities was provided by ex-rural Americans.

These trends were closely associated with changes in class and political relationships.

Strong trends toward oligopoly capital appeared in transportation (for instance, railroads), raw materials crucial to heavy industry (iron and oil), utilities (electricity), and a variety of other areas. Concentration in these areas paralleled concentration in banking; although complete monopoly was only occasionally achieved, the large concerns "could often exercise a decisive influence over the cost of raw materials, the prices of finished products, and the fortunes of independent competitors." [2]

As we have seen, the federal administrations of the first half of the nineteenth century aided industrial capitalism in a variety of ways; thus, the increasing support for business in the period after the Civil War was not a novelty, but, quantitatively, was so much greater that it verged on subservience. Among the many actions of support were the granting of public land to railways for very favorable terms, federal protection (under the Fourteenth Amendment) for corporations against efforts by the states to regulate them, and the use of the injunction as an instrument of control of movements and unions. Meanwhile, the measures that might have been used to curb corporations—the Interstate Commerce Act of 1887, the Sherman Anti-Trust Act of 1890, and the natural resource bill of 1891—remained unenforced.

At the ideological level, a number of earlier themes continued to be developed even though they had partially lost their meaning. One has come to be called the Horatio Alger myth; by preaching the petty-bourgeois virtues of hard work and thrift and at the same time portraying its hero as suddenly becoming fabulously wealthy through a stroke of luck it played a twofold trick on those who believed it. Evidence indicates that young native-born rural in-migrants to the city, rather than foreign immigrants, were the chief consumers of the literature of the American Dream. A second ideological theme was Americanism, linked to the final solution to the Indian problem and to the emerging imperialism of the turn of the century. A third theme, enunciated by university professors but widespread in popular forms as well, was social Darwinism, which provided the biological symbolism for two social phenomena: the exploitation of proletarians (at the bottom of the social structure) and the trend toward monopoly capital. Both the poor and the unsuccessful smaller corporation could be dismissed as unfit in the struggle for existence.

These ideological themes were influential, even if they were not universally accepted. At the level of the industrial laborer, tenant farmer, and freeholder, most men stayed quiet and resigned simply because the daily round of toil left so very little time for questioning, much less for radical movement activities. But at more middle-class levels, even dissenting opinions incorporated substantial portions of ideological themes. For instance, movements of reform often directed some of their efforts at inculcating the poor with the dominant values of thrift, hard work, sobriety, and individual success; the leaders of agrarian movements were also unable to break away from the myth of entrepreneurship as a means to success. No section of the native-born white population of northern European background was entirely free of hostility toward eastern and southern European immigrants, Indians, blacks, and foreigners.

LABOR MOVEMENTS

The best strategy for discussing labor movements in the post-Civil War period is first to offer the reader a descriptive chronology that can then be used as the basis of analysis.

1860   Dispersed local craft unions with a total of about 250,000 members.

1864–66   The National Labor Union, a nationwide association, was formed. The NLU was both a representative of labor in its fight for union recognition, higher wages, and reduced hours, and a general reform pressure group with a strong emphasis on monetary reform. Eschewing the strike (in part because of the disastrous strike experience of founder Sylvis' Molders' Union), the NLU attempted to create arbitration procedures and cooperatives. Some gains were made toward achieving the eight-hour day for federal employees in a few states (where the legislation was rarely enforced), but virtually no success was attained by the cooperative workshops or the monetary reformers.

1869   The Noble Order of the Knights of Labor, a local union of Philadelphia garment workers, was formed.

1872   The NLU and the related National Labor Reform Party, primarily a middle-class organization that suffered an overwhelming defeat in 1872, disintegrated.

1875   A national convention of a variety of eastern urban unions, including the Noble Order, resulted in the founding of the Knights of Labor.

1860–75   The "Molly Maguires" (properly called the Ancient

Order of the Hibernians), a secret terrorist organization in the anthracite region of Pennsylvania, was started parallel to the reformist and limited-demand urban craft labor movement. Efforts to organize unions among the primarily Irish miners in the 1840s and '50s had been met by violence on the part of state troopers and private police forces. The Order acted against mine superintendents, strikebreakers, and occasional union leaders and socialists who aroused local hostility. In this period, the depression of 1873, the futile starvation that caused the "long strike" of 1875, the counterterror of the "Modocs" (vigilantes organized to aid the private police forces) began. Infiltration of the Order by a Pinkerton agent and subsequent executions of twelve men broke the power of the Order and left the coal miners in scarcely improved working and living conditions.

1877   The "Great Railroad Strike" climaxed a series of strikes that began in the depression of 1873. Wages had been cut repeatedly in all enterprises, and the July 16 walkout of forty men employed by the Baltimore and Ohio railway line precipitated two and a half weeks of nationwide strikes, demonstrations, burning of roundhouses, and mass meetings and confrontations with the police, the state militias, federal troops, and private vigilantes. The Great Lakes region from Buffalo and Reading to St. Louis was the hardest hit. Demonstrators paralyzed midwestern transportation, emptied mines and factories, and held Chicago for a day and St. Louis for several days. This was made possible by the Marxian Socialist Working Men's Party (founded in 1876), which provided organization and strategies in these two cities. Although the strikers destroyed property, they committed little violence; violence, in the sense of attacks on human beings, was committed *against* the strikers, most notably when the Philadelphia militia fired into a Pittsburgh crowd and killed twenty demonstrators. The Philadelphians had been sent to Pittsburgh because the Pittsburgh militia had refused to act against the strikers; such an insurrection in armed forces is usually symptomatic of a fundamental breakdown in the legitimacy of the elite—it suggests the magnitude of the crisis.

1880   Terence Powderly became head of the Knights of Labor, then near the peak of its power with 700,000 members. Like the NLU, the Knights of Labor experimented with cooperatives and shunned strikes. Unlike the craft unions that coexisted with it and were soon to overshadow it, the Knights of Labor tried to organize women, the unskilled, the blacks, and middle-class professionals. Many themes were blended in the program of the Knights of Labor: an attractive but perhaps unrealistic petty-bourgeois dream of small-scale cooperative and individual control; a cautious emphasis on education rather than on strikes; a radical willingness to organize all proletarians (that is, those who live by selling their labor); and occasional experimentation with political action. By the late 1800s, the Knights had failed because of their unwilling involvement in unsuccessful strikes, their failure to attain concrete changes in wages and hours, and the competition of the craft unionists.

1873–86   Rise of socialist and anarchist organizations:
    1876   Marxian Working Mens Party forms.
    1877   WMP becomes Socialist Labor Party.
    1878   SLP elects two Chicago aldermen and gains three seats in the Missouri Legislature.
    1881   Paramilitary squads of the SLP form nucleus of Revolutionary Socialist Labor Party, which shunned electoral politics.
    1883   Anarchists and leftwing socialists form International Working People's Association—the "Black International," which emphasized force.

Many of these movement organizations remained quite small and confined to German immigrants.

1886   The Federation of Organized Trades and Labor Unions was enlarged and renamed the American Federation of Labor. The AFL was based on city assemblies of unions and national or state unions of crafts; only rarely were local craft unions allowed to become members. Under Samuel Gompers, a cigar maker, the AFL pursued economic gains, fended off socialist efforts to capture it, lobbied for legislation but did not become a party, and generally functioned to ameliorate the impact of capitalism on the individual worker without questioning the overall system. For crafts workers, it helped to obtain standard hours and wages, better working conditions, collective bargaining, emergency benefit funds, some safety and injury compensation legislation, and the abolition of child labor. Only an inveterate revolutionary elitist could deny that skilled workmen's lives were made more secure and more bearable. But although it was rational and immediately gratifying to the individual, it postponed—perhaps made impossible—any fundamental change in the system of production and ownership. As we shall see in the next chapter, the AFL was an essential ingredient in the emerging social order of corporate capitalism.

1886   The Chicago Haymarket incident gives some insight into police techniques for controlling the most radical dissidents—the anarchists. The dramatic events of May 4 must be understood against the background of the events of May 3: four men had been killed when police opened fire during the clash of locked-out McCormick Harvester employees and strikebreakers. On May 4, a crowd of 3,000 attended a protest meeting in Haymarket Square; a bomb thrown at the police by an unknown individual set off indiscriminate shooting by the police, which resulted in scores of dead, including seven policemen. This incident provided an excuse for police invasions of the homes and offices of suspected anarchists, the destruction of the anarchist organization in Chicago, and the deaths (by execution and preexecution suicide) of five undoubtedly innocent anarchist leaders.

1886   New York Police attacked a crowd of ten thousand during a streetcar strike.

1886   The Independent Labor Party of New York and Vicinity was formed. It backed Henry George (author of the demand for a single tax on land, *Progress and Poverty*) who ran for Mayor and almost won, beating Theodore Roosevelt and losing to the winning Democrat possibly only because of fraud. A variety of other third labor parties won local offices elsewhere.

1888   Defeat of most of the labor parties.

1889   In the Homestead strike against Andrew Carnegie, strikers battled Pinkertons and drove away strikebreakers, only to lose in the face of the Pennsylvania National Guard, legal proceedings, and specially protected strikebreakers.

1891   The Idaho National Guard is used to defeat the Coeur d' Alene mineworkers' strike.

1894   The Pullman strike in Chicago is suppressed by President Cleveland's use of federal troops and the federal district court's issuance of an injunction (for whose purported violation Eugene Debs, president of the American Railway Union, was imprisoned without jury trial for contempt of court).

In short, the labor movement of this period was active and diverse. In almost every one of its constituent movement organizations, a number of the major themes appear: extra-legal violence, efforts at third-party organization, economic demands, lobbying as a pressure group, and the strike as a political weapon as well as an economic weapon. The gains made for individual laborers were great, but as a radical movement, proletarian organization had failed by the end of the century.

Perhaps the Socialists and Wobblies of the following twenty-five years were organizationally sounder movement organizations than were the movements that preceded them, but they developed in an environment in which the societal structure was already less fluid, defenses against radicalism were more advanced, social control was more effective, and the potential mass base was better integrated into the society. From 1890 to the present, American radicalism would be increasingly confined to the margins of the society. The labor movement in America had failed to achieve either of the prerequisites for a revolutionary movement: the creation of a dual organization or the injection of an unresolvable issue into the machinery of the state. As we have seen, the American Revolution and the southern counterrevolution of 1875 succeeded by the construction of local coercive structures, the revolutionary dual organization. The Abolitionist movement succeeded by developing an issue that could be introduced into electoral politics but never was resolved in that arena because it grew out of substructural cleavages that were uncontainable in the bourgeois liberal state.

The labor movement failed to develop a dual structure at all; what it produced in this attempt was so small and so geographically and ethnically confined that it could not be the basis of the transformation of the society. The Molly Maguires were willing to use violence and were sufficiently tightly organized, but they had neither an ideology that could be spread beyond the Irish coalminers nor a structure open enough to expand into a mass movement; they remained too conspiratorial, too local, too ethnic. The anarchist and revolutionary socialist groups had broader ambitions and a more modern ideology but were also limited by ethnicity; where the Molly Maguires were excessively specialized by region and skill group, the revolutionary socialists and anarchists were forced to operate in the city, the most hostile possible climate for revolutionary movements.

In theory, the urban guerrilla has access to the large urbanized portion of the proletariat; in practice, the city is too permeable and too integrated—there is too little relief from the police and too many individuals who have not been, and perhaps cannot be, brought under the control of the revolutionary organization. The urban guerrilla can succeed in organizing these persons and holding the city only if there is a massive breakdown in police and military power. Thus, in Russia in February 1917, a number of regiments stationed in St. Petersburg refused to move against the demonstrators just as the militia in March of 1848 refused to attack the Parisian workers and, as in 1871, the defeated French armed forces were unable to prevent the Commune's seizure of Paris. But in post-colonial America there has never been a similar breakdown in control of the legitimate practitioners of violence other than the militias in the Revolutionary War, the southern armed forces in the Civil War, and a few isolated incidents. One of these was the military vacuum in the south in the early 1870s that permitted the southern counterrevolution; another more relevant to the present discussion was the refusal of the Pittsburgh militia to fire on Pittsburgh demonstrators during the Great Strike of 1877. This failure of disciplined violence was met by replacing the resisting units by members of the Philadelphia militia who *did* open fire in indiscriminate, bloody, but effective shooting.[3]

Thus one important factor in the history of American radical labor movements was the continued loyalty of the rank and file of the wielders of violence—policemen, militiamen and National Guardsmen, federal troops, and private police and vigilantes. In order to create a revolutionary labor movement in most industrialized countries, the organizer must work in the cities.[4] In the cities, he has little time or space for experimentation with dual structures, liberated zones, and so on. In the face of a reasonably effective police force and a populace that was partially hostile, at least, he cannot establish distinct areas under revolutionary control. What revolutionary structure there is must be put into effect under emergency conditions of widespread spontaneous strikes, demonstrations, rioting and looting; it can succeed only if there is a breakdown in the discipline of the forces sent against these outbreaks. This sequence of events occurred in Chicago and St. Louis during 1877, but the rapidly mustered radical workers could not hold out against the loyal armed forces within a city that was not entirely within revolutionary control. This is precisely the dilemma of the revolutionary in an industrial country; the bulk of the population is in cities and must be organized there, where the dual structure is particularly vulnerable, the population is integrated into the central institutions of the society much better there than it is in a rural area and the armed forces are fairly likely to remain loyal. In short, where the substructural conditions generate a large urban proletariat, they *also* generate a high degree of loyalty to and integration into the central institutions of the society. In slightly different terms, modern urbanized industrial countries have strong ideologies and strong structural integrating mechanisms: the ruling class and its ideas enjoy a hegemony, as defined above.[5]

To some degree, American ideology with its themes of success and nationalism inhibited radicalism among American workers, especially among rural born native Protestants. Equally important, what radical organization did develop among proletarians could be suppressed by the ideologically committed groups—namely, the urban middle class as a whole (composed of a petty-bourgeoisie and clerical and professional workers) and individuals who staffed the police forces, the National Guard and the militias in particular. Unlike these strata in France, for instance, where they had a history of insurrection, the American middle strata remained committed to the ideology as a whole and to the legitimacy of political institutions; these conditions of integration were actually strengthened by urbanization and the decline of regionalism—by the growth in cultural and political power of the society's center.[6]

Figure 1 can be used to summarize our discussion of the failure of radical proletarian movements in America. On the other hand, the moderate labor movements that sought improved wages and working conditions *within* the capitalist framework were effective, and the AFL which at the ideological level was most accepting of capitalism and at the structural level most in tune with the trends away from self employment succeeded best. (The Knights of Labor ultimately

Figure 1 Social Integration and the Failure of Radical Proletarian Movements

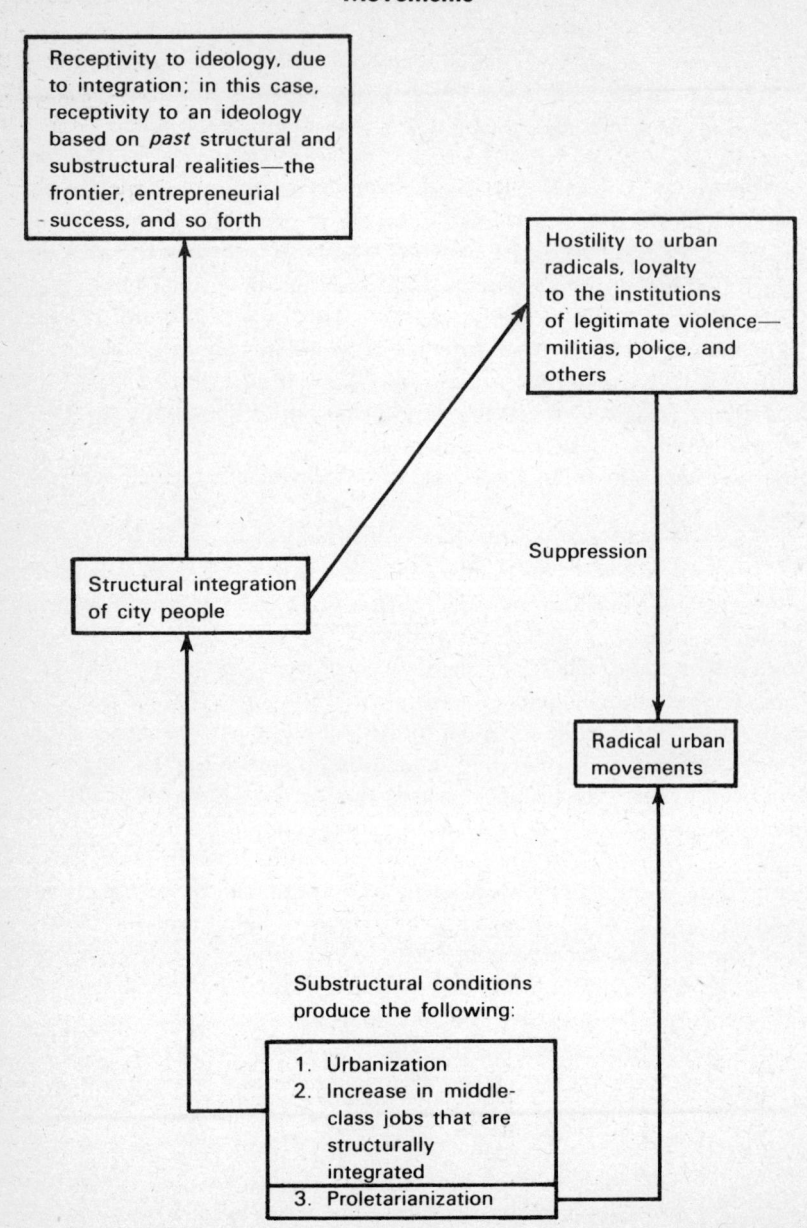

```
┌─────────────────────────────┐
│ Receptivity to ideology, due │
│ to integration; in this case,│
│ receptivity to an ideology   │
│ based on *past* structural and│
│ substructural realities—the  │
│ frontier, entrepreneurial    │
│ success, and so forth        │
└─────────────────────────────┘
              ▲
              │              ┌─────────────────────────┐
              │              │ Hostility to urban       │
              │              │ radicals, loyalty        │
              │              │ to the institutions      │
              │              │ of legitimate violence—  │
              │              │ militias, police, and    │
              │              │ others                   │
              │              └─────────────────────────┘
              │                         │
   ┌──────────────────────┐             │
   │ Structural integration│            │ Suppression
   │ of city people       │─────────────┤
   └──────────────────────┘             │
              ▲                         ▼
              │              ┌──────────────────┐
              │              │ Radical urban    │
              │              │ movements        │
              │              └──────────────────┘
              │                         ▲
   Substructural conditions             │
   produce the following:               │
   ┌─────────────────────────────┐      │
   │ 1. Urbanization             │      │
   │ 2. Increase in middle-      │      │
   │    class jobs that are      │      │
   │    structurally             │      │
   │    integrated               │      │
   ├─────────────────────────────┤      │
   │ 3. Proletarianization       │──────┘
   └─────────────────────────────┘
```

could not accept the diminishing chances of individual or small cooperative control and lost out to the unions that *did* accept these realities).

The year 1886 superbly symbolizes these two centrally related aspects of the American labor movement: the shattering of the revolutionary movements by middle-class hostility, the problems of urban organization, and the steadfastness of the police are exemplified in the Haymarket affair; the success of the moderate union movement with its limited demands and its acceptance and acceleration of an ameliorated corporate capitalism is exemplified in the founding of the AFL.

One avenue remained open to movements that were neither revolutionary nor acquiescent: the effort to transform themselves into political parties or to inject fundamental issues into political campaigns. This effort on the part of labor movements can only be understood in conjunction with the parallel and often intertwined political efforts of the agrarians.

AGRARIAN MOVEMENTS OF THE LATE NINETEENTH CENTURY

> Prairie avenger, mountain lion,
> Bryan, Bryan, Bryan, Bryan.
> Gigantic troubadour, speaking like a siege gun,
> Smashing Plymouth Rock with his boulders
>   from the West.
>
> In a coat like a deacon
> In a black Stetson hat
> He scourged the Elephant plutocrats
> with barbed wire from the Platte . . .
> . . . plutocrats . . .
> with dollar signs upon their coats
> and spats upon their feet.
>   ———Vachel Lindsay

I can think of no better summary of the position of the smallholding farmer than the description offered by Arthur Stinchcombe in his analysis of the relation between agricultural enterprise, rural class relations, and political movements.[7]

> Family smallholding has the same sort of enterprises as does family tenancy, but rights to the returns from the enterprise are more heavily concentrated in the class of

farmers. The "normal" property holding is about the size requiring the work of two adults or less. Probably the most frequent historical source of such systems is out of family-tenancy systems by way of land reform or revolution. However, they also arise through colonization of farmlands carried out under governments in which large landlords do not have predominant political power, for instance, in the United States and Norway. Finally, it seems that such systems tend to be produced by market forces at an advanced stage of industrialization. There is some evidence that farms either larger or smaller than those requiring about two adult laborers tend to disappear in the industrial states of western Europe.

Perhaps the best way to begin analysis of this type of agricultural enterprise is to note that virtually all the costs of production are fixed. Labor in the family holding is, in some sense, "free": family members have to be supported whether they work or not, so they might as well work. Likewise, the land does not cost rent, and there is no advantage to the enterprise in leaving it out of cultivation. This predominance of fixed costs means that production does not fall with a decrease in prices, as it does in most urban enterprises where labor is a variable cost. Consequently, the income of smallholders varies directly with the market price of the commodities they produce and with variability in production produced by natural catastrophe. Thus, the political movements of smallholders tend to be directed primarily at maintenance of the price of agricultural commodities rather than at unemployment compensation or other "social security" measures.

Second, the variability of return from agricultural enterprise tends to make credit expensive and, at any rate, makes debts highly burdensome in bad years. Smallholders' political movements, therefore, tend to be opposed to creditors, to identify finance capital as a class enemy: Jews, the traditional symbol of finance capital, often come in for an ideological beating. Populist movements are often directed against "the bankers." Further, since cheap money generally aids debtors, and since small farmers are generally debtors, agrarian movements tend to support various kinds of inflationary schemes. Small farmers do not want to be crucified on a cross of gold.

Third, agrarian movements, except in highly advanced societies, tend to enjoy limited intraclass communication, to be poor in politically talented leaders, relatively unable to put together a coherent, disciplined class movement controlled from below. Contributions to the party treasury tend to be small and irregular, like the incomes of the small farmers. Peasant movements are, therefore, especially prone to penetration by relatively disciplined political interests, sometimes Communist and sometimes industrial capital. Further, such movements tend to be especially liable to corruption, since they are relatively unable to provide satisfactory careers for political leaders out of their own resources.

Moreover, at an early stage of industrial and commercial development in a country without large landowners, the only sources of large amounts of money available to politicians are a few urban industrial and commercial enterprises. Making a policy on the marketing and production of iron and steel is quite often making a policy on the marketing and production of a single firm. Naturally, it pays that firm to try to get legislation and administration tailored to its needs.

Fourth, small-farmer and peasant movements tend to be nationalistic and xenophobic. The explanation of this phenomenon is not clear.

Finally, small-farmer and peasant movements tend to be opposed to middlemen and retailers, who are likely to use their monopolistic or monopsonistic position to milk the farm population. The co-operative movement is, of course, directed at eliminating middlemen as well as at provision of credit without usury.

Under normal conditions (that is, in the absence of totalitarian government, major racial cleavage, and major war) this complex of political forces tends to produce a rural community with a proliferation of associations and with the voting power and political interest to institute and defend certain elements of democracy, especially universal suffrage and universal education. This tends to produce a political regime loose enough to allow business and labor interest groups to form freely without allowing them to dominate the government completely. Such a system of landholding is a common precursor and support of modern liberal democratic government.

In smallholding systems, then, the upper classes of the rural community are not distinct in legal status and relatively not in style of life. Social mobility in such a system entails mainly a change in the amount of property held, or in the profitability of the farm, but not a change in legal status or a radical change in style of life.

A politically enfranchised rural community is characterized by a high degree of political affect and organization, generally in opposition to urban interests rather than against rural upper classes. But, compared with the complexity of their political goals and the level of political involvement, their competence tends to be low until the "urbanization of the countryside" is virtually complete.

Incidentally, Stinchcombe contrasts this setting to the family size tenancy setting, which is also volatile but produces considerably more sophisticated, disciplined, and skillfully led movements.

Family smallhold agrarian movements have had a long history in America, beginning in the colonial period. However, the movements of the late nineteenth century were movements of commercial farmers, not of subsistence farmers (who organized during the colonial era and provided some of the popular support for Jackson). In the early 1870s, farmers of the Midwest—Iowa, Illinois, and Wisconsin—felt hard pressed by the general economic slump and by the expanding power of the railroads and middlemen. Their efforts had taken the form of the Granger movement, farm associations that pressed for state legislation to regulate railroad rates and generally curb enterprises that exploited the commercial farmer; this was a reasonable strategy as long as the states wielded control over property rights (that is, until the Fourteenth Amendment was used to protect corporations from state regulation).[8] In 1876, farmers entered the national political arena with the Independent National Party (the "Greenbacks"), which demanded national inflation through the issuance of federal paper money, the perennial demand of agrarian debtors. The Greenback Party was neither successful as a political party nor as a pressure group that could force a major party to adopt its stand on specific issues.

By the 1880s, the midwestern farmers had achieved some stabilization of railway rates (which actually declined slightly during this period) and a fairly prosperous local market in dairy products, corn and hogs. Meanwhile, the western wheat and southern cotton regions were plunged into the worldwide farm depression of the late nineteenth century.[9] Wheat and cotton farmers were especially dependent on exports, that is, on the world market. (As a matter of fact, American entry into the world farm products market on a large scale had been one of the causes of the devastating drop in prices.) These regions lacked the diversification of the Midwest. The structural impact of the agricultural depression was to drive marginal farmers off the farms, either into the cities or into tenancy (which increased sharply during the 1890s).[10] Even so, farming remained one of the most competitive sectors of the economy. Because of this competitiveness and the inelasticity of the demand, the problem of predictable handling of the surplus was virtually insoluble.

At first, agrarianism in the wheat and cotton regions was expressed through the organization of Farmers' Alliances, which were educational and social associations. As has been the case with so many American movements (and is generally so in a liberal political system), politicization as a party occurred rapidly; in the 1880s, the Alliances expanded and coalesced into the People's Party. Heartened by success in state and congressional races in 1890, the People's Party (or Populists) ran General James Weaver as its presidential candidate against the two business-supporting major party candidates.[11] Democrat Cleveland won and Weaver polled 8.5 percent of the total vote. Only in nine sparsely populated states of the wheat, cotton and silver mining regions did Weaver get more than a third of the vote. In 1896, the Democrats swallowed up the Populists (or conversely, the silver forces within the Democratic Party gained control of the convention), and ran Bryan, a quasi-Populist candidate who lost to McKinley. The Populists received a fair amount of support from black voters but little from urban voters and virtually none from the ethnic blocs.[12]

The brief history of agrarianism as a third party underlines the points Stinchcombe made. Most striking is its ideological primitivism. When it was insightful in its analysis of the society, its insights were generally borrowed from Socialism. Its own uniquely agrarian contributions were often superficial (as in the demand for currency inflation) and all too easily soured into nativism and antisemitism. The more whimsical and even repulsive aspects of Populist ideology have three sources. First, the pressure that all radical movements in America feel towards reducing their program to single-issue reform is the major source. Thus, when Populism joined radical labor movements in attacking the capitalist system of production and distribution, intellectually, it was at its soundest, but it faced the certainty of losing the votes of an alarmed petty-bourgeoisie. Such a broad analysis is reflected in the simplistic, yet not incorrect, assertion that the charge that overproduction caused the farmer's troubles was ridiculous as long as "tens of thousands were going hungry, and that the only overproduction admitted by all, was millionaires" [13]—in short, that agricultural overproduction was a by-product of capitalist distribution and not an inherent quality of agriculture. When Populism aimed its demands at a middle level of structural and political reforms, it abandoned its radical analysis but tried to attain realistic concrete gains such as regulation of corporations, direct election of Senators, the initiative, referendum and recall, the subtreasury plan (low-cost federal loans issued against stored crops), and, a little more daringly, public ownership of railroads, telephones, and telegraphs. At this level, it might have remained ideologically sound and no less politically vigorous than it finally was. Unfortunately, despite serious misgivings, the Populist leadership could not resist the impulse to base its appeal on the issue of silver, that is, of currency inflation. This issue had three advantages: it appealed to the American Bimetallic League and opened the coffers of the silvermining interests to the financially desperate Populists; second, it caught the imagination of the public and provided the rich imagery of Populism ("you shall not press down upon the brow of labor this crown of thorns, you shall not crucify mankind upon a cross of gold"); and third, the leaders themselves were attracted as members of the petty-bourgeoisie to a self-image as debtors and victims of an international monetary conspiracy. The more the issue of silver predominated, the more populism lost intellectual vigor. Ultimately, there is little evidence that bimetallism gained populism more votes than a more fundamental analysis and diversified demands would have. As we shall see, many radical movements in America lost their larger goals as they reduced their general analysis to a single-issue demand; Populism was not alone in this respect, but its tendencies toward the single issue of currency inflation were particularly primitive and eventually politically useless because the issue had no proletarian appeal and thus could not contribute to a broad coalition.

A second source of Populism's uneven ideology and eventual defeat was the position of farmers in American society. Farmer's movements are often affected by the "idiocy of rural life." The petty-bourgeois traits that everywhere militate against movement success are especially concentrated in rural areas; among them are isolation, competition, suspicion of outsiders, and a primitive conspiratorial world view. In tenants' movements, these traits are ameliorated by a clearer understanding of the concept of class, but in freeholders' movements, a spirit of enterpreneurship, individualism, and property ownership pervades the movement. Populist ideology was torn between a self-image of farmers as producers (which would have linked them to labor) and farmers as a hard-pressed class of indebted property owners. The repeated choice of the latter image was perhaps not itself unrealistic but prevented any broader analysis of the petty-bourgeoisie in capitalist society and opened the door to bizarre fantasies of an international (usually Anglo-Jewish) gold conspiracy. Farmers, like the rest of the petty-bourgeoisie, were a declining class in America in numbers and in power; out of this declining position grew not only Populism, but also other far more grotesque movements with a stronger nativist tinge, which we shall mention later. Related to the class position of farmers (simultaneously rural and petty-bourgeois) was the peculiar nature of the leaders. Some were farmers; others were rural editors, journalists, veterans of repeated inflationary movements—a sort of cracker barrel intelligentsia that shared its constituency's entrepreneurial identity and its enjoyment of conspiracy theories. Given this background, it is not surprising to find that in their later years, these leaders were involved in nativist and obscurantist movements; for instance, Tom Watson of the Southern Populists who had courageously worked with blacks eventually supported the Klan, and Bryan attacked the teaching of evolution. Essentially, these soured movements are also attacks on modernity and corporate capitalism, but attacks of a primitive and mistaken nature in their lack of a sound analysis of the social structure.

A third source of the nativist elements of Populism is their general presence in the soceity; virtually no stratum of native-born white Protestants were free of the prejudices that Populism harnessed to its special class interest of currency inflation.

Some comments on Populism as a third party are in order. It is commonly asserted that Populism was a successful third party, that within a few years, its reform measures had been made into law by the major parties. It is true that some of its proposals were enacted, but the most radical aspects of its program were never attained and the elements that did make their way into political legitimacy did so in circumstances very different from third-party victory. In this sense, there can be no third-party success through forcing reform legislation; the reforms are torn from their broader context and their structural support base and are often interpreted for altogether different ends. Specifically, we shall see how the Populist's opposition to laissez-faire was accepted as a federal stand primarily in the form of governmental cooperation with corporations—hardly what the Populists had in mind.

We have analyzed Populism as essentially a failure, a movement of a declining propertied class and hence totally unsuitable as the partner in a coalition with proletarians. But in what sense could farmers be said to be a declining group, except numerically, when they were yet to enjoy their most prosperous years—1900 to 1914? As we shall show elsewhere, all petty-bourgeois groups were losing power over national decisions in the late nineteenth and early twentieth centuries. More specifically, farmers were a declining class in the sense that never again would they equate their interests with the interests of the society as a whole; never again would they enter the political arena as a group with universal demands and an ideology that could speak of liberation for all. After the 1890s, the more prosperous farmers were transformed into a special interest group overtly pursuing narrow goals and demanding specific pieces of legislation that were often detrimental to the rest of the nation. This tendency was further strengthened in the 1920s and '30s, when hardships pruned the ranks of the farmers down to a still smaller more prosperous core, and again in the '60s, when farm production was increasingly integrated into corporate enterprise. For the 1890s, we can speak of an agrarian movement; thereafter we must use the phrase "farm lobby." Meanwhile, the more marginal farmers, insofar as they did not flee to the cities, pursued another but no less anti-universalistic course in joining nativistic movements of reactionary opposition to both corporate liberalism and urban proletarians—the Klan, the Temperance Movement, the opposition to evolution, and so on.

MIDDLE-CLASS MOVEMENTS

The turn of the century marks a reasonable end point for our discussion of labor and agrarian movements. Agrarian movements were transformed into pressure groups or into nativist rancor; labor movements were to undergo a resurgence in the first two decades of the twentieth century, but in altered form in an effort to cope with some of the problems we diagnosed above. But there are no such breaks in the continuity of middle-class movements. Their pattern of change is much more gradual.

We must return to mid-nineteenth century for the roots of middle-class movements. Their class and ethnic sources were similar to those of Abolitionism and individuals tended to sort themselves into one or the other of these movements, according to personality, life experiences and life style more than to class or ethnic group membership. To some degree, movement adherence was interchangeable, and just as utopian experimenters became Abolitionists or vice versa, so was there free circulation among the movements of the later nineteenth century. (This fact is also a characteristic of working-class movements, especially among the leaders.)

Among the oldest and most narrow of the middle-class movements were the Know-Nothings (the American Party) of Massachusetts in the 1850s. This was an alliance of conservative Whigs, who were motivated by hatred of immigrant Irish Catholics, with liberals of both parties, who were distressed at Irish support of conservative Democrats. It already contains many of the peculiarities and contradictions of later middle-class movements. Its most important planks were designed to extirpate the political power of immigrants by extending the waiting period for naturalization from five to twenty-one years and by excluding the foreign born from public office. Ironically enough, the Know-Nothing legislature of Massachusetts in 1855 did not pass these measures but achieved protection for runaway slaves and free blacks, improvements in the jury system, extension of the rights of women, and expansion of public education. The Civil War swept away the American Party; the nativism of the late nineteenth century, in the form of the Anti-Catholic American Protective Association, the antiimmigration lobbies and upper-class academically legitimated racism were its soured descendants. In the Know-Nothings can be found the cooperation of disgruntled Anglo-Saxons and genuine reformers, a combination that coexisted not merely within the party but also within individuals. Mingled in it were the following: a not unrealistic opposition to political participation of groups who lacked experience with local self-government (and remained indifferent to it as long as it failed to better their lives materially), and were violently anti-black; a genteel distaste for working class immigrant life style and especially for drinking and sexual mores that differed from the Protestant-Puritan ones; anti-Catholicism, with traditional Protestant roots; ambivalence about whether to exclude foreigners or transform them into "Anglo-Saxon" Protestants. Structurally these sentiments arose from the loss of power of urban middle-class groups (mercantile entrepreneurs and professionals) to industrialists on the one hand and proletarians on the other. In some sense, this response was a more militant and harsher counterpart of the flight of the intellectuals from Jacksonianism into utopianism and away from politics, in this case exacerbated by the foreignness and Catholicism of the working-class groups. In part, the immigrant working-class was being used as the scapegoat for the loss of political democracy that could not have survived anyway under conditions of increasing population, urbanization and the growth of the power of industrialists; in part, class power, rather than political democracy, was at stake for the nativist reformers.[14]

The mingling of a desire to ameliorate the lot of workers, to destroy a less genteel life style and perhaps unconsciously express frustration at the loss of political power, was also present in the Temperance movement, another important middle-class movement of the nineteenth century. More readily understandable to the reader is the middle-class movement to ameliorate working conditions, to limit and abolish the toil of women and children and to generally provide support for the labor movement. Some but not all of the organizations formed for these goals were committed to Protestant "social gospel" doctrines (which had a far more radical counterpart in the revolutionary leveling Protestantism of much of the working class during the Gilded Age[15]); thus in 1887, New York City Episcopalians organized the Church Association for the Advancement of the Interests of Labor. The YMCA, youth organizations, the work of women volunteers, the settlement house, the Salvation Army were all parts of the movement to better the lot of the worker, generally through changing his life style and self-image, although sometimes also by changing his working conditions.

Perhaps the most radical and widespread middle-class movement was the women's movement. As with other movements that have not primarily transformed themselves into a political party, the women's movement ideologically and structurally had a radical core and a large generally very moderate penumbra.

Political party movements presuppose the right to vote, impose a minimal amount of consensus within the movement and exercise at least one clear demand on their penumbras—voting; the women's movement lacked all these elements and thus was characterized by heterogeneity of goals and tension between the core and the penumbra. The penumbra is easier to explain than is the core in terms of the substructural changes and the class-base approach. As larger numbers of women were freed from the domestic chores that once only the wealthiest had escaped, middle-class women involved themselves in a variety of ameliorative activities that were quite in keeping with the Victorian image of women as nurturant, merciful and moralistic.[16] Among these activities were support for reforms that would improve the lives of the poor (including temperance legislation and child labor laws), volunteer work of various types, and cultural concerns of a more or less genteel sort. As early as the 1830s women were developing these interests in church associations and literary societies. One can only view them with ambivalence. On the one hand they led a large number of women out of the home and into an atmosphere of political and cultural problems that was potentially liberating. On the other hand, they removed middle-class women further from any participation in production, and expanded rather than diminished some of the worst aspects of the nineteenth century stereotype of women. In some respects, these portions of the women's movement tended to fill political reform and artistic endeavor with the gooeyness, sentimentality and naivete that a sexist society ascribes to womanly activities. In the 1830s Harriet Martineau wrote about women's literary societies: "in my progress through the country I met with a greater variety and extent of female pedantry than the experience of a lifetime in Europe would afford . . . not to be despised in an oppressed class as it indicates the first struggle of intellect with its restraints; and it is therefore a hopeful symptom." [17] The very contemporaneity of her words—"oppressed class"—suggests that she was wrong in her judgment; unfortunately the terms of women's liberation arguments have remained virtually unchanged for almost a century and half—attesting to a complete failure of the movement, so far.

By the end of the nineteenth century, this penumbra included a number of nationwide organizations of women, including the nationalist ones (Daughters of the American Revolution, Colonial Dames of America), the professional, and the civic and reformist.

Set aside from this penumbra, although touching it at various points (especially in the Women's Christian Temperance Union under Frances Willard and the suffrage movement) was the feminist core of the women's movement. Some of the women in it had become feminists after the experience of discrimination in anti-slavery and temperance work. Unlike the sentimental penumbra of middle-class women whose activities were legitimated by the imagery of nurturance and the home, the feminists were radical in attacking Western domestic arrangements as enslavement of women. They demanded economic and educational rights and sought transformation of family structure. Their tactics included agitation for legal reform (for instance, the liberalization of divorce), as well as the propaganda of living one's life outside the confines of the prevailing norms. Throughout the writings, speeches and actions of the radical feminists appears the realization that the patrifocal family is the source of women's socialization to an ideal of submission, and is the structural vehicle of the total exclusion of women from political and economic power. Therefore Elizabeth Cady Stanton described marriage as "opposed to all God's laws"; and the Claflin sisters openly and dramatically practiced free love for as long as nonmarital sexual relations remained surreptitious and shameful their prevalence merely lent support to the norms. Only a publicly and proudly admitted crime, which thus became a political act, could reverse the legitimacy that secret crimes bestow on norms. So forceful a blow did the revelations of the Claflin sisters strike against public morality and middle-class pretensions that their acts proved counterproductive and the feminist movement was forced to withdraw to the no doubt safer but less central issue of civil rights.

By the second half of the nineteenth century, the feminist movement was beset by exactly the same three problems that women's liberation is now facing. The first is that most women are so bound by conventional ideology that they cannot accept the innovations in familial arrangements that are a prerequisite to women's liberation. Few groups have remained so socialized to participate in perpetuating the institutions in which they are oppressed. Because of socialization patterns, women are especially vulnerable to ideological sanctions against participation in feminist movements, sanctions which in the nineteenth century took the form of appeals to "decency" or religion and in the twentieth century appeals to psychotherapeutic belief systems; in both periods, women were subjected to the argument that sexual oppression was natural—it is this assumption of the "naturalness" of present sexual arrangements that exposes feminists to laughter, to charges of abnormality, and to efforts to debunk women's attempts at structural transformations by reducing oppression to a "personal trouble." All movement participants to some degree are "abnormal" in the sense that cognitive liberation is not the universal condition and in the sense that they come to reject prevailing norms. The therapeutic explanation of movement behavior is basically an attempt to present this statistical and normative deviance as a personality defect, to reduce cognitive liberation to an illness. Since women's movements (and those of homosexuals) must confront the questions of socialization experience, body image and sexual activity more directly than any other movement they are particularly vulnerable to these cognitive counterploys. A second perennial problem of women's movements is that they are strongly middle class. Under present conditions, on the one hand, the freedom of the middle-class woman depends on the exploitation of working-class women as domestics and babysitters and on the other hand, working-class women cannot separate themselves easily from class-based as opposed to sex-based loyalties. Third, in American history women have been continually pitted against blacks in the struggle for crumbs—the women's suffrage organizations were pressed to withdraw their demands to allow white male America's small stock of liberalism to be devoted to supporting the vote for freedmen. This issue was one of the factors that split the suffrage movement into the Boston-based American Woman's Suffrage Association and the Anthony-Stanton-led National Woman's Suffrage Association, which did not give in to these pressures. Until women develop an analysis that can unite women and ethnically- and class-oppressed groups, and overcome the very deep-seated attachment to present arrangements of sexuality and child-rearing, the movement is doomed to repetition of its nineteenth century history. In no other movement is there quite the same sense of *déjà vu*, of having made so few changes and having profited so little from the substructural transformations. The feminist movement failed like other nineteenth century movements by narrowing its radical goals to single-issue reform—in this case, suffrage. But unlike the other movements, its failure was even greater, its impact on social and political structure less, because of the extraordinary structural (and ideological) difficulties in organizing women. Women are an oppressed group that is totally integrated into the existing structure of society; second, women's socialization experiences mean exposure to the prevailing ideology from birth, which presents formidable obstacles to efforts at implanting cognitive liberation.[18]

By the end of the century, this whole array of predominantly middle-class movements was poised at the edge of a new world: in the following decades the coalitions that had worked in the late nineteenth century were to split apart and portions of the movements were to narrow their goals and attain specific demands, other portions were to become the soured nativistic movements of the early twentieth century and yet other smaller portions were to become radical or Bohemian.

In reviewing the middle-class movements of the late nineteenth century one must very carefully sort out three factors: the "objective conditions" of the times, the hardships suffered by so many under the new regimen of industrial capitalism, which moved the more sensitive and aware members of the middle class to seek reforms; secondly, the "objective conditions" of women and of the professional and entrepreneurial middle class itself which was less economically exploited than laborers but nevertheless politically threatened by societal changes; and thirdly, the subjective world of the reformers, comprising the personal experiences that sensitized some more than others and the interpretations of social reality that enabled them to act as they did. (These three conditions are, of course, present for every movement, but for movements of the "objectively oppressed" the first two factors coincide, whereas for radical and reform movements of the more or less advantaged each factor appears to be more independent of the others.) To examine only the subjective world of the reformers is to reduce them to guilty masochists; to examine only the conditions of the urban Protestant middle class is to fail to understand the reformist nature of the movements; and to refuse to look beyond the objective conditions of the proletariat is to lose sight of the mechanisms by which oppression generates society-wide resistance.

Most of these middle class movements enjoyed some measure of success and gained some specific changes in legislation or custom. But success was made possible only by a narrowing of goals.

THE INDIAN RESISTANCE

It is appropriate to begin an examination of the Indian resistance movements in this chapter because the late nineteenth century was the period of the closing frontier; from the Indian's point of view the closed frontier meant his reduction to an encircled and segregated remnant, deprived of his lands and at the mercy of the numerically and militarily superior white. Henceforth the history of Indian resistance to whites is no longer the history of wars between two nations but the history of movements of a persecuted minority whose suffering in terms of theft of lands, cultural destruction and genocide at the hands of the White American is impossible to exaggerate. At the time of this writing, the theft continues unabated, for instance in the land development schemes in the Southwest (for example, the Cochise Land Development Corporation) and the proposed coal works on the Navaho reservation in which Peabody coal company plans to ravage the Navaho's land as it has helped to destroy Appalachia.

The movements of conquered peoples during the period of Western imperialism frequently have three phases: a phase of realistic armed opposition to the invader, which depending on terrain, numbers and military traditions of the defenders may last from a few days to several generations; a phase of nonpolitical quasi-religious movements, a revitalization period of individual and collective working-through of the shock of conquest; and finally a period of political and often military movements of protest, resistance, terrorism and—when possible—national liberation. This pattern seems to occur in a wide variety of colonial and quasi-colonial areas, including those where the population is enslaved, indentured, proletarianized or otherwise exploited in the extraction of raw materials, and those where it is subjected to genocide because of its resistance to white settlers.

In the period under consideration we will be primarily concerned with the quasi-religious phase of Indian movements. They are shaped by the following conditions:

1. Irreversible military defeat.
2. The persistence of religious, magical and shamanistic perspectives on the social order, that is, metaphors for conceptualizing a social structure. The movements are often quite realistic in their understanding of historical events but turn to a richer more imaginative symbolism to present their interpretations of it.
3. The normal processes of cultural diffusion resulting in the borrowing of white religious and technological culture traits and their incorporation in the revitalization movements (cultural borrowing of course also occurs in the opposite direction, especially in the learning of indigenous ways of handling the environment and in agricultural production).
4. Individual cognitive disorganization as a result of war, death or deportation of friends and kinsmen, forced resettlement, exploitation as a worker, and deliberate cultural destruction. In this respect, the revitalization movement provides a new cognitive order in place of the damaged old one. Its "irrational" elements—that is, religious metaphors—not only represent resistance to accomodation to a technological secularized society but perhaps also a kind of dreaming phase in which otherwise individually shattering cognitive destruction can be transformed into fantasy. (Just as in dream-sleep, daily events are processed into fantasies without which individuals can be driven into daytime hallucination.)[19]

Within this broad sequence of movement types there are a number of smaller cycles. Short-run fluctuations in economic conditions can set off a wave of movement activity (as Peter Worsley has shown for Melanesia where cargo cults have been related to the business cycle of copra production).[20] Second, religious movements can touch off armed resistance as was the case in the Pontiac rebellion of the Delawares, the Tecumseh revolt, the long march of the Nez Perces in 1877, and Ghost Dance uprising of the Sioux in 1890 (which was suppressed at the Wounded Knee massacre of 300 unarmed people, largely Sioux women and children).

An especially interesting aspect of revitalization movements are the personalities and conversion experiences of the prophets which reflect characteristics similar to those of shamans on the one hand and the Protestant sectarians on the other. The theme of death (from a physical illness or as a symbolization of a state of intense depression), journey to another world, and rebirth appear frequently, sometimes with Christian borrowings; the imagery of rebirth is applied directly to the prophet but has wider implications for the collectivity he represents. The movements of Native Americans are particularly important because they provide a cognitive framework for opposition to the prevailing ideology whose sources are largely outside of that ideology. Movements of groups which are historically a part of the larger society can not present a complete cognitive liberation; the movements' rejection of the ideology is in many ways shaped by the ideology and the movement belief systems are necessarily related to the ideology. The movements' belief systems are a distortion and reversal of the ideology's elements. Thus, Marxism shares many features of nineteenth century bourgeois materialism and the contemporary American counterculture contains an exaggeration to the point of satire of American culture. But the nineteenth century Indian movements attack white America at an ideational level with an imagery and a value system that are non-European-based and wholly outside of the liberal consensus; literally, they do not speak the same language and, for these reasons, they present to the contemporary reader a unique vantage point for viewing white American society.

I have arranged a brief chronology of Indian revitalization movements, giving the date and location for each, and whenever possible trying to capture the symbolism by short quotes from doctrine and liturgy. Many of these movements no longer exist; they survive better in their poetry than in a detailed account of their doomed history.[21]

1799–1972   Handsome Lake movement among the Iroquois, properly known as Gai'wiio or "Good Message." Iroquois-Quaker syncretism. "If an Inner Light from the Great Spirit could shine into the soul of the believer it would separate good from evil."[22] Revision of the traditional ceremonial cycle. Assimilation of the sacramental eating of the white Dog at the Great Festival of the New Year to the Eucharist.
1762   Delaware Indians of Michigan. Nameless prophet of intertribal unity, new healing rituals, and open warfare with native weapons against British, leading to Pontiac rebellion.
1805   Ohio Valley. The prophet Tenskwatawa is looked upon as the incarnation of the Algonquin hero Manabozo, and preaches

intertribal unity in rebellion against white efforts at deportation. His brother Tecumseh became the military and political leader of the large but ultimately defeated federation of Shawnees, Delawares, Wyandottes and others. "The Great Spirit has given this great island to his red children. He placed the whites on the other side of the big water. They were not contented with their own but came to take ours from us, they have driven us from the sea to the lakes, we can go no further." [23]

1819–52   Movements among the Kickapoo of Illinois. "My father, the Great Spirit, holds all the world in his hands and I pray to Him that we may not be removed from our lands. Take pity on us and let us remain where we are." [24] The Kickapoo were finally forced to migrate to Kansas, where their prophet Kanakuk and most of his followers died of smallpox.

1880–1900   The Dreamer Movement. Columbia River tribes—Wanapum, Nez Perces, and Yakima. The conflict of white and Indian ways has never been better stated than in the words of Smohalla, the reborn prophet and adamant opponent of acculturation, whose preaching touched off the 1877 rising of the Nez Perces and whose followers "dreamed" in ecstatic dances: [25]

>   My young men shall never work. Men who work cannot dream, & wisdom comes in dreams.
>   You ask me to plow the ground. Shall I take a knife & tear my mother's breast? Then when I die she will not take me to her bosom to rest.
>   You ask me to dig for stone. Shall I dig under her skin for bones? Then when I die I cannot enter her body to be born again.
>   You ask me to cut grass & make hay & sell it, & be rich like white men. But how dare I cut off my mother's hair?
>   It is a bad law, & my people cannot obey it. I want my people to stay with me here. All the dead men will come to life again. We must wait here in the house of our fathers & be ready to meet them in the body of our mother.
>
>   (Statement by Smohalla, Nez Percé Indian)

1870–80   Early Ghost Dance. Started by the preaching of Wodziwob, a Paviotso (Western Nevada) and soon spread to all western tribes. The earth would open up to swallow the whites, leaving their material culture behind for the Indians. The Great Spirit and the risen dead would come to live among the cult followers.

Earth Lodge Cult, Dream Dance and Bole Maru. Ghost Dance offshoots among the Klamath, Pomo, Wintu, and other tribes of California and Oregon. Circle dances, trance, healing cults, symbolic games, some Catholic elements and emphasis on the imminent end of the world.

1870s–1930   Kolaskin's movement among the Sanpoil and other Washington State tribes. The paralysis, coma, and apparent death of Kolaskin were followed by a sudden rebirth; the faithful composed songs, entered into a silent trance, and at one point, built an ark which the federal government destroyed. Like almost all of the preceding movements, Kolaskin's sect strongly fought against the use of liquor and other forms of personal disorganization.

1873–75   Isatai's movement among the Comanche (Southern Plains). Militant and antiwhite, it resulted in daring punitive attacks on white buffalo hunters and was suppressed by the massacre of the Comanches.

1879–1972   The Dream Dance of the Menomini (Upper Wisconsin). Explicitly and self-consciously traditional and anti-Christian. Ecstatic dancing. Stress on intertribal unity.

1881–1972   The Shakerism of the Puget Sound tribes. Prophet John Slocum was reborn from a coma and death. Sect includes shaking during rituals, healing rites, recognition of Jesus, and many Roman Catholic elements.

1886–93   (Still extant in modified form.) The Second Ghost Dance, started by Jack Wilson (Wovoka), a Nevada Paiute ranchhand whose death vision coincided with an eclipse of the sun. There was mutual borrowing with the Mormons (some of whom accepted Wilson as the Messiah), although most elements of the Ghost Dance are traditional or directly adopted from the First Ghost Dance. Ecstatic dancing is accompanied by newly composed songs. The Ghost Dance cult spread throughout America west of the Mississippi in a number of variant forms and was resisted only by the Navajo and southwestern groups. Ghost Dance cultists were persecuted by the federal government persistently, leaders were imprisoned, and followers killed. Some Ghost Dance Songs follow:[26]

A Sequence of Songs of the Ghost Dance Religion

1
My children,
When at first I liked the whites,
I gave them fruits,
I gave them fruits.
　　　　　——Nawat, "Left Hand" (Southern Arapaho)

2
Father have pity on me,
I am crying for thirst,
All is gone,
I have nothing to eat.
　　　　　——Anon. (Arapaho)

3
The father will descend
The earth will tremble
Everybody will arise,
Stretch out your hands.
　　　　　——Anon. (Kiowa)

4
The Crow—*Ehe'eye!*
I saw him when he flew down,
To the earth, to the earth.
He has renewed our life,
He has taken pity on us.
　　　　　——Moki, "Little Woman" (Cheyenne)

5
I circle around
The boundaries of the earth,
Wearing the long wing feathers
As I fly.
　　　　　——Anon. (Arapaho)

6
I'yehe! my children—
My children,
We have rendered them desolate.
The whites are crazy—*Ahe'yuhe'yu!*
　　　　　——"Sitting Bull" (Arapaho "Apostle of the Dance")

7
We shall live again.
We shall live again.

——————Anon. (Comanche)

1870s–1972   The Peyote Cult, including the Big Moon (Christianized), Little Moon (non-Christian), and Native American Church variants. Widespread but centered in Southern Plains. The white opposition to the central sacrament of peyote was countered in the twentieth century by organization of "Churches," a structure acceptable to whites.

John Rave described his conversion as follows: "During 1893–94 I was in Oklahoma with peyote eaters. In the middle of the night we were to eat peyote. We ate it and I also did. It was the middle of the night when I got frightened, for a live thing seemed to have entered me. 'Why did I do it?' I thought to myself. 'I should not have done it for right at the beginning I have harmed myself. Indeed, I should not have done it. I am sure it will injure me. The best thing will be for me to vomit it up.' " But his efforts failed and he lamented, " 'I am surely going to die.' " As the day broke he was able to laugh with the others. "The following night we were to eat peyote again. I thought to myself, 'Last night it almost harmed me! . . .' 'Well, let us do it again,' they said and I replied, 'Alright, let us do it.' So there we ate seven peyote apiece." On the third night he ate eight peyote, and his account relates the visions he had on each of three nights. On the first he was terrified by a big snake crawling toward him; on the second a hideous creature with legs and arms and a long tail ending in a spear jumped on him and, failing to strike him, jumped again. On the third night, says Rave, "I saw God. To God living up above, our Father, I prayed: Have mercy upon me! Give me knowledge that I may not say and do evil things! To you, O God, I am trying to pray. Do Thou, O Son of God, help me too. This religion let me know. Help me, O Medicine! Grandfather, help me! Let me know this religion!" . . . "Now I know," says Rave, "that I had taken the wrong road and I shall never take it again. I was like blind and deaf . . . the Peyote is life, the only life, and only by eating peyote will you learn what is truly holy." [27]

JINGOISM AS A MOVEMENT WITHOUT MOVEMENT ORGANIZATIONS

> "The Spanish War finished us. The blare of the bugle drowned the voice of the Reformer." Tom Watson[28]

The juxtaposition of the sections on middle-class movements and on the resistance of the Indians brings us to a brief consideration of sentiments in support of American military and economic ventures abroad, for this rather unorganized support had a predominantly petty-bourgeoisie source and developed around the notions of mission or manifest destiny that had added the element of moralistic efforts at cultural destruction to the campaigns to remove the Indians from their lands. The best short summary of the turn of the century mixture of economic and moralistic justifications for imperialism is to be found in an article by Lloyd C. Gardner. "United States leaders identified colonial and undeveloped countries as neo-frontier wastelands—wasted in the sense that their resources were not being developed and used by the industrial nations for the benefit of the whole world economy. . . . America's mission, or New Manifest destiny, was to bring to 'Waste Areas' political democracy (as much as such peoples could absorb) and stability. In this view, selfish exploitation (such as colonial monopoly systems), which did not contribute to the overall system, was almost as bad as not making use of the area at all." [29] In other words, simple economic motives of gain, more complex economically generated value judgments (such as "stability," "efficient use of resources," and "development"), and a moralistic rhetoric are all inextricably mixed and cannot simply be reduced to any one of these motivational sources of foreign policy.

This mixture occurred in the general populace as well—rarely among workers, but quite frequently among the urban middle-class and agrarian entrepreneurs. It is not strictly speaking a movement since it had little structure and remained at the level of sentiment rather than action except for a small number of missionaries, Spanish War volunteers, and members of a flurry of patriotic societies. More importantly, we cannot consider it a movement because it was so strongly in support of the goals of political and economic elites. Yet nationalist sentiment was a movement-related phenomenon in three ways: it was given a great impetus by the depression of 1893, just as the movements were and was in this sense co-related; second, it drew support away from the movements, by overarching class frustrations with nationalist ideology (and perhaps at the individual level providing channels for aggressive feelings); and third, it was even absorbed into some movement belief systems—in a pacifist "Americanist" form into Populism, and in an ambivalent form in the middle-class movements that developed into the core of Progressivism.

NOTES

[1] Charles Beard and Mary Beard, *A Basic History of the United States* (Philadelphia: Blakiston, 1944), Chapters XVIII–XX.

[2] Beard and Beard, *op. cit.*, p. 309. This statement has been disputed by Gabriel Kolko, *The Triumph of Conservatism* (New York: Free Press, 1963), who claims that important industries—including those that we have mentioned—were in a state of competitive chaos. In short, the reader should recognize that oligopoly was only partially achieved and real monopoly was not.

[3] Sidney Lens, *Radicalism in America* (New York: Crowell, 1966), p. 146.

[4] The situation may be quite different among industrial but nonurban segregated workers in a number of countries. Such workers include Bolivian and South African miners, Cuban sugar cane workers, and Malaysian rubber plantation workers; here, there is a combination of the modern proletarian work force and the nonurbanized setting.

[5] Very strong support for this view comes from an article by Kerr and Siegel showing that wildcat strikes are far more numerous among isolated occupational groups—loggers, miners, sailors, and others—than among workers whose jobs are physically and structurally integrated into the central (urban) institutions of the society, for example, communication workers. This finding holds cross-culturally. In the next chapters, we will discuss how the substructural trends toward urbanization, and structurally integrated and integrating occupations (in education, the media, sales, communication, for instance) are a necessary element of the establishment of political and ideological corporate hegemony. The latter is not the result of conspiracy between business and political leaders (although cooperation is doubtless present, usually overtly) but of conditions of material life. Clark Kerr and A. Siegel, "Inter-Industry Propensity to Strike," in Robert Dubin, Arthur Kornhauser, and Arthur Ross, *Industrial Conflict* (New York: McGraw-Hill, 1954).

[6] Although a revolutionary movement often begins in a city, generally, it cannot win without spreading to the countryside. The integrating and pacifying impact of urbanization has been recognized by the intellectual advisors of the Pentagon who have directed their efforts at the forced migration of the Vietnamese peasantry to the cities as well as to other areas of population concentration. Samuel Huntington, cited in Noam Chomsky, "After Pinkville," *New York Review of Books* 13, no. 12 (January 1970): 40.

[7] Arthur Stinchcombe, "Agricultural Enterprise and Rural Class Relations," *American Journal of Sociology* 67 (1961–1962): 165–76.

[8] Beard and Beard, *op. cit.*, p. 318.

[9] Carl Degler, *Out of Our Past*, rev. ed. (New York: Harper & Row, 1970), p. 323.

[10] Beard and Beard, *op. cit.*, p. 332.

[11] Another view of this election was offered by the industrialists: Frick to Carnegie (1892) "I am very sorry for President Harrison, but I cannot see that our interests are going to be affected one way or the other by the change in administration." "Cleveland! Landslide" Carnegie replied. "Well we have nothing to fear and perhaps it is best. People will now think the Protected Manufacturers will be attended to and quit agitating. Cleveland is pretty good fellow. Off for Venice tomorrow." Gabriel Kolko, *Triumph of Conservatism* (New York: Free Press, 1963), pp. 62–63.

[12] Eric Goldman, *Rendezvous with Destiny* (New York: Knopf, 1956), p. 54.

[13] "Coin Harvey," quoted in Degler, *op. cit.*, p. 331.

[14] It is perhaps not too farfetched to note the parallels between contemporary middle class reform movements and the late nineteenth century movements that blended class interests, efforts to reform the poor and efforts to reform the institutions that perpetuated the oppression of the poor. Nowhere is this confusion of motives, ambivalence toward the oppressed and confusion of programs more visible than in the present contact of Jews and blacks in New York City. Richard Scott, a Columbia University student, has gone so far as to suggest the interesting but debatable proposition that radicalism among Jews in the 1960s was primarily a response to the ceilings on Jewish professionals' upward mobility into the ranks of the power elite.

[15] Herbert Gutman, "Protestantism and the American Labor Movement," in Alfred Young, ed., *Dissent* (DeKalb: Northern Illinois University Press, 1969), pp. 137–74.

[16] William L. O'Neill, "Feminism as a Radical Ideology," in Young, *op. cit.*, p. 273; and Christopher Lasch, *The Agony of the American Left* (New York: Random House, 1966), pp. 23–27.

[17] Quoted in O'Neill, *op. cit.*, p. 278.

[18] Aileen S. Kraditor, *Up From the Pedestal* (Chicago: Quadrangle Books, 1968); and William O'Neill, *Everyone Was Brave* (Chicago: Quadrangle Books, 1968).

[19] Anthony Wallace, "Revitalization Movements," *American Anthropologist* 58 (April 1956); and Vittorio Lanternari, *The Religions of the Oppressed* (New York: Knopf, 1963).

Note also Robert Lifton's treatment of the psychological integration of a collective disaster through works of creative imagination in *Death in Life* (New York: Random House, 1969).

[20] Peter Worsley, *The Trumpet Shall Sound* (New York: Schocken, 1968).

[21] Based on Lanternari, *op. cit.*, Chapters II and III.

[22] *Ibid.*, p. 103.

[23] *Ibid.*, p. 109.

[24] *Ibid.*

[25] Jerome Rothenberg, ed., *Technicians of the Sacred* (Garden City, N.Y.: Anchor Books, 1969), p. 361.

[26] *Ibid.*, pp. 98–99.

[27] Lanternari, *op. cit.*, pp. 72–73.

[28] Tom Watson, quoted in Goldman, *op. cit.*, p. 55.

[29] Lloyd Gardner, "American Foreign Policy 1900–1921," in Barton J. Bernstein, *Towards a New Past* (New York: Random House, 1968), p. 214.

7

The Rise of the New Industrial State: 1900–1929

Political capitalism is the utilization of political outlets to attain conditions of stability, predictability, and security —to attain rationalization in the economy. Stability is the elimination of internecine competition and erratic fluctuations in the economy. Predictability is the ability, on the basis of politically stabilized and secured means, to plan future economic action on the basis of fairly calculable expectations. By security I mean protection from the political attacks latent in any formally democratic political structure. I do not give to rationalization its frequent definition as the improvement of efficiency, output, or internal organization of a company; I mean by the term, rather, the organization of the economy and the larger political and social spheres in a manner that will allow corporations to function in a predictable and secure environment permitting reasonable profits over the long run. My contention . . . is not that all of these objectives were attained by World War I, but that important and significant legislative steps in these directions were taken, and that these steps include most of the distinctive legislative measures of what has commonly been called the Progressive Period.[1]

INTRODUCTION

Chapters 7 and 8 will be concerned with the movement phenomena accompanying two phases of the rise of the new industrial state; the first phase spans the Progressive Era of the first two decades of the century and the Jazz Age, and the second phase covers the recent past of the New Deal, World War II, and the Cold War. Movements of this period can be arranged in a spectrum from those that actively and intentionally fostered the rise of political capitalism to those that totally opposed it. Most movement organizations fell somewhere in the middle, frequently lending unintentional support to political capitalism because of their premise that government regulation of corporations was necessarily a step toward curbing the power of economic elites. Somewhat independent of the dimension of support for political capitalism was the dimension of support for political democracy. A third and also partially independent dimension that we will consider is the degree of realism in the assessment of substructural trends—specifically, some movements of opposition to political capitalism were futile efforts to restore the lost world of the early nineteenth century. Finally, cultural movements play an important role during this period.

The overall impact of movements during the progressive period was similar to that of the Jeffersonian and Jacksonian phases: they established a closer cooperation of economic and political elites at the national level while attaining some economic relief and political democracy at the local levels.

An interesting aspect of this period is that some movements split into a liberal [2] wing that continued to press for sociopolitical reforms to ameliorate modern capitalism in a soured and futile form and a cultural wing experimented with life style changes. This separation into wings had three important characteristics: the wings interchanged personnel; potential movement members tended to sort themselves into the wings on the basis of personality and personal experience more strongly than on the basis of social background; and the cleavage into wings occurred most dramatically, after the reforms had been achieved, when success had removed the goals that had provided consensus within the movement. Cleavage into wings also occurred in earlier movements (for instance, in the tripartite division of New England dissidents into Abolitionists, Know-Nothings, and Utopians in the mid-nineteenth century), but it can be observed most clearly after the reforms of the Progressive Era.

THE PROGRESSIVE ERA: 1900–1916

I believe it is erroneous to speak of a Progressive movement or of *the* Progressives. There are two types of inconsistencies within this phenomenon, one is the inconsistency between the hopes of participants and the unanticipated and unintended accomplishments of their movement organizations; the other is the inconsistency between the interests of the participating groups. Therefore, it is more correct to speak of a reform era, a period in which a number of movements were linked by their simultaneity, their common sources as responses to the substructural change of large-scale industrialism, and their agreement on a single negative ideological feature—namely, their rejection of contemporary Marxian or Anarcho-Syndicalist movements.

The ideology appears to be fairly cohesive and can be summarized as having the following goals and means:

1. Regulation of corporations for the public benefit in the form of trust-busting, product regulation, and curbs on the rapacious use of natural resources.
2. An end to corruption in government, particularly at the municipal level. This goal had two components:
    (a) Introduction of mechanisms for allowing wider participation in local decision-making and for thereby circumventing the power of the "boss," through the referendum, initiative and recall provisions.
    (b) A demand for efficiency, professionalization and expertise in government, expressed in the commission and city-manager plans for city government and the introduction of "rational" business-derived norms, such as cost-accounting and quanti-

fication of evaluation procedures, into public education and other administrative systems.

3. Integration of immigrants into American life *structurally* by improving their working and living conditions and by providing skills for upward mobility and *ideologically* by providing a variety of learning programs and protecting them from habits that led to personal disorganization.

A slightly different aspect of the integrationist impact of the Progressive movements was the political integration of women by national female suffrage.

4. Support of labor legislation that would raise the living standard of workers and improve job safety and compensation measures.

5. Strategies of moral suasion, legislation, and the establishment of middle-class outposts in immigrant ghettos.

So far, so good. This list may seem quite familiar to the reader since it overlaps in such large measure with those reforms and welfare measures now peculiarly referred to as "liberal"; it is a series of primarily legislative acts and legal procedures to reduce the laissez-faire aspects of the American State, to create welfare administrations and to integrate the excluded and alien into American life. Substitute "ecology" for "conservation," "blacks" for "immigrants," "drug abuse" for "intemperance" and bring the housing and labor laws up to date and you have a contemporary "liberal" program. Closer examination of this ideology, its supporters, local variation in its implementation and its overall impact destroys the appearance of uniformity and raises the question in what sense these measures were progressive.

Let us begin with the support base for reforms of the Progressive era. There was a fair amount of popular support, as evidenced in the frequency of local government reforms, the passage of legislation at state and national levels, and the repeated election—or if not election, a very strong showing—of presidential candidates (as well as more local ones) who were broadly identified with the "Progressive Movement." These concrete achievements, combined with the general sentiment attested to in the mass media (which presumably depended on and also shaped their readers' Progressive attitudes), suggest that Progressivism was a very widespread phenomenon, especially when compared to the perhaps more intense but much smaller support for Populism, and nineteenth and twentieth century radical movements.

Four strata seem to have contributed to Progressivism: the elite associated with the largest corporations; a new middle class of corporate managers and professionals; an older middle class of professionals and smaller entrepreneurs; and the working class. That each of these groups *contributed* support does not mean that their contributions were equal nor that their entire stratum supported Progressivism. It does however suggest that support and opposition to Progressivism does not fall simply along class lines. In this respect, the Progressive Era has some of the characteristics of Jacksonian Democracy, which also drew very diverse and widespread support. (In Jacksonian Democracy, we found a shared element of self-identification as a rising entrepreneurial class, although even in this case, subsistence farmers who did not share this self-image supported Jackson.) But further examination shows that the apparent unity of the Progressive ideology disintegrates when each stratum is associated with a particular set of reforms.

Let us begin with the "old" middle class. Its association with reform has the oldest roots, as we have seen in the preceding chapter where we discussed middle-class movements of the nineteenth century. This component of the Progressive Era produced the most vocal and zealous leaders, many of the fulltime movement members (intellectuals, journalists, community workers and politicians) and provided the Progressive movement with much of its imagery. Much attention has been devoted to their movement as a "status" revolt, an unrest caused by the loss of political power and ethnic-regional prestige.[3] This unrest in turn found two modes of expression within this old middle class—the strongly nativistic efforts to reform the immigrants (best exemplified by Prohibition) and the effort to curb the other new and threatening force, the giant corporation. But it would be cynical to assert that merely frustration was the psychological driving force behind these endeavors; a humanitarian spirit, to some degree based on Protestant doctrine, also informed these activities and the observer, no less than the participants, could witness the transmutation of frustration into generous feeling. But the curious ambiguity of "status revolt," of class problems translated into cultural reform projects, remained; where a clear understanding of one's own social position was repressed, concern easily deteriorated into a puritanical nativism on the one hand or manipulation of the young and the poor into adjustment on the other hand.[4] That this manipulation into conventional behavior was carried out in order to help the poor does not change the fact that it closed off the exploration of alternative paths of social change. Ultimately, the combination of the Puritan heritage and the liberal dream of opportunity meant that American reformers could not tolerate a situation of cultural pluralism under conditions of general welfare. That is, they could not conceive of a society in which ethnic or proletarian subgroups exist that are assured a comfortable standard of living without acquiring a bourgeois or petty-bourgeois life style, values and ambitions. The neocapitalist states of western Europe have moved toward this welfare state model of a pluralist society in which the working class holds few illusions about upward mobility (inter- or intra-generational) and maintains distinct values, kinship patterns and even speech while sharing in a fairly high degree of affluence. The example of these states suggests that a high level of welfare is possible within a society that maintains a distinct working-class subculture and that has not become entirely socialist; the model for this social order comes from the European synthesis of feudal corporatism, capitalist class structure and socialist welfare demands. The result is a society that has a capitalist stratification system, in which substantial parts of the population accept a fixed status but are not penalized for their lack of aspiration by being kept at a low living standard. In America, the lack of a feudal past, the Puritan penchant for moral homogeneity and the Horatio Alger myth of liberal competitive uniformity have made such an outcome exceedingly unlikely for largely ideological reasons. The nature of the middle-class impulse in Progressive reform (when contrasted to the socialist-inspired reform movements of Europe) underlines the ideological limitations on outcomes for neocapitalism in America. The present animosity against the unassimilated and consequently unambitious poor, expressed in the extreme resistance against welfare payments, reflects the survival of this demand for assent to the American Dream. The contrast between Western European welfare capitalism (in which capitalism is modified by a feudal past, strong socialist movements, and relatively little ethnic diversity) and American neocapitalism illustrate the postulate that a similar substructure and structure (in this case, industrial corporate capitalism and representative democracy) can be accompanied by diverse ideological systems with very tangible consequences for the population.

We can quickly examine working-class support for portions of Progressive legislation; it can be summarized as realistic and selective. Where Progressive leaders sought legislative support for job safety measures, workingmen's compensation, widows' pensions, wages and hours standards, and tenement laws, working-class and immigrant constituencies in the Northeast voted for them. Furthermore, workers were not particularly opposed to the Federal regulatory measures that stabilized the economy and drove small enterprises from the field, since the marginal entrepreneur was often more exploitive than his large rival. Few persons of urban working class background can be identified as Progressive leaders, however.[5]

A third stratum involved in the Progressive movement was a new middle class of corporation managers, engineers and a variety of professionals. It is often very difficult to sort this level out from the old middle class; then as now the two groups are analytically different but actually very overlapping in occupations and social backgrounds.[6] Let us therefore apply the "new" label only with great caution, and rather stress that the stratum was new in its ideology as much or more than in its structural position—it repeatedly appealed to the values of expertise and efficiency. This was the stratum that can be shown to have exerted most of the influence for civic reforms, especially the push for commission or city-manager municipal governments. The movement organizations that acted as carriers for these reforms were the Municipal Research Bureaus, the Voters' Leagues, the Civic Clubs, the Commercial Clubs and the National Municipal League. The core membership of these movement organizations were industrialists and corporation officials associated with major post-1870 wealth in iron, steel, electrical equipment (comprising 52 percent of the members of the Pittsburgh Civic Club and Voters League, for instance) and professional men.[7] For these groups, official goals of efficiency, business principles, professional qualification for office, civic responsibility, budgeting, centralization of civic government and "clean-up" coincided with class interests in rationalization of enterprise, systematization and accountability in the business climate, professional control of welfare functions, the application of expert analysis (described as "scientific"), and so on. Civic reforms thus established legitimate channels between these rising business and professional groups and the city administration; in this legalistic sense, "corruption" was swept away for it was no longer necessary. The genuinely populistic measure—initiative, recall, referendum, and direct primary, for instance—were used more to clear away the former holders of power and to open administrative positions to the professionally qualified than as part of an ongoing movement to involve individuals in political decisions. These civic reforms by and for a new managerial and professional class were often bitterly and successfully resisted by working and petty-bourgeois city neighborhoods; this has led to labeling the working class as conservative and boss-manipulated, which is true but only in a short-run way. In larger cities, with a numerically strong working class, especially in the Northeast, the city-manager movement generally failed.[8] Much as one might deplore the city boss and the existence of corrupt (that is, nonlegitimate) channels of influence, the older mayoral pattern left open more possibilities for a genuinely informed populistic future; the professionalization and centralization of city administration removed the boss, legitimized business control over political decision-making, and removed any future chance of alert and competent community control. It is the author's opinion that the narrow-mindedness and even reaction that have in the past and present accompanied popular control should not be used as an excuse for avoiding the risk of democracy. The cult of efficiency had particularly devastating effects on American public education, where professionalism and business principles took hold even in cities where the city manager or commission plan was defeated;[9] for instance, the lock-step of age-grading is one of the products of these reforms. As I shall argue in my last chapter, the reforms of "new" Progressives at the civic level have been re-opened as a battleground for social movement in the '60s and '70s; at present radical intellectuals are generally on the side of working-class opposition to professionalism, efficiency and "rationalization" in the businessman's sense. Acting as professionals themselves in health care, law, education, social work and other fields, they are attempting to reduce the helplessness of the client that resulted from bureaucratization and professionalism; at the same time, of course, they do not advocate a perpetuation of the equally helpless, albeit less impersonal role which the political machine imposes on its flock.

Goals of efficiency, professionalization and stabilization of relations between the government and the corporations were sought also at the national level by the fourth stratum under consideration, the national economic elite associated with large corporations.[10] At the national level there was much less effective opposition to these innovations than at the local levels where the conflicts were more open and more subject to the electoral process. At the national level the movement to regulate product quality (exemplified by the Pure Food and Drug Laws and the FDA), to curb trusts (for example, the Clayton Act of 1914) and to conserve natural resources had in a more complex and sophisticated way an impact similar to the civic reform movement: the economic situation was stabilized in a variety of ways, most dramatically in the Federal Reserve Act; channels between industry and the federal government were created through the regulatory agencies so that standard methods of communication and bargaining replaced the older more haphazard "corrupt" techniques of personal influence; in many areas, for instance, meatpacking, small competitors who could not meet regulatory standards were destroyed; resources were used more efficiently, that is, according to professional and technological standards that could not be met by the small untrained entrepreneur. Despite occasional busting of trusts, the economic situation began to be more favorable in the long run for the large bureaucratically organized, scientifically managed corporation with its desire for stable predictable conditions. Through a shift yet further away from laissez-faire (which had never really been an American government policy anyway) business gained a favorable climate for profits, growth, and vertical and horizontal expansion, while losing only the potential chaos of the free market. Its relation to the government was also legitimized; in the past, it had to some degree been a suppliant (albeit one that was rarely refused) which depended on politicians' favorable inclination to it; it now was included in the workings of the state—the state defined itself as having a responsibility toward the economy, that is, toward the incumbent economic elite rather than the small entrepreneur. This growing-together of state and capitalism is the most fundamental fact of the twentieth century; it was made possible—even likely—by the substructural changes of industrial capitalism, but the specifically political component of the "New Industrial State" came about only as part of the Progressive Era, as the result of conscious political effort. In no sense am I suggesting that a *conspiracy* occurred; any conspiracy theory is made ridiculous by two facts: the weight of the substructural conditions which made the appearance of political capitalism more than the result of a chance plot; and the overt commitment of elected Progressive leaders to the fusion we are calling political capitalism.[11]

This discussion should clarify my contention that any claim that Populism was fabulously successful in its anti-laissez-faire demands is nonsense; anti-laissez-faire measures demanded and enforced in the theoretical case of victory, by a more or less radical third party cannot be equated with similarly worded measures by which an existing elite innovates and strengthens its control. The Populists—and the Progressive trustbusters and muckrakers—wanted to use the political system *against* the economic elite; the unanticipated and unintended end result of the reforms they had proposed was an important step toward the *fusion* of these two sectors of the society. Where in the past the political elite had frequently aided the economic elite on the basis of ad hoc decisions, there now appeared an ongoing structure of connecting agencies. (The difference between the two stages is like that between grafts or blood transfusions on the one hand and the tissue connecting Siamese twins on the other.)

Thus, we see how the apparent unity of Progressive goals falls apart totally when the interests of different strata are sorted out and ideology is separated from actual impact. We have seen also how when a movement permits some of its goals to be taken from their original context and adopted as part of a general program of social change, the subsequent reforms are necessarily transformed into a completely unanticipated and undesired consequence; meanwhile, the movement that has narrowed its goals in the hope of attaining one or two of its more "realistic" goals is not only disappointed in their effect, but also drained of energy and drawing power.[12] "Partial incorporation" (and hence complete transformation) of its goals into the existing distribution of wealth and power is one of the worst fates that can befall a movement.

If we assess the various themes of Progressive thought in terms of the dimensions suggested above, we find that overall, it hastened the rise of political capitalism—perhaps made possible what was *not* inevitable—although this end was not the goal of the "old" middle-class reformers who formed its ideological center. Even the partially successful efforts at integrating immigrants into the central institutions of American society contributed to the hegemony of political capitalism.

The performance of Progressives in support of democratic political participation is mixed. Political capitalism is an obvious obstacle to attaining this value. Professionalism and efficiency in public administration are ultimately damaging to democracy. But those tools of Progressive reform that are used only sporadically—referendum, recall, initiative and direct primary—may yet be of value; in a country in which radicalism cannot now resort to violence, any populist piece of legislation must be carefully protected and judiciously used by radical movements.

One may conclude by noting that except in some nativist pieces of legislation, Progressivism was eminently rational in strengthening and establishing within the political system some major substructural characteristics of advanced industrialism like stabilization, rationalization, and acculturation of subgroups into a culturally homogeneous proletariat.

To some degree, we can apply a market place model to social movements and conceptualize each one as competing for time and funds with other organizations and pursuits. In this sense, Progressivism was very hard to "sell" to the working class. At the middle class levels it had to compete with cultural movements among the more alienated middle class. Some of the latter involved itself primarily in movements of nativist souring, such as Prohibition. Other portions experimented with a Bohemian life style. This period saw the development of Greenwich Village as a center and symbol of these efforts —and sometimes with socialism.[13] The intimate but uneasy alliance of radical life styles and radical politics during the Progressive Era repeats the relation of utopians and abolitionists in the pre-Civil War period and foreshadows the liaison between "hippies" and political radicals in the '60s. In any case, both Bohemians and Socialists remained only at the fringes of the Progressive movements. Progressivism also had to compete with more overtly class-based organizations such as the National Association of Manufacturers.

In the following pages, we will briefly examine some competing movements: two working-class movements, the Socialists and the International Workers of the World; and the middle-class movement alternatives, many of which gained support as the Progressive impulse was absorbed by the existing social order.

THE AMERICAN LEFT

A General Post Mortem on the Left

For the period before the Great Depression we will glance at a variety of strategies of radical movements. None of them can be said to have been successful.

Radical groups in *any* society have to face the problem of pulling themselves up by their own bootstraps—by definition, class structure, the political and legal system and the ideology are all obstacles to them. Their resources of money, members, military capability, and control over media and educational institutions are exceedingly limited. In a *modern* society these problems are enormously greater because one of the characteristics of modernity—one of the correlates of economic-technological growth—is the increase in the power of the central institutions;[14] politically, culturally and economically the society is drawn into the center. The periphery weakens, corporate groups tend to disappear, the population is proletarianized and the culture becomes a mass culture. More people live in cities; the media and means of communication are technologically improved and less locally oriented; power moves from the local to the national level; the means of social control are more subtle, more pervasive, more national, and more professionalized; bureaucracies are larger and penetrate more deeply into the society; people are more politically mobilized and educated in more uniform institutions. I do not wish to appear to be insisting on a mass society model that applies completely to every modern society, but these statements do hold in a broad comparative way. They are not logically determined, but empirically probable. It is fairly safe to state that a randomly selected individual is more in touch with central institutions in the United States, the Soviet Union, France or China than he is or was in Ethiopia, Byzantium, Medieval England, or modern India. The import of this proposition for radical movements is that the creation of "liberated zones," physically and/or socially isolated bases that are secure from social control and can function as starting points for radical organization, is difficult. The radical movement must therefore either wait for a massive breakdown in central institutions (as occurred in European countries during the world wars) or must very slowly and patiently build a mass movement which can either engineer such a breakdown itself (this being the somewhat dubious myth of the general strike) or can gain power through legitimate channels (as in Chile at the time of this writing, in Guatemala before the CIA coup, and so forth).

It is simply a fact that since the Civil War there has been no major breakdown of American central institutions. Even the economic disaster of the Great Depression left the political and legal institutions functioning, a majority of persons pursuing economic routines, and the police and the schools still in operation. There has been no breakdown of central institutions in post-Civil War America comparable to German defeat in World War I, the chaos of China in the warlord period and World War II, and the occupation and liberation of Greece prior to the post WW II guerrilla war, and so on. On the contrary, we have seen—and will show in our discussion of the depression—that American central institutions have grown stronger and more legitimate.

Given the lack of any massive deroutinization of life, American radical movements had to turn to the more laborious techniques of organizing mass movements. To continue our deroutinization model a bit further, we can categorize radical organizing by whether it builds on individual deroutinizing experiences or works to create such experiences for whole local groups. The first is essentially the technique of the Socialist Party in its peak years; it reached out to and was able to involve people who felt touched by experiences (of urbanization, of declining entrepreneurial opportunity, of exploitation as workers, of disgust at mass culture) and/or by contact with progressive reforms. A number of dislocated people were able to understand their personal troubles as the results of structural transformation, and felt that action within the legitimate channels was not entirely futile: that is, they voted for the Socialists because they believed that voting outside the conventional party system had educational value, avoided the backlash effects of nonlegitimate acts, and in some localities and in the long run, might actually bring about political change by election of officials. This first strategy, the "educating the alienated" model of radical organizing, involves personal or —as a very poor second—media contact with individuals who have undergone dislocations in order to help them understand their experiences and take some kind of action. It is of necessity a slow process. One way of speeding it up is to begin by contacting individuals who are not merely alienated but also deroutinized. For the Wobblies, this target population was the itinerant laborers; for the 1960s and '70s these have been the young poor, the gang members of the ghetto, the barrio, and the poor-white neighborhood.[15] For a variety of reasons, the intellectual proletariat and adolescents are also already deroutinized and hence a favorite starting place for radical movements. The problem with this strategy is that it is difficult to spread organization from the deroutinized pockets of youth, intellectuals and gangs to the rest of society; furthermore, some of the deroutinized may be too involved in subsistence problems to be organizable—thus, the deroutinization of the addict and the migratory laborer makes participation in a movement difficult rather than easy. A third strategy therefore is to create deroutinizing situations for normally integrated people; herein lies the importance for radicals of strikes and "mass action." These tactics can of course also be used by nonradical unions as a bargaining weapon and to create small crises that are used to strengthen regular union leadership,[16] but when applied by a radical movement organization they create tiny socially, spatially and temporally liberated zones. The Columbia uprising of 1968 no less than the IWW-organized Lawrence and Paterson strikes of 1912 and '13 established situations that were totally nonroutine, that were suspended in revolutionary time, that were totally divorced from and opposed to the central institutions.[17] The chief problem of beginning by organizing the deroutinized in the timber camps, the pool halls or the coffee shops is to spread the organization beyond the spatial confines of these environments; the chief problem of beginning by organizing through deroutinizing experiences is to sustain the organization beyond the temporal confines of the crisis. Neither the IWW in Lawrence, nor the Strike Steering Committee at Columbia (nor for that matter, Billy Graham in his religious movement organization) could successfully maintain a radical organization beyond the crisis period itself. Once the episode ended, the local representatives of the central institutions once again rushed in to fill the vacuum in a variety of ways—by punishing strikers once they had lost widespread public support, by re-imposing the daily routines of factory (or classroom), by playing on the recurrent and inescapable physical needs of the strikers, by making small concessions in order to gain the larger victory of a return to normalcy. The strategies of organizing the deroutinized and creating deroutinization were the strong points of the IWW. But they were unable to spread and sustain the new ways of thinking and acting.

The language of deroutinization should shed some further light on the problems of political versus economic action, dual unionism versus boring from within, and immediate demands versus long-term goals. As long as any one of these strategies failed to change individual (and group) self-images, daily routines, and life styles they could not succeed as organizing strategies. Long-term goals were ineffective because they appealed only to those who were convinced by radical programs in the first place and seemed senseless to everyone else. Immediate demands worked only when they led to crisis episodes; if employers made concessions individuals benefited a little but the movements gained nothing—and we must remember that the Progressive Era was one of general willingness to make concessions; boring from within was very unlikely to produce results—even when it was as widespread as was Communist participation in the CIO in the 1930s, it seemed to leave individual workers untouched; political campaigning was effective in that it *did* lead many individuals to make small moderate commitments to radical ideology and participation but did little to weaken the central institutions because it recognized their legitimacy. All of these strategies together might have produced a viable movement which combined the creation of cadres of the deroutinzed to produce deroutinizing incidents, whose participants would then be further organized to work in campaigns and to "bore from within." But such a coordination of efforts was never effected. The mutual compatibility and interdependence of these strategies was subordinated to short-sighted hairsplitting and arguments over which *one* was the best. Any radical movement in America *must* begin with the fact that American central institutions are strong, that they are not likely to break down in the near future, that there exists a prerevolutionary situation only in the most abstract sense. Once it has accepted these premises, an American radical movement can build a base only by a combination of strategies aimed at first prying people away from their ideological convictions and daily routines and sustaining this perspective and activity over a long time; obviously these are two distinct tasks and require cooperation as well as division of labor between movement organizations (or sections within a movement organization). Division of labor has rarely been a well-developed strategy among the movement organizations within a movement perhaps because the scarcity of money and members has encouraged competition; ideational rigidity—a useful defense against partial incorporation—has also led to efforts to nullify rival movement organizations.

Our conclusion about the American left between 1900 and the Depression must be that it suffered failure because of *preventable mistakes* and not because of the operation of some inevitable substructural demiurge or because of the inherent pragmatism of American national character—whatever that may be. It is true that American ideology *has* made radical organization exceptionally difficult but not necessarily logically impossible. One must also take into account that radical movements—like Protestant sects—attract individuals who rebel against routine and/or demand doctrinal purity, so that a movement which must be both flexible and willing to undertake day-to-day organizing tasks tends to be staffed by precisely those individuals who are neither. If they were cognitively casual and willing to do routine work they would very likely not have become radicals in the first place. Perhaps this self-selection process coupled with the strength of central institutions in a modern society really does make the growth of a radical movement impossible.

We will now examine the various small successes and large failures of radical movements between 1900 and the Depression.

The Socialists

The most useful way to begin a chapter on self-identified "left" movement organizations is to begin with a family tree (see Figure 2).[18]

The reader should note that left and right on the chart do not necessarily correspond to left and right ideologically. Notice that during the period under consideration there was a single strong trunk—the Socialist Party. It had two main roots: the socialist parties with an urban and European support base and a more native base in the American Railway Union and Populist splinter groups. Parallel to the Socialist main trunk was the slim but tough growth of the Industrial Workers of the World, historically based on the organization of Western metal miners, and more or less anarcho-syndicalist in style and goals. Where the Socialists operated within the electoral process and by organizing within the AFL, the IWW attempted to create in-

168   SOCIAL MOVEMENTS IN AMERICA

Figure 2

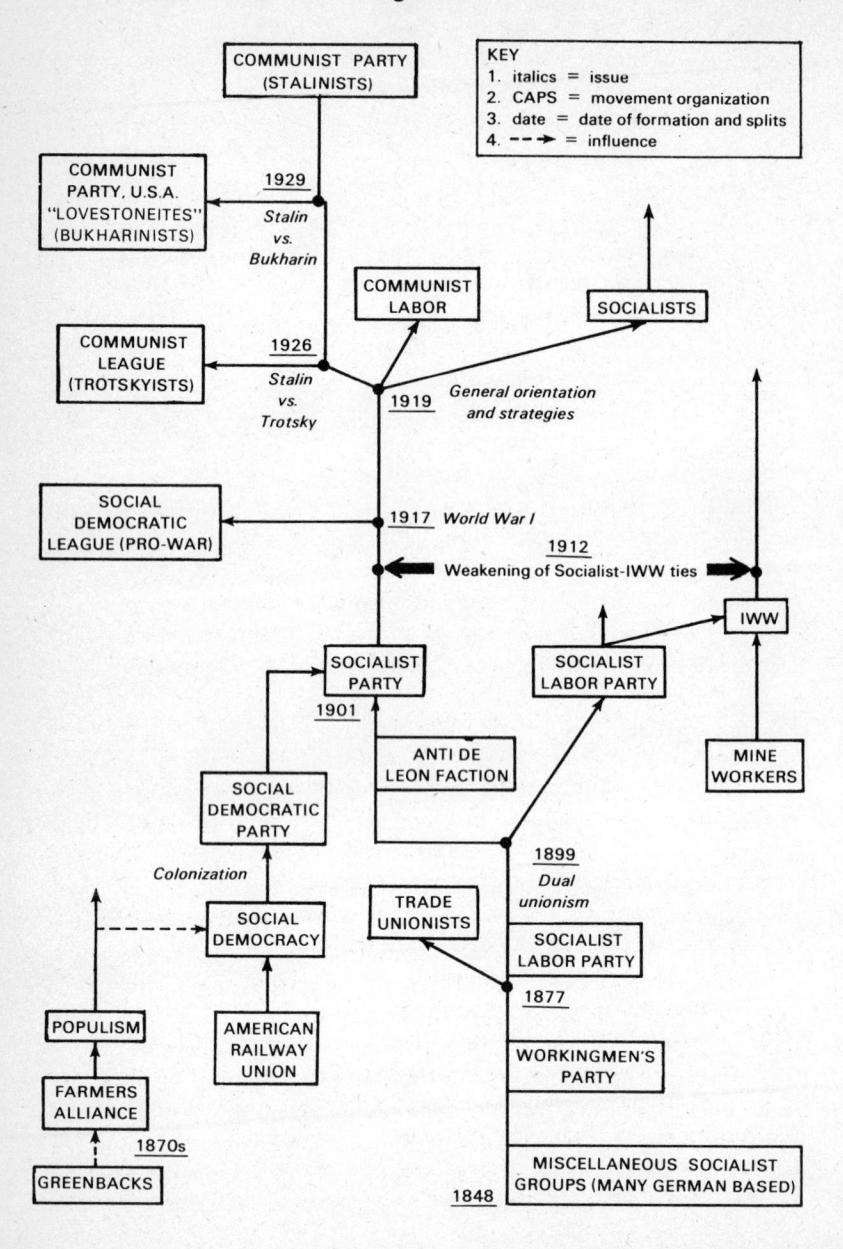

dustry-wide unions with the ultimate goal of seizure of the means of production by loosely linked collectives of workers. The chief branches of the Socialist "tree" were the thin proliferating growths of communist parties of the 1920s.

A summary of key splits, coalitions and factionating issues follows.[19]

1848–73 Marxian, Lassallean and Anarchist movement organizations, some of which ran candidates in local elections. Some cooperation and shared membership with Knights of Labor and farm groups.

1877 Formation of Socialist Labor Party, Repudiation of trade unionism. Headed by Daniel DeLeon, editor of its journal, brilliant but rigid, and little concerned with organizing a mass proletarian movement. Nevertheless, the SLP does make efforts to capture the support base of Knights of Labor and AFL, by organizing "dual unions."

1899–1900 Splits in Socialist Labor Party over issues of dual unionism and immediate demands; DeLeon faction attacks support for immediate demands as "kangarooish"—that is, primitive.

Meanwhile, back in the Midwest . . . .

1897 American Railway Union merges with other labor union representatives, some Socialist Labor Clubs, cooperative movement organizations and religious groups to create the Social Democracy, with railway man Eugene Debs as chairman. In addition to the usual radical demands of public ownership of monopolies, utilities and resources, public works for the unemployed, reduction of hours, postal savings banks, proportional representation, and initiative-referendum, and recall, this body called for control of a state to be developed as a cooperative commonwealth—the colonization plan.

1898 After an influx of urban Jewish and German socialists who opposed colonization, Social Democracy split over the colonization issue and died in the process of bringing forth the anticolonization Social Democratic Party.

1900–01 The Social Democracy Party and the anti-DeLeon forces of the Socialist Labor Party unite to form the Socialist

Party. In 1900, the new group's candidate Eugene Debs, polls 96,878 votes to the SLP's 32,751 votes in the Presidential election.

1901–17   These are the peak years of American Socialism as a growing body that could overcome its internal ideological splits (between a left and a right) and could elect numerous local officials.[20] A Socialist (Max Hayes) poses a formidable challenge to Gompers—one-third of the vote—in the 1912 campaign for the presidency of the AFL. The only serious splits are over the role of the IWW, a syndicalist body that was developing a very different but also potentially successful form of radical labor organization.

1917–19   The war years indirectly contribute to the Socialist Party's de-decline in that Federal persecution and vigilanteism hit the southern and western sections most heavily and give the foreign language federations a proportionately stronger role within the party. These bodies draw the Socialists into the discussion of whether Bolshevik strategies can be adopted in the United States and whether such a policy will benefit Soviet socialism; the foreign language federations and a small number of English-speaking socialists are purged from the Socialist Party and the Communist Party and the Communist Labor Party are founded.[21]

1920–30   The Communist splinter groups undergo further factionalism, while the Socialists briefly support the rather successful third-party movement of Robert La Follette Progressives but never again are able to regain a mass working-class base.

Early twentieth century American radicalism is important for at least three reasons: it demonstrates the potential for successful development of a mass base, for effective political work and industrial organization; secondly, it presents a case study of factionalism in radical organizations; thirdly, it brings to our attention some earlier formulations of issues that are now once again plaguing American radicals—that is, the issues of strategy, of cooperation and/or infiltration of conventional labor organizations, of work in political campaigns, of sustaining support during noncrisis phases, and of relationships to revolutionary movements abroad.

Radical organization in America has tended to be linked chronologically to reform movements because ultimately both are efforts to come to terms with the same substructural trends and the economic and social manifestations of these trends—industrialization, depression, migration, and so on. To understand the relationship between movements during the Progressive Era we must return to our marketplace model of movement organization. Mass movements that lack elite sponsorship and eschew the romantic tactics of terrorist conspiracy must establish a base that either includes the mobilization of substantial numbers of people (be it for elections, general strikes, paramilitary action, and so forth) or the penetration of key institutions (army, conventional unions, political structure, for example); it is often difficult to specify where "mobilization" ends and "penetration" begins. Both endeavors require the recruitment and involvement over a period of time of fairly large numbers of people; for each committed movement member, there must be many formally uncommitted individuals who are at least mildly sympathetic—the penumbra that we have mentioned several times. One of the chief problems for radical movements in America has been the creation of a "penumbra." For the Progressives—even for those who were not themselves members of the local or national business elite—the creation of a penumbra of partially or potentially mobilized persons was relatively easy since the Progressive movement organizations had access to the media and expressed views that were not altogether novel to Americans. The Progressives were thus quite successful in staking a claim for reform among the middle class; as we have seen, although they had occasional support from the working class they left it essentially unorganized.

A second possible competitor with radical class-conscious movements was the AFL. But for ideological reasons (Gompers' goal of junior partnership for labor in a capitalist society) as well as the exigencies of obtaining gains for its skilled base, the AFL made little effort to organize the mass of American workers; it had organized about 3 percent of the total number of employed nonfarm workers in 1900 and 5 percent in 1910.[22] It had more or less deliberately left unorganized unskilled and semiskilled workers, blacks, immigrants (many of whom were unskilled), a variety of southern and western workers, farm laborers, and railwaymen (whose organization antedated the AFL). All these were a potentially vast support base for movements that were more radical than the AFL and the Progressives, that is, those that were at all radical. The degree to which these workers were organized and the reasons why so many of them were not are a key question for this period.

The question cannot be answered without raising another question: How were they to be organized, and for what short-range purposes (postponing for the moment the broader issue of the vision of the good society)? Three basic strategies occurred to radical leaders: first, dual unionism, in which large-scale inclusive unions would be a radical alternative to the AFL and could win immediate improvements for proletarians, educate them toward larger goals, incubate indigenous leaders, and ultimately act as the structure for a general strike or revolution and as the building blocks of a new social order; second, "bore from within," that is, penetrate the existing unions and, thus, capture the support of skilled workers and the established labor media;[23] third, build a political base rather than an economic one and—at least in the foreseeable future—operate as a political party. In retrospect, one can remark that the dual unionism and "boring from within" strategies seem perfectly compatible considering the small size of the AFL and the small number of firmly committed workers that would be gained even if it were captured. Nevertheless, the limited resources of radical movements forced these movements to assign priorities to strategies and, eventually, to view such strategies as mutually exclusive for specious doctrinal reasons. These three strategies—dual unionism, boring from within and electoral participation—were the three major options, although they received a little competition from other strategies such as the anarchist-terrorist propaganda of the deed and the slightly ludicrous colonization scheme. Somewhat related to the problem of strategies but partially independent was the question of whether or not "immediate demands" should be issued. The affirmative position (supported by virtually all except DeLeon) was that aside from any humanitarian benefits workers would gain from struggles for immediate demands, such a struggle would be an educational experience in which the nature of the capitalist elite would become clearer and also an excellent way to develop leaders of proletarian background. The counterargument that the pursuit of immediate demands led to reformist contentment with trivial victories may have been abstractly correct, but when put into practice (chiefly by the DeLeonists), this strategy produced an unrealistic movement, hopelessly distant from a proletarian base.

The problem of strategy proved to be the greatest source of factionalism in the prewar years; undeniably, it was aggravated and also crosscut by differences of personality and background among the leaders, by adherence to or deviation from "orthodox Marxism," by one's vision of the good society, by nuances of rhetoric, and so on.

Despite the supposed split into a left wing and a right wing,[24] the prewar Socialists were fairly united in their preference for political action, despite occasional flirtations with the IWW dual unionists and some very impressive intrusions into the AFL.[25] The years of Socialist vigor correspond to diversity, willingness to experiment and an unforced unity. These were also the years during which Socialism had a working-class support base. There are two pieces of evidence for this contention—their strength within the AFL and the nature of their local political victories. In 1912, a Socialist, Max Hayes, received almost one-third of the vote in his campaign against Gompers for the presidency of the AFL; the Socialist Vice Presidential candidate received almost two-fifths of the vote.[26] Socialist strength was especially great among the Machinists, Brewery Workers, Bakers, United Mine Workers, Western Federation of Miners, Painters, and Quarry Workers, a majority of whose delegates voted for the Socialist candidates. After 1912, the Socialists gained control of the International Ladies Garment Workers Union and later it and the Amalgamated Clothing Workers Union were the only unions that wholeheartedly supported the Socialist antiwar stand. Socialists also won the presidencies of state labor federations in Pennsylvania and Illinois.

In local and state politics, Socialists also demonstrated working class roots. Weinstein remarks of the eighty to eighty-five Socialists elected to state legislatures from 1912 through 1918: "Approximately 62 percent of them, for example, were workers at the time of their elections, or had been workers for most of their lives, while another ten percent were farmers." [27] Socialist administrators were elected more frequently in towns than they were in cities; in towns, they were likely to be workers, while the rarer city Socialist officials were more often ministers, lawyers, editors and other professionals.

Let me clarify the purpose of introducing this evidence for

working-class support for Socialism. The fact that many supporters of Socialism were workers (which is true) should not be confused with the statement that many workers were supporters of Socialism (which is false). Even at its peak, Socialism attracted only a small percentage of the national vote and only a minority of the AFL vote, which itself represented only a tiny fraction of American labor. Nevertheless, Socialist support does suggest that viewing the Socialist Party as a potential forerunner of an American Labor Party (with all the realistic strengths and reformist weaknesses of its European counterparts) is not wholly ludicrous.

I also want to emphasize that I am concerned with working-class support not because of a doctrinaire faith in the proletariat or the conviction that only manual workers can be radicals, but simply because Socialism could not have competed successfully with Progressivism for middle-class votes. As a matter of fact, when Socialism turned to reformist goals and lost sight of its end goal of organizing workers to control the means of production, it could not capture the Progressive support base. Progressive reforms undercut local Socialist strength insofar as both sought better government and improved conditions for labor and the Progressive tickets seemed to be more realistically able to carry out their programs since they were better funded and received more support from economic and national political elites. Thus appeals to and support from manual workers was essential to the distinctness and survival of socialism.

The discussion of long-run chances for socialism deteriorates into idle speculation because the Socialist Party declined with the war and split over the Russian Revolution. More than ever before (with the exception of the French decision to back the American revolutionaries in order to strike at the British) events abroad were to shape the course of American social movements. World War I did not lead to a substantial numerical decline in membership in American radical movement organizations; despite some drops in membership, caused partly by fear of government and vigilante repression and partly by the splitting off of pro-war groups, both the Socialists and the IWW were almost at full strength again by 1919.[28] But the composition of the Socialist party had changed; the western branches had been harder hit by local repression and federal postal censorship so that the Party's center of gravity shifted toward the foreign-language federations. These bodies were partly composed of recent immigrants from Eastern Europe (Russia, the Ukraine, the Baltic countries) and understandably were attuned to events in Europe and Russia; the revolutions and disorders that swept Europe in the postwar years were personally vivid to the members in a way that they could not be to the rank and file in small cities and mining towns in the Midwest and West. They were also exciting for a substantial number of radical intellectuals who chafed under the political minority-party strategy and the AFL penetration strategy of the Socialist Party. Men and women who had participated in the Bolshevik Revolution could not commit themselves to working for the success of the Socialist candidate for assessor in Sheboygan, Wisconsin. The nebulous left-right schism of the prewar years became sharper and rapidly less bridgeable; in 1919 came the inevitable purge in which the purging right wing kept the party name and about one-third of the membership while some of the left wing took with it into the Communist Party (primarily based on the foreign language federations) and the Communist Labor Party (more heavily American intellectuals) the radical immigrants and the romantic theorizers. In some sense, the old issue of "immediate demands," ostensibly interred with the DeLeonists, had come back to haunt the American left as the issue of "orthodoxy" versus "opportunism." Despite some initial flirtation with IWW notions of industrial unionism, One Big Union and the general strike, the orthodox faction eventually cleaved to Leninist principles and the effort to create a small, disciplined pure party that would transfer Russian experiences to American soil. For the time being, such a party could do little to gain mass support in America. Its fossilization in this rigid Moscow-oriented form allowed Communism to survive the years of reaction and general privatization in the twenties but also weakened its ability to respond realistically to the thirties.

The Industrial Workers of the World

> The lake dries up at the edges.
> ———(Bantu reflection)

In the non-Euclidean geometry of radical movements, parallel lines do occasionally meet and so the Socialist Party and the IWW touched at several points but rarely produced the cooperation that was necessary.

The IWW was committed to socialism in a broad sense, hoped to attain it by dual unionism with industrial (rather than craft) unions using the weapons of the strike and eventually the general strike. Their goal was the creation of unions for each type of enterprise in which skilled and unskilled workers would cooperate eventually to paralyze the capitalist productive system and then to seize the means of production and use them by and for the producing majority. Not opposed in principle to political action, most IWW leaders saw it as rather pointless. Their organizing efforts were primarily directed at workers at the geographical, social and economic margins of society: timber workers in the Northwest, Great Lakes area and the South; metal miners; migrant farm workers in the West; unskilled and semi-skilled immigrant textile workers; migratory harvesters in the plains states; seamen; black dockworkers in Philadelphia and Baltimore. The IWW were eager to organize precisely the majority of workers that the AFL refused to include. They demonstrated that recent immigration and ethnic diversity were not necessarily obstacles to labor solidarity. While the Progressives hardly improved the black man's lot at all, the AFL deliberately excluded him, and the Socialist Party offered a lukewarm vacillation, the IWW was beset by neither prejudice nor "practical considerations" and organized black workers, often into integrated locals even in the South.

Contrary to contemporary charges and present romantization, the Wobblies did not use violence. Although their final split with the Socialists came in 1913 over the issue of the Socialist anti-sabotage clause (and the consequent recall of the IWW's Haywood from the Socialist Party's National Executive Committee because he refused to support it), the IWW used little sabotage and virtually no violence against human beings. Despite their occasional violent class struggle rhetoric almost all of the violence associated with the IWW organizing campaigns was committed by the police, by troops and by vigilantes *against* the IWW and the workers they tried to organize. This contention should not be unfamiliar to readers who remember how scores of blacks were killed by undisciplined National Guardsmen during the Watts-Newark-Detroit riots, while the "sniper fire" of the rebels not only took no white lives but proved to have been grossly exaggerated.[29] The Wobblies were violent only in the sense that they generated demands and situations that could be met within the system only by violent suppression. When faced with violence, IWW organizers responded with the techniques of non-violent resistance.

Tactics almost always grew out of the strategy of organizing men as workers. They included the following: strikes for better living conditions and decent wages in mining towns and the textile centers of Lawrence, Mass., and Paterson, N.J.; organizing itinerant "timber beasts" and farm laborers into the only grouping that provided stability and solidarity; civil disobedience and nonviolent resistance in Spokane, Fresno, San Diego, and other Western cities in 1909-11 in order to win the right to public speaking and organizing, a prerequisite for access to the wandering homeless laborers who sought day work in the city labor markets. The ultimate goal was always the destruction of capitalism and the state and the creation of a society of producers; but pragmatic considerations and the relentless pressing of immediate demands were not subordinated to the development and imposition of an ideology.

Structurally, as well as tactically and strategically, the IWW remained open, decentralized, antibureaucratic and sometimes disorganized. While the leadership of the SLP, the Socialists, and the Communists was heavily middle class or upwardly mobile, the IWW had largely proletarian leaders, men and women who practiced the unskilled manual work of their support base. Yet the openness of the IWW prevented a satisfactory confrontation with the problem of sustaining movement participation; even while it continued to organize a variety of industries successfully in the short run, the IWW often failed to sustain and consolidate its organization after the deroutinizing crisis and the ensuing burst of enthusiasm and solidarity.

The end of the IWW came as a result of federal suppression that began during the war years and continued unabated into the early twenties; not only did employers, local governments, and vigilantes add their persecution to that of the federal government, sometimes in coordinated fashion, but the IWW was plagued by agents provocateurs also. The unrest among workers that had provided the IWW with a support base was absorbed in a variety of ways: employers made concessions and either established company unions or submitted to AFL organizing; technological change wiped out the marginal and deroutinized worker—especially in the lumber industry—and permitted a shift to a smaller, stabler, more skilled work force; among IWW leaders the newborn Communist parties offered some a new path, although many resisted absorption into a Leninist party;

finally, a reduced but still substantial number of workers were left as exploited as before and remained unorganized till the union drives of the '30s or, in the case of migrant farm workers, until the present.[30]

So far, we have discussed two radical movements that enjoyed a small measure of success by using very different strategies during a period of reform and upheaval. Neither was numerically strong—the IWW failed to hold more than 100,000 members even in its peak years and the Socialist vote was not impressive at the national level, despite local victories. But both remained flexible and potentially complementary, and reasonably realistic in their assessment of American conditions; in tactics and organizational style, they were at least partially decentralized and able to bridge internal conflict. Recent historians have unfortunately come to use "pragmatic" to mean "submissive to the status quo"; one should go beyond this usage and speak of a pragmatic radicalism that remains in touch with local conditions and acknowledges national variations in the relation of substructure to superstructure. Both the Socialists and the IWW attempted to adapt themselves to American conditions in tactics and structure. But both prematurely had to face the problems posed by the war, suppression and—especially in the case of the Socialists—the European revolutions. Neither survived; both became small becalmed remnants.

Meanwhile their successor, the Communist Party in its various forms and guises, coped with the very harsh environment of the twenties by the peculiar stratagem of becoming as rigid structurally and unrealistic strategically as possible. (Its greatest successes—meager as they were—came with the effort to work within the AFL, chiefly by amalgamating craft unions into industrial unions.) This style allowed it to survive the twenties but weakened it for the thirties for once the rationale and structure for obedience to Moscow were set they proved impossible to reverse. In the thirties, a pragmatic radical movement might have succeeded in establishing a large base either as a party or as a dual union. The Communists almost succeeded in doing the latter, but having been unable to link their organizing activities in the building of the CIO to comprehensible American-oriented radical goals, they were easily purged from the CIO and fell back into sectarian paralysis again. The failure of American Communism in the '30s and '40s must be understood as partly a result of the party's initial foreign orientation and unrealistic assessment of American conditions.

THE RETURN TO NORMALCY

Contrary to customary views, the return to normalcy began with the war. For among other meanings, normalcy meant the end of both reform and radicalism and their weakening began during the war years. A national war effort can be understood as a movement phenomenon (though clearly not a movement, by our definition) in which an elite mobilizes a large portion of the population, exciting them ideologically and deroutinizing them. As such wartime nationalism not only directly affected radical movements by government suppression and vigilanteism but also indirectly by providing an alternative outlet for aggression, adventurousness and idealism, by drawing on some of the same personal qualities and experiences that could lead into rank and file membership in a reform or even radical movement. But nationalism as an ideology and nationalist mobilization stressed the opposite of radical principles—that is, submergence of class differences to a national goal.

One of the chief causes of the reaction of the late teens and the twenties must, therefore, be war mobilization. High prices and other economic dislocations, urbanization, the revolutions in Europe, the continuing presence of the immigrant—all these induced popular frustration that came to be expressed in nativist attitudes and actions; but without the incentive, example and provision of enabling structures by the government in 1917 (the Sedition Act), 1919–20 (the Palmer raids, mass deportations, state legislature restrictions on free speech, and appointment of known reactionaries to key posts), and 1924 (the restrictionist National Origins Act), it is unlikely that the private movements of intolerance would have been as virulent or well supported.

Of these movements, the expansion of the Klan into the Midwest is best known. It is used as the chief example of the small-town working or petty-bourgeois Protestant sources of reaction; this and the increasing irrational nativism of the Prohibition forces are used as arguments for the case that American suppression of civil liberties has the same support base as the Populism and other reform agitation of the turn of the century. But the Klan was atypical in that it solicited funds only from private individuals and therefore remained in a precarious financial condition. By 1927, the American Civil Liberties Union no longer cited it as a leading threat.

Far more characteristic of the period were the American Legion, the War Department (which initiated and funded anti-radical action) and the professional patriot societies. During their peak years, 54 such societies were listed as members of the American Coalition of Patriotic Societies. Among their activities were pressuring civic bodies to blacklist reform speakers (Jane Addams, for one), harassing reform groups (such as the American Birth Control League, the American Civil Liberties Union, the liberal church groups, the National Child Labor Committee, and the Consumers League) and providing data and manpower for attacks on radicals (for example, by compiling and circulating a data sheet on individuals and organizations).

The interrelationships between these movement organizations, businessmen's interest groups, and branches of the government indicate that in large part this was an elite movement, sponsored by groups with wealth or power to rid themselves not only of radicals but also to block or undo moderate Progressive reforms. Some examples follow:[31]

William Burns, head of the Bureau of Investigation, found that his new office stimulated business for his Burns International Detective Agency.

In August 1922, the Bridgeman raids against radicals were instituted by Burns but the work of publicity and organization of mass support was carried out by leaders in the National Civic Organization (a businessman's organization), the American Defense Society and the National Security League.

The National Civic Federation funded a large number of the patriotic societies.

In 1923 General Amos Fries, head of the Chemical Warfare Service of the War Department tried to establish Preparedness Day and sponsored and circulated the "Spider Web Chart" a document that linked women's peace organizations to the Communists and was widely relied upon until the 1930s.

By 1927, the ACLU named the American Legion, the patriotic societies, and the War Department as the chief threats to civil liberties.

Thus we see a pattern of military, federal-civilian, national-corporate and local cooperation. The nature of reaction in the 1920s is important as a key to a clearer understanding of McCarthyism and Cold War hysteria in the late forties and early fifties. It suggests that while normalcy and McCarthyism drew on popular frustrations and petty-bourgeois and working class fears (American labor unions were eager to cut the flow of immigrants, and Gompers participated in the Civic Federation),[32] they cannot be explained as heirs of the Populist tradition; they are understandable only as elite-sponsored movements that are partly extensions and displacements of wartime mobilization, partly efforts to curb a growing radicalism, and partly efforts to limit middle-class reformism. As such they were at least temporarily quite successful and in this sense also cannot be dismissed as a futile struggle against inevitable change (like the post-Prohibition Temperance movement).

Incidentally, narrow economic motives were merged with broader class interests as the case of Burns and his detective agency as well as the following quote from a letter by the head of the American Vigilant Intelligence Federation, suggest:

> We cooperate with over thirty distinctly civic and patriotic organizations. . . . It would take me too long to relate how I "put over" this part of our activities, namely "trailing the Reds." Should you ever be in Chicago, drop in and see me and I will explain. That it has been a paying proposition for our organization goes without saying.[33]

In this climate, as we have seen, radicalism became fossilized. Reform was however more tenacious and in 1924 rallied insurgent midwestern Republicans, railroad brotherhoods, part of the AFL and the moderate Socialists behind La Follette's third party candidacy; with seventeen percent of the vote, he lagged well behind Roosevelt's 27 percent third-party vote in 1912, but was of course well ahead of any Socialist candidate during the peak years of the Socialist Party. Yet much of what was left of the Progressive Era represented either the interests of the upwardly mobile new middle class (which was now in the prosperous '20s far less interested in regulation for economic stabilization) and the sourer aspects of the movement—as manifested in the nativist immigration laws and Prohibition.[34]

Under these circumstances, intellectuals once again deserted the *political* arena and consequently generated a broad unorganized *cultural* movement of protest against American conditions. In part this cultural movement developed themes that had already been present before the war, for it was then that Greenwich Village had become the chief refuge of Bohemian and alienated young intellectuals;[35] these experiments in life style were continued and sometimes joined to expatriation. Where intellectual cultural nonconformity overlapped with the spread of mass culture (powerfully amplified by technological developments in radio and cinema) the Jazz Age, the flapper, pop-Freudianism, and a very marked change in sexual mores made their appearance—earlier counterparts to the recent blending of Bohemian life styles and mass culture in the "hip counterculture." Prohibition assigned to liquor a role similar to that of marijuana now. But the analogy cannot be carried too far; the sixties was also a period of political activity while in the twenties politics was expressed largely in muted deliberately apolitical forms.

At the margins of these cultural movements were more esoteric dabblings in oriental religion, not of great importance to American social institutions but an interesting commentary on the disposition of energy during an apolitical phase.

At least as profound in its structural impact as middle-class life style experimentation was the organization of ethnic defense groups among Jews, Catholics, and blacks, as well as among other minority groups. Most of these set the pattern for the present mode of integration of white ethnic groups: increasing economic integration, political integration as a bloc in areas where the group is numerous, disappearance of a distinct life style or culture, and a strong measure of continuing structural separatism. Thus for instance among Catholics in the 1920s the National Catholic Welfare Council spearheaded a drive to duplicate Protestant organizations in a way which had few uniquely Catholic features and simply replicated the most conventional Protestant institutions in the form of Catholic Boy Scouts, Catholic Daughters of America, a Catholic Total Abstinence Union and the election of a Catholic Mother of the Year.[36] A similar although slightly more defensive pattern of separation and duplication of institutions within the context of vanishing economic and cultural differentiation began to appear among Jews. (For blacks, as we shall see, this pattern of duplication and integration was not carried out.) These organizational activities were not really a movement, by our definition; neither was the increase in strength of existing occupational associations (the Farm Bureau, the AMA), for neither set of organizational activities really challenged the developing ideology and social structure. Nevertheless they share some movement features.

MOVEMENTS AMONG BLACKS

Segregating black movements in a special section is a somewhat questionable procedure. Yet despite the parallels between white movements and black movements in the early twentieth century the sources of black movements seem to me to be quite different. The similarities are in style and of course in the general social context in which the movements took place. Thus there are resemblances between the NAACP and the Progressive movements in their style of moderation, integrationist aims for all ethnic groups, emphasis on legal reforms and appeals to elites, and so on; similarly there are resemblances between the Jewish, Catholic and other white movements of defensive duplication of structure and the Marcus Garvey movement. But despite these similarities in form and historical context, the position of blacks in American society was unique; and their oppression which developed through slavery, the Civil War, and the southern agrarian system, always in the ideational context of white prejudice, can not be equated to the problems of the white poor or of white minority groups.

The ferment of the 1890s and the turn of the century that generated both reform and radicalism, also marked one of the many low points in the history of blacks in America. The political reforms of Reconstruction were virtually undone; the *Plessy vs. Ferguson* decision of 1896 legitimated the informal practices of segregation; the turn of the century was the peak period of lynchings; violence against blacks was northern as well as southern, with riots in Springfield, Ill. and elsewhere in northern urban areas (where, incidentally, attacks on blacks had been endemic throughout the nineteenth century and had culminated in the anti-draft riots in New

York City during the Civil War). The migration of blacks to the North during the First World War was the beginning of large-scale integration of blacks into the industrial urban economy—an integration that almost always placed them at the bottom of the labor force, in the least desirable jobs and as the most subject to unemployment. Two exceptionally bloody riots against blacks took place in East St. Louis (1917) and Chicago (1919); they continued the anti-draft riot pattern of white working class violence against blacks in that the East St. Louis riot was provoked by local union leaders and the Chicago attacks were spearheaded by Irish working-class "athletic clubs" with the tacit approval of ward politicians.[37]

Response to these conditions was organized around several themes: integration, cultural nationalism, and black duplication of white institutions were the three major thrusts. These ideational positions were in practice often intertwined in the program of movement organizations and were occasionally embellished with more or less symbolic goals such as emigration, that served to sharpen and bring into focus the broader themes. Like most movements, the movements among blacks involved only fairly small numbers of people in the organizations—although the Garvey movement is an exception to this—but included many who unselfconsciously carried out the programs of the movement organization without formally being members.

The white movements were relatively indifferent to blacks. From their initial position of willingness to organize blacks, the Southern Populists lapsed into attacks on them sometimes limited to campaign rhetoric but sometimes extending to support for the Klan and other white supremacist groups and to opposition to black appointees to federal positions. The more urban middle-class Progressives gained legislation that incidentally benefited blacks (such as the abolition of child labor and convict leasing) but sponsored virtually no reform for blacks per se, and remained thoroughly patronizing. The major parties had little to offer beyond promises (in the case of the Republicans) and the astonishing statement, "To revive the dead and hateful race and sectional animosities means confusion, distraction of business, and the reopening of wounds now happily healed" (issued by the Democrats in 1904). The presidents reflected this general vacillation and indifference. Even the Socialists were split over the issue, with some of the right-wing Socialists (specifically

Victor Berger) being openly racist and the left-wing calling for an end to all discrimination but taking few steps toward implementing its goal.[38]

Under these conditions blacks found the most widespread support from northern philanthropists for the program of economic development, social separation, and acceptance of the value premises of white culture that is associated with Booker T. Washington. According to this theme in black sociopolitical thought, blacks were to prepare themselves for entry into the economy at a level higher than that which was currently open to rural migrants, were not to challenge political and social segregation, and were to adopt the cultural norms of the white petty-bourgeoisie. A fundamental premise of this view was "No race that has anything to contribute to the markets of the world is long in any degree ostracized." [39] Its accomplishments were the rise of Tuskegee Institute and the attraction of northern philanthropy to black development projects; a less well-known but perhaps more impressive achievement of this movement (formally embodied as the National Negro Business League) was the Afro-American Realty Company which despite lack of capital and an early demise was instrumental in opening up Harlem to black buyers and renters and in establishing it as a black community—a ghetto yet also a capital.[40]

A second major effort of the prewar period was directed at integration and civil rights. It began formally with W.E.B. DuBois' Niagara Movement of 1905, essentially a conference which issued a statement of protest and demand whose premises in part overlapped Washington's emphasis on economic development, education and general agreement with American ideology but went far beyond the "Tuskegee Machine" in calling for political rights, civil rights, the end of discrimination in public transportation and accommodations, the end of discrimination by both employers and unions, government efforts to provide schooling and to police the courts, and vigorous protest to attain these demands.[41] Following the 1908 Springfield riot, a number of white reformers and black leaders formed the National Association for the Advancement of Colored People that continued to work for complete equality; it was met with far more hostility and much less financial aid than Washington's efforts. DuBois himself eventually despaired of attaining his goals within American capitalism and first joined the Socialists and later the Communist

Party. What is especially interesting about DuBois' later years is his effort in 1940 to propose a program of new economic institutions, neither capitalist nor state socialist, that "were to be initiated and engineered by Negroes themselves," and were generally to take the form of cooperative consumer and producer enterprises.[42]

A third basic theme of black movements in this period was formulated by Marcus Garvey, a Jamaican who came to the United States in 1916 (the influx of West Indians coincided with southern black migration northwards) as the founder of the Universal Negro Improvement Association. Drawing to some extent on Washington's circle and ideas (for example, Washington's secretary, Emmett J. Scott, worked closely with Garvey),[43] Garveyism revived the ideology of a Return to Africa which had first been proposed in the mid-nineteenth century by a Harvard-trained physician, Martin Delany. In Garvey's case the Back to Africa rhetoric can be understood largely as the symbolic focus of a strongly nationalist ideology. At the ideational level, Garvey's movement extolled the beauty of black peoples, rescued African and Afro-American history from contemporary white neglect and contempt, and reworked Christianity around a black God, a black Jesus and a white devil. Structurally, Garveyism followed a similar route as the other ethnic voluntary associations, in proliferating institutions that duplicated those of middle-class white Protestants: Garveyism's replicating bodies included the Black Cross Navigation and Trading Company, the Negro Factories Corporation, the African Legion, the Black Cross Nurses, and the African Orthodox Church (with a liturgy closely modeled on the Roman Catholic and the Episcopal ones). The movement was highly centralized. Strategically Garvey envisioned an independent African state that might not necessarily attract every black individual as an immigrant but that could nevertheless serve as a source of pride and focus of nationalism for blacks everywhere. Tactically, Garvey had to face the indifference of most whites, the colonial status of virtually all of Africa, and the hostility of American integrationists. While white supremacist groups in the States generally were favorably inclined towards Garvey because of his indifference to integration and civil rights, his call for racial purity, and his description of the Klan, the Anglo-Saxon Clubs and the White American Societies as honest rather than hypocritical, black integrationists saw him as endangering their very precarious efforts for civil rights and political, economic and social participation. A. Philip Randolph, DuBois and a number of others attacked him publicly in print, while his most persistent opponents—those who sought to have him jailed for fraud in connection with financial irregularities in the Black Star Line—were West Indians. Eventually, Garvey was jailed for a five-year term, had his sentence commuted after two years by Coolidge and was deported as a convicted felon. After unsuccessful efforts to revive his movement in Jamaica, which eventually did contribute to the rise of the violent guerrilla-like Rastafarians there, he died in London. At the peak of his success in the States, his movement probably numbered 75,000 to 80,000 members and had a broad penumbra of perhaps millions.[44] His base was among poor urban blacks, although the central core of the movement remained West Indian.[45] The UNIA split, weakened and ended with virtually no immediate structural impact. Yet the effort to reorganize the cognitive universe of blacks had long lasting effects, both in its general impact on present black nationalism and in its specific impact on the life experiences of individuals. For instance, Malcolm X's father was a member of Garvey's movement who was killed for his participation in it;[46] this fact suggests that despite its end as a movement organization, Garveyism had ideational effects in the expression of black pride and black solidarity that could contribute to a second generation movement, this time of course more radical and politicized.

If the successes of Garveyism were long in unfolding themselves, so was its shortcoming—the failure to link cultural nationalism with noncapitalist economic ventures. Given that Garvey's African vision was symbolic rather than realizable, his movement must be understood in terms of the actual institutions that were to offer the structural underpinnings for black identity; for a number of reasons (chief of which is the West Indian background pervaded by the same liberalism as the North American fragment of bourgeois Britain), Garvey agreed with Washington in his hopes for black capitalism. But by the 1920s, small-scale private enterprise had ceased to be a path of group upward mobility—it might be a ladder for individuals to attain a comfortable life and even a wealthy one but it was unlikely to be satisfactory either economically or culturally as a route of economic upward mobility for a whole group, particularly one as poor as blacks. The hope that blacks could create a separate but economically and politically equal capitalism is unrealistic; the more realizable goal of structural differentiation and separate *modest* economic enterprises that do not compete with modern corporate capitalism is *culturally* one-dimensional, an acceptance of permanent exclusion from the center of society. Integration meant inclusion in the center but only on the cultural terms of the dominant white society.

The alternative of black commitment to European-derived socialism foundered on white dominance of the parties that were the main movement organizations of socialism; in particular, Communism with its vacillation between integration and separatism as the correct "line" and its white leadership, was an unproductive vehicle for black aspirations. For these reasons, the effort by DuBois to formulate and transform into a movement a program for culturally autonomous black cooperative economic institutions was so extraordinarily important.

In these movements of the first three decades of the twentieth century many of the important issues for contemporary black movements had already been raised: integration in some form vs. separatism in some form; the difficulties of formulating a position of cultural nationalism after the deculturating experience of slavery; the conflicts and shared interests of black Americans, West Indians and Africans; the hopes for black capitalism in a society in which small-scale entrepreneurial capitalism had long since become a marginal endeavor; the difficulties in formulating alternative economic programs; the relationship to white elites and the relationship to white radicals; the relationship between the "talented tenth" for whom integration into central institutions in something other than a menial capacity might be a reality, and the urban and rural masses who had turned to Garveyism not merely as a "compensatory escape" [47] but as an effort to resolve the central ideational issue of identity. Harold Cruse in his discussion of these antecedents of the present crisis of black intellectuals makes the following comments:

> American Negro history is basically a history of the conflict between integrationist and nationalist forces in politics, economics, and culture, no matter what leaders are involved and what slogans are used. After Malcolm X's death, the Black Power slogan was actually a swing back to the conservative nationalism from which Malcolm X had just departed. The pendulum swings back and forth, but the men who swing with it always fail to

synthesize composite trends. W.E.B. Du Bois came the closest of all the big three to understanding this problem, when he wrote in *Dusk of Dawn*: "There faces the American Negro therefore an intricate and subtle problem of combining into one object two difficult sets of facts:"

The "two difficult sets of facts" DuBois refers to are integrationism (civil rights, racial equality, freedom) versus nationalism (separatism, accommodationist self-segregation, economic nationalism, group solidarity and self-help). This was truly the first theoretical formulation of the historic conflict between tendencies, but DuBois never developed his basic theoretical premise. He failed to go beyond this first principle into a greater synthesis of all the historical ingredients of Afro-Americana, which he knew better than all the Washingtons and the Garveys combined.[48]

The white movements could not count on the existence of a stratum of intellectuals who could act autonomously and remain sociopolitically involved; instead intellectuals alternated between supporting existing elites by their roles in the cultural apparatus (the media, advertising, the universities, and the arts and entertainment) and withdrawing from political behavior altogether. Similarly black American movements have lacked leadership that was simultaneously culturally creative, politically involved as intellectuals and at least to some degree structurally as well as culturally free from subservience to white institutions; there have been many individuals who attained most or even all of these characteristics but no accumulated organizational tradition. In the case of blacks, a precarious economic position and the pervasive problem of survival were added to the same factors that retarded the development of an independent intelligentsia among American whites.

Our section on black movements of the pre-Depression period ends where our section on white movements ended—with a rather outwardly apolitical burst of literary activity and life style experimentation—the Harlem Renaissance, which reached its peak in the 1920s. This relatively unformalized movement of cultural nationalism received little financial support from the black bourgeoisie, and thus was opened to exploitation by white publishers and the white theater. Like movements of intellectuals generally in America, it had relatively little impact on the masses but temporarily at least it drew the attention of white intellectuals and some of the black middle class to the possibility that black culture might represent a totally different artistic and cognitive order from white American culture—that it could be an alternative to the prevailing ideology. Furthermore black culture could be recognized as having been a key factor in the transformation of American culture into something other than a fragment of European liberalism. In this sense, there was truth to James Weldon Johnson's assertion in 1922 that the black man was "the creator of the only things artistic that have yet sprung from American soil and been universally acknowledged as distinctive American products." [49] (He later amended this statement in a footnote with the concession that skyscrapers were perhaps both distinctive and a white invention.) But like all insights in an ahistorical society, the potential of the Harlem Renaissance to be the core of a cultural alternative was lost, so that while the works of McKay, Johnson, Weldon, Toomer and others are still read there is virtually no continuity or cumulative effort in associations and media between that period and present efforts to generate a cultural revolution. (Again, these remarks can also be directed against the white literary movements, the women's movements, and so on; Americans have always been condemned to act in the farce of repeated history.)

NOTES

[1] Gabriel Kolko, *The Triumph of Conservatism* (New York: Free Press, 1963), pp. 2–3.

[2] Here I am using "liberal" in its present-day meaning—that is, "in favor of state intervention in the economy but not opposed to private ownership." This is obviously not the original meaning of the word.

[3] Richard Hofstadter, *The Age of Reform* (New York: Random House, 1955).

[4] This is a complicated charge; rather than attempt to support it here I refer the reader to Christopher Lasch's essay, "Politics as Social Control," and especially his remarks on Judge Lindsay, Jane Addams, and John Dewey in *The New Radicalism in America 1889–1963* (New York: Random House, 1965), pp. 154–68.

[5] J. Joseph Huthmacher, "Urban Liberalism and the Age of Reform," in Barton J. Bernstein and Allen J. Matusow, eds., *Twentieth Century America* (New York: Harcourt, Brace & World, 1969).

[6] C. Wright Mills, *White Collar* (New York: Oxford University Press, 1951).

[7] Samuel P. Hays, "The Politics of Reform in Municipal Government," in Bernstein and Matusow, *op. cit.*, p. 41.

[8] *Ibid.*, p. 51.

[9] Raymond E. Callahan, *Education and the Cult of Efficiency* (Chicago: University of Chicago Press, 1962).

[10] Kolko, *op. cit.*

[11] Martin Sklar, "Woodrow Wilson and the Political Economy of Modern United States Liberalism," in James Weinstein and David Eakins, eds., *For a New America* (New York: Random House, 1970).

[12] Christopher Lasch, *The Agony of the American Left* (New York: Random House, 1969), Chapter One.

[13] Caroline Ware, *Greenwich Village, 1920–1930* (New York: Houghton Mifflin, 1935).

[14] Edward Shils, *Selected Essays* (Chicago: Center for Social Organization Studies, University of Chicago, 1970).

[15] Todd Gitlin and Nanci Hollander, *Uptown* (New York: Harper & Row, 1970).

[16] Elinor Langer, "Inside the Hospital Workers' Union," *New York Review of Books* 16 (May 17 and June 3, 1971).

[17] F. W. Dupee, "The Uprising at Columbia," *New York Review of Books* 11, no. 5 (September 26, 1968): 20.

[18] Based on: Daniel Bell, "The Background and Development of Marxian Socialism in the United States," in Donald Egbert and Stan Persons, eds., *Socialism and American Life* (Princeton, N.J.: Princeton University Press, 1952); James Weinstein, *The Decline of Socialism in America* (New York: Random House, 1969); Harry Laidler, *History of Socialism* (New York: Crowell, 1968), Chapter 37; and Sidney Lens, *Radicalism in America* (New York: Crowell, 1966).

[19] See note 18 above.

[20] Weinstein, *op. cit.*, Chapters 1 and 2.

[21] *Ibid.*, Chapters 4 and 5; Theodore Draper, *The Roots of American Communism* (New York: Compass Books, 1963); and Irving Howe and Lewis Coser, *The American Communist Party* (New York: Praeger, 1962).

[22] Draper, *op. cit.*, p. 20.

[23] When William Z. Foster proposed this strategy to the IWW in 1911, the following criticism was made: "Within craft unions we are told to bore; to form an apple from a rotten core; yet boring till we find ourselves outside, we will have built a hole—but nothing more." Quoted in Melvin Dubofsky, *We Shall Be All* (Chicago: Quandrangle Books, 1969), p. 225.

[24] Close examination suggests that these labels correspond but little to reality till after World War I—neither background (since both wings included proletarians and middle class, western "natives" and eastern immigrants) nor fundamental questions distinguish the two wings, although the left wing had a greater commitment to Marxian terminology and a greater propensity for cooperation with the IWW.

[25] Weinstein, *op. cit.*, Chapters 1 and 2.
[26] *Ibid.*, p. 36.
[27] *Ibid.*, p. 42.
[28] *Ibid.*, p. 172.
[29] *Report of the National Advisory Commission on Civil Disorders* (New York: Bantam Books, 1968).
[30] Dubofsky, *op. cit.*
[31] Paul Murphy, "Sources and Nature of Intolerance in the 1920s," *Journal of American History* 51 (June 1964): 60–74.
[32] Ronald Radosh, "The Corporate Ideology of American Labor Leaders from Gompers to Hillman," in Weinstein and Eakins, *op. cit.*, pp. 125–52.
[33] Murphy, *op. cit.*, p. 67.
[34] Arthur S. Link, "What Happened to the Progressive Movement in the 1920s?" *American Historical Review* 64 (July 1959): 833–51.
[35] Ware, *op. cit.*
[36] Eric Goldman, *Rendezvous with Destiny* (New York: Knopf, 1956), p. 232.
[37] St. Clair Drake and Horace Cayton, *Black Metropolis* (New York: Harper Torchbooks, 1962).
[38] Dewey W. Grantham, Jr., "The Progressive Movement and the Negro," in Bernstein and Matusow, *op. cit.*, pp. 63–74.
[39] Booker T. Washington, "Atlanta Exposition Address," in Joanne Grant, *Black Protest* (Greenwich, Conn.: Fawcett, 1968), p. 195.
[40] Harold Cruse, *The Crisis of the Negro Intellectual* (New York: Apollo, 1968).
[41] "The Niagara Movement," in Grant, *op. cit.*, p. 206.
[42] Cruse, *op. cit.*, p. 333.
[43] *Ibid.*, p. 19n.
[44] Edmund Cronon, *Black Moses* (Madison: University of Wisconsin Press, 1955).
[45] Malcom X, *The Autobiography of Malcolm X* (New York: Grove Press, 1965).
[46] Cruse, *op. cit.*, p. 124.
[47] The phrase appears in August Meier and Elliot Rudwick, *From Plantation to Ghetto* (New York: Hill & Wang, 1966).
[48] Cruse, *op. cit.*, p. 564.
[49] Quoted in Goldman, *op. cit.*, p. 234.

8

The Rise of the New Industrial State: 1929–1960

ON WRITING ABOUT THE RECENT PAST

The past of the depression is still alive; because it has not yet lost its presence in flesh and blood or been transformed into nothing but books and archives, it is very difficult to write about. One of the central facts of movement history in the 1930s is the dominant role of the Communist Party. Few who lived through the period can write about the Communist Party as anything other than participants and partisans, one way or the other. A historian of the postwar generation who was unborn when the banks closed and Pearl Harbor was bombed, an infant when Hiroshima burned, and a child when Reds and ex-Reds were purged from every walk of life must perform a juggling act in order to balance three considerations: her own present commitments necessarily color her judgments of the past and lead her to prefer some of history's lessons to others; sufficient value-freeness to be able to interpret historical accounts and identify the multiple layers of fancy that surround each fact—that come to constitute the fact itself, that create facts and that annihilate other facts; and finally, an effort to understand the events of the past as they were understood by the participants, regardless of "facts," for ultimately the events of ideological phenomena exist only in the minds of contemporaries. As we read the accounts of intellectuals' continuing commitment to Communism we are shaken by our own response that surely no one could be so subservient to a distant capital and an inner party core and so mistaken in their understanding of America; would those who call themselves radicals today have acted differently? We are repulsed by the Party line, by justifications for Stalinist purges, and by every phenomenon connected with anti-Communism from the righteousness of those who never fellow-traveled to the abnegation of the ex-Communists to the zeal of the witch hunters. We must struggle against being drawn into this moral and cognitive morass. We must not succumb to accepting the language that is forced on us by Cold War intellectuals. We must not embroil ourselves in the issues. We must avoid identifying ourselves with those who joined the party out of the best of motives, and who felt that humanitarian as well as revolutionary reasons forced them to play their almost preordained roles more and more docilely and mechanically. The era must be cold and dead to us; yet we must learn from it. And we can do so only by refusing to think in terms of its false choices.

A second and obviously related historiographical problem is that foreign developments have come to play such a key role in the vicissitudes of American social movements. To some extent, this has always been true: there would have been no gallant Marquis de Lafayette fighting for the American Revolution if that incident had not been part of France's hot and cold war with Britain; and as we have seen, the French Revolution of 1793, the emigrations from Germany in 1848, the South's dependence on the British textile industry, and the Spanish-American and First World Wars were events that had important consequences for American social movements. But the impact of events abroad became more continuous and insistent with modern means of communication, the victories of communism in Europe and Asia, America's rise to a position of international power, and the disintegration of the western European colonial empires. America is no longer the historian's delight—an at least partially sealed laboratory for the study of social movements. Movements are no longer indirectly affected by international events (as the Populist wheat farmers had been by the worldwide farm depression) but are direct self-conscious responses to such events. The Communist Party in America as well as McCarthyism and related phenomena can only be understood in terms of international events and Americans' interpretations of them.

THE DEPRESSION

Introduction

By the end of the twenties, both small and large businessmen had enjoyed a period of prosperity, manual workers were actually in a somewhat weaker position than they were at the beginning of the decade despite several waves of strikes (AFL membership was proportionately down in comparison to the peak prewar years), farmers had undergone yet another depression, and the percentage of white-collar employees in the labor force was rising dramatically. For a while, it had seemed as though the reforms of the Progressive Era were enough to stabilize capitalism and resolve its contradictions (although the latter phrase was hardly the one in current use).

The bubble burst in 1929, but only after several years had passed did either elites or masses take decisive action. For the adjustment to a depression came slowly and unevenly. Since groups and individuals felt the impact of the Depression at different rates, in different forms, and often in isolated circumstances, mass actions were unlikely; furthermore, collective action (by the government) required emotional and cognitive acceptance of the shattering of prosperity. Pragmatic optimistic America resisted: the *Saturday Evening Post* informed its readers after the crash, "Wall Street may sell stocks but Main Street is buying goods," and cheerful billboards queried "Wasn't the Depression Terrible?" [1]

The unemployment of a fifth to a quarter of the labor force could not long be ignored or met by the hesitant measures of the Hoover administration. By 1932, organization was proceeding in three directions: in the newly elected Roosevelt Administration itself; in a variety of proto-fascist movements; and in the primarily Communist left (the Socialists remained unable to develop a mass base). In many respects it is correct to approach the New Deal as a social movement; in terms of our definition, it did not use nonlegitimate channels for changing structure and ideology but certainly *did* use the existing channels innovatively and above all, created many new channels. Viewing the New Deal as an elite revolution is by no means an exaggeration. Approaching it as an elite revolution in which capitalism and the state were fused suggests parallels to European developments and in particular a resemblance between the eventually discarded NRA legislation and the fascist corporate state.[2] That it was a mild, benign, democratically instituted, and only partially realized approximation to a corporate state should not allow us to skim over the similarities.[3] At the same time, there was much in the New Deal—especially in welfare programs—that was pragmatic, ad hoc and unideological; but pragmatism itself can be ideological. Corporate-bureaucratic, populist and professional-expert modes of decision making were fused in the New Deal—sometimes fused within an agency or even within an individual.

It resembled Progressivism in many respects. Like the earlier movement it was an effort to save capitalism from its worst enemies —the capitalists; in other words it attempted to stabilize the economic climate (the Securities Exchange Commission is an excellent illustration of this aspect) and to develop a productive, politically moderate, independently organized and prosperous work force (illustrated by New Deal labor legislation and social security measures). It went much farther than the Progressive reforms in this latter direction. Like Progressive reforms, it reached local as well as national levels, was supported for different reasons by different strata, and combined artificial respiration for capitalism with genuine humanitarian concern. We will not examine the New Deal as a social movement; rather, we will accept it as the context of social movements and as a powerful competitor of social movements.

The New Deal proved too strong a competitor for a series of movements that we can call proto-fascist movements. We will discuss these first and then turn to the left.

The Proto-Fascist Independents: "Every Man a King"

Now we are concerned with a series of movements that are connected to each other and share a number of features, as follows:

1. Strength in the Midwest and South Central area, partially overlapping the old Populist strongholds, but actually drawing more support from corn and hog areas than the Populists had;
2. Class support from a varied base, including hard-pressed farmers and Midwestern urban workers;
3. Ideologies supporting a corporate state in which private enterprise continued under rather stringent government regulation, in which extensive welfare legislation is in effect, in which currency is regulated, in which large fortunes are taxed, and in which labor is organized as a partner under state control; and
4. Initial organization as a mailing list and lobby under the aegis of a strong leader but later transformation into a political party.

These movements had multiple beginnings in the early thirties and later fused into a single effort to enter the political arena—the Union Party of 1936.

One beginning was the Farmers' Holiday Movement in the corn and hog area of Wisconsin and Iowa. As we have seen, farmers have been traditionally volatile and had suffered longer than other groups had (the Depression hit them as early as the 1920s). The midwestern movements involved interference with foreclosing courts, disruptions of sheriffs' auctions, and crop destruction.

Meanwhile, in Detroit, a Basilian priest of Irish working-class background, Father Charles E. Coughlin, was devoting his weekly radio program more and more to political and economic issues. He rented time from Chicago and Cincinnati stations, and when he was dropped by CBS and snubbed by NBC, he created his own radio network of eleven stations. His discourses on popular controversial topics attracted large amounts of mail; his discourse, "Hoover Prosperity Means a New War" brought in 1,200,000 letters, a comparison of Morgan, Mellon, Mills, and Meyer to the Four Horsemen of the Apocalypse garnered 600,000, and his normal volume of mail was 80,000 letters a week—many including donations for his Saint Theresa of the Little Flower building campaign. His discourse on "Russia and the Red Serpent" brought a call to Washington to give expert testimony on Communism to a House committee. By the mid-thirties he began a national lobby with state and local conventions (that is, with the potential to be transformed into a party), called the National League for Social Justice. Its sixteen plank platform follows; note how heavily it is weighted with currency demands.

1. Liberty of conscience and education;
2. Living annual wage;
3. Nationalization of banking, currency and natural resources;
4. Private ownership of all else;
5. Control of private property for the public good;
6. Government banking;
7. Congressional control of coinage;
8. Steady currency value;
9. Cost plus fair value for agriculture;
10. Labor unions under government protection;
11. Recall of non-productive bonds;
12. Abolition of tax free bonds;
13. Social taxation;
14. Simplification of government;
15. In war, conscription of wealth; and
16. Human rights preferred over property rights.[4]

In the South, Huey Long had won the governorship of Louisiana and had transformed that state in a number of ways—by shifting the weight of state taxation from the poor to large corporations (with special measures designed to punish his *bête noire*, Standard Oil), improved schooling, medical care and the development of Louisiana State University, a two percent "tax on lying" on newspaper gross receipts from advertising, and so on. His support in the 1928 primaries correlated .62 with the Louisiana Populist vote of 1892, by area—in other words, his support was strongest in the upcountry parishes inhabited by smallholders.[5] By the mid-thirties, Long and Gerald L. K. Smith (a minister) launched the Share Our Wealth movement, essentially a mailing list with several million names and a program similar to Coughlin's, but with stronger welfare planks and less emphasis on currency and the corporate state.

This is set forth in a pamphlet entitled "Share Our Wealth," compiled by "Huey P. Long, United States Senator, Washington, D.C." On the cover is the quotation from St. John, Chapter 8, verse 32: "And ye shall know the truth and the truth shall make you free." Under the title is the subtitle: "Every Man a King"—part of a phrase of William Jennings Bryan's, "Every man a king but no one wears a crown." This is followed by a six-line quotation from Goldsmith, and under this: "Containing authorities, laws, statistics, and published comments of Leaders of all times." On page 1 is the following statement of principles and platforms:

1. To limit poverty by providing that every deserving family shall share in the wealth of America for not less than one-third of the average wealth, thereby to possess not less than $5,000 free of debt.
2. To limit fortunes to such few million dollars as will allow the balance of the American people to share in the wealth and profits of the land.
3. Old-age pensions of $30 per month to persons over sixty years of age who do not earn as much as $1,000 per year or who possess less than $10,000 in cash or property, thereby to remove from the field of labor in times of unemployment those who have contributed their share to the public service.
4. To limit the hours of work to such an extent as to prevent overproduction and to give the workers of America some share in the recreations, conveniences, and luxuries of life.
5. To balance agricultural production with what can be sold and consumed according to the laws of God, which have never failed.
6. To care for the veterans of our wars.
7. Taxation to run the government to be supported, first by reducing big fortunes from the top, thereby to improve the country and provide employment in public works whenever agricultural surplus is such as to render unnecessary, in whole or in part, any particular crop. Go ye into all communities and preach the Gospel to every living creature.[6]

By 1936, these forces had allied themselves into the Union Party, which ran William Lemke of North Dakota for President. (Long, the more obvious choice as a third-party candidate, had been assassinated.) The Union Party won some votes in wheat-growing areas of North Dakota, among the Russian-Germans (Germans who had once settled in Russia) who lived in the poorer farm areas, and in some German and Scandinavian areas of Wisconsin.[7] Like most third-party candidates, he did not gain a large percentage of the vote and his party had virtually no direct impact on federal policies. This was essentially the last bid of agrarians for national status, although it was dominated by urban-based Coughlin. With Coughlin, a good many authoritarian elements were infused into what was otherwise a straightforward agrarian radical economic program. The agrarian radical program was shared by the radical wing of the Farmers Union, which had supported Lemke although the rest of the union did not; the Farmers Union was strong in the corn areas, while the Union Party was strong in the wheat areas. The radical wing continued strikes and prevention of foreclosure sales, which were illegal but effective tactics.[8]

These movements have several important aspects. First of all, they show that Populist strength had waned since the turn of the century as farmers became numerically weaker; while Populism had developed active local-level associations, the movements of the thirties retained some of the characteristics of lobbies and mailing lists, with the possible exception of the almost spontaneous Farmers Holiday and the radical wing of the Farmers Union. Second, the Populist issue of political democracy—so very central to the Populist platform—had become very muted by the thirties; Coughlin seemed rather uninterested in mass participation in decision-making and offered no proposals to extend it, and the Farmers Union radicals had little to offer but hostility toward the government. This marked deterioration in concern for political democracy and Populist participation cannot simply be ascribed to the priority of economic issues during a depression; the Populists had after all also organized during a depression. I would suggest two reasons for the turn to authoritarianism in the 1930s. One is that the medium of the radio tended to reduce the public to a mass in a way that newspapers could not, that it led to adulation of a leader (particularly Coughlin) and a consequent centralization in the movement and loss of local participation—the media-accelerated trend toward centralization and passivity was after all a nationwide phenomenon and in turn linked to a general decline in local power. The second reason for authoritarianism in the popular movements of the thirties is the loss of contact—and growing enmity—between the "independents" and the left. Unlike the early Socialists, the Communists (and the non-Communist left of the thirties, as well) had relatively little interest in the farmers; Coughlin in turn was explicitly hostile to Communism (as was the Church as a whole during the twenties and thirties).

These movements force us to sharpen our definitions of authoritarianism, fascism, and a variety of other terms which have generally deteriorated into meaningless epithets. Fascism may be defined as a system of beliefs and institutions that structure a society in which the state and business elites are fused, in which the state becomes sovereign but the business elite remains identifiable and separate, and in which the institutions of profit and private ownership are maintained. Fascism is a program for a society structured around the existence of a capitalist class, a class of employed propertyless workers organized into unions that are subservient to the state, and a large network of agencies connecting business enterprises to the state; the state explicitly assumes responsibility for the stability of the economic climate. Business and state elites may be interlocked by exchange and rotation of personnel as well as by mutual responsibility and channels of communication. Ideology tends to be all-encompassing and propagated by media that may or may not retain formal independence. Formal democracy is weak or nonexistent. In this sense, the Coughlinite program was undoubtedly fascist. All modern neo-capitalist societies share some of these elements, although the strong labor organizations and multiple-party political systems of the western European democracies reduce the authoritarian side effects of the fusion of the state and the economic elites.

Authoritarian describes a political system in which most individuals are not permitted to participate in decision-making. Power is voluntarily or involuntarily relinquished in a variety of ways: by bureaucratization and hierarchization on the job, by passivity vis à vis media, by transfer of political decision-making from mass meetings or elected bodies to appointed agencies, by the transfer of power to national levels during more or less phony foreign affairs crises (Gulf of Tonkin!), by witch hunts, pogroms, and terrorism, by the rule of experts, by the pressure of a secret police force, by the extraordinary power of charismatic leaders, and so on.

All of these devices may operate simultaneously. Ethnic scapegoating and witch hunts are especially quick and efficacious devices and are thus prominent—but not necessarily so—in most authoritarian states. Concentration of power is of course not only compatible with but even expedited by plebiscitary elections and other signs of (meaningless) mass participation. More or less by definition, all fascist societies are authoritarian; so are state socialist societies, although conceivably socialism without the state could be nonauthoritarian. Authoritarianism must not be confused with physical coercion which may contribute to the former but is in the long run less effective than structural and ideological constraints.

Movements of the thirties showed authoritarian tendencies in their adulation of leaders, their mode of media use, their lack of concern for the issues connected with political participation, and their lapses into ethnocentrism. In this sense, the Populists were clearly *not* authoritarians, despite their occasional ethnocentrism. That there is some continuity in class and regional base is however not to be denied; we have already suggested two reasons (changes in the media and loss of contact with the left) for the shift from populism to authoritarian proto-fascism in the programs that were addressed to this support base.

Populism is an ambiguous word referring simultaneously to efforts to transfer power from existing elites to other groups *and* to efforts to really lessen the concentration of power. The Populists of the 1890s were keenly aware of the fact that a shift of power from capitalists to the federal government would be meaningless unless legal devices were developed to disperse power (such as the referendum, recall, and so forth); for this reason, their program could not be fragmented without severe damage to its purpose.

The word totalitarianism has now gone out of fashion, one of the fossils of the Cold War period. Just as "fascism" all too often represents an effort to lump together the United States and Nazi Germany so "totalitarianism" frequently represented an effort to lump together the USSR and Nazi Germany. I would like to suggest a more useful meaning: totalitarianism is a form of authoritarianism in which ideological uniformity and the disappearance of subcultural (or other) sources of heterogeneity are important features. In this sense certain traditional states were authoritarian but not totalitarian—for instance, late-nineteenth century Germany. In the totalitarian societies, the public (political) and private (cultural, familial and economic) sectors are largely fused. One troubling problem is that it might be very difficult to distinguish a completely consensual totalitarian society from a completely perfect democracy (although careful structural analysis would reveal differences not apparent at the ideational level). This question was already posed in the eighteenth century by Rousseau and Robespierre in their model of a society ruled by the *general will*, in which hypocrisy had ceased to exist and in which the despotism of liberty prevailed.[9]

As long as Americans think in the outmoded rhetoric of laissez-faire liberalism in terms of concentration of power in the state *or* in the business elite, they will simply not be able to get power back from either of these groups. For this reason programs of economic regulation[10] are pointless without demands for political changes; vice versa, attacks on the power of the state remain authoritarian unless they are coupled with a challenge to the power of economic elites.[11]

Movements that were similar to Midwestern and South Central proto-fascism but less interconnected appeared in California, which had a large population of elderly persons and an attraction for the uprooted of the rest of the country. Whatever propensities for movement activity may have been present for sociological or psychological reasons in its population were strengthened by the sources of California's political institutions in the Progressive Era, which simultaneously left a heritage of reliance on the expert and—almost paradoxically—legal arrangements that furthered popular political experimentation. Thus for instance, party patronage jobs were fewer than in other states, a system which encouraged ideologically based factionalism and lack of party discipline. Present also was the tool of the referendum. The presence of a mass media center may also have contributed to a colorful ideologized style of political behavior. In this propitious climate flourished Dr. Francis Townsend's National Recovery Plan, a financially preposterous scheme to provide $200 a month pensions for the elderly by means of a tax on business transactions; this plan, which would raise consumption as well as aid the elderly, was organized into a petition campaign and a network of clubs. At its height it drew enough support to lead to the recall of an Oregon state legislator who refused to endorse it. With the introduction of social security measures, the Townsend plan lost some of its appeal to the old—a neglected and politically weak group—and the clubs gradually transformed themselves from movement bodies to social clubs and money-making enterprises.[12] The elderly are not an easily organized group even though many have been faced with de-routinizing experiences of bereavement, sudden loss of income, and loss of stabilizing integrating jobs; ill-health and fatigue make movement participation difficult. For a while, some links were established between the National Recovery Plan and Coughlin's movement, but came to little.

We may briefly mention Upton Sinclair's EPIC (End Poverty In California), the Technocrat Movement, the "Ham and Eggs" Movement that promised $30 a week to every unemployed person or resident over fifty, the Utopian Society, and so on.[13] Most of these organizations sought the welfare measures that the New Deal eventually produced; yet they conceived of themselves as movements that would contribute to history and not simply reap the benefits of federal decision-making. Bizarre as some of them were, it is difficult to fault them for their desire to develop and propagate an independent solution to the problems of the decade.

Mention in passing may also be made of Brown-Shirt style paramilitary groups, such as the Detroit-based Black Legion. Lack of elite support led to a rather rapid and quiet demise of these groups.[14]

The Communists and the CIO

A very different challenge to the New Deal came from the Communist left, which awakened from its sectarian slumbers. It made gains among intellectuals (who have therefore perhaps given Communism a more important historical role—as both hero and villain—than it deserves[15]), among the unemployed, in the media, and, rather more feebly among blacks and in the federal agencies; its major effort was, however, its attempt to "bore from within" in the labor movement. The two most important movements of the thirties are bound together—Communism and the rise of the CIO, the industrial unions.

The Communists had made several efforts at organization within the union movement during the 1920s; as we noted, that had been an inauspicious period for unions and the Communists made few gains. When the Depression came, the first major organizing thrust of the Communists (by now purged of its Trotskyists and its Lovestoneite [Bukharinist] majority) was among the unemployed. (Minor attempts were addressed to union organizing and breaking up the meetings of other left-wing groups.)

The nation's attention was captured by the Bonus Marchers, twenty thousand veterans who were members of the Communist-dominated Workers Ex-Servicemen's League, and who marched on Washington to demand bonuses of $50 and $100 that had been promised them in 1923, but were not due until 1945. The Hoover administration met them with ambivalence and a stalemate persisted during June and July of '32, while the marchers camped at Anacostia Flats, across the Potomac. On July 21, they were issued an ultimatum to leave by August 4th from government quarters in which they had been permitted to squat; when they refused to leave a building a week later, the police attempted to seize it, killing two marchers. Finally, Hoover ordered General MacArthur to drive the veterans away by force.[16]

The marchers remind us of the symbolic significance of Washington, the target of a number of marchers, none with any realistic hopes of seizing the capital, few with even the minor success of alleviation of misery: Coxey's Army of the Unemployed in 1894, the Bonus Marchers, A. Philip Randolph's March on Washington for black civil rights in 1940, the Civil Rights March of '64, the Poor Peoples' March, and the Antiwar demonstrations. Of these, only the Civil Rights March met with identifiable success, perhaps because its goals were relatively closely linked to specific legislation and less identified with the radicalism of the poor; in other words, its demands were more compatible with political liberalism. The symbolic importance of Washington is heightened by the city's total orientation to political power and its lack of any non-political central institutions.

More useful to the poor of the Depression although less spectacular was the Communist organization of the Unemployed Councils which not only organized demonstrations for jobs (such as the Hunger March on Ford in '32 at which the Detroit police killed four marchers and wounded fifty) but also provided local relief measures without the indignities meted out by private charities.[17]

Meanwhile, efforts were made to organize blacks; the Communist Party never gained a great deal of support from blacks despite their attempt to appeal to black nationalism by the slogan "self-determination for the Black Belt" (that is, establishment of a black state in the South), their defense of the Scottsboro boys (nine young blacks sentenced to death for two rapes of which they were almost doubtlessly innocent), the creation of a special Negro Department (variously named in accord with the party line), and the drawing of blacks into formal positions of party leadership. But blacks never composed more than 8% of the party.[18]

The affinity between intellectuals and Communists was much greater. Peculiarly enough, intellectual involvement with the party was at a peak during the party's closed and aggressive years in the early thirties, not its Popular Front and union organizing period of the later thirties. Reasons for this withdrawal of intellectuals are manifold; intellectuals' disdain for the cruder forms of wooing the proletariat, intellectuals' rapidly growing disillusionment with Stalin, intellectuals' support for Roosevelt once the New Deal was launched, among others.[19] Mass media intellectuals (especially in Hollywood) continued their support for Communism somewhat longer than the literary elite, although it is difficult to perceive how —if at all—their affiliation influenced their media work beyond a mild advocacy of racial tolerance and New Deal perspectives. This lack of a clear relationship between political sentiments of writers and media output is extraordinarily interesting. It suggests that "boring from within" the media is not a policy that is immediately productive for radicals; rather, the economic and political commitments of media elites sweep the radical along.

The uneasy relation of the dissident intellectual to the cultural apparatus of the society is a widespread and relatively old phenomenon; the intellectual contributes to generating and propagating an ideology about which he is cynical or angry. His position in the media, in advertising, in the arts and educational institutions is alienating in the strict original sense of the word—he must be disassociated from his work. His alienation is not merely the dissatisfaction and boredom of the factory worker but centers on his constant, voluntary, ingenious and even creative contribution to a hegemony that he entirely sees through. The power, subtlety, and pervasiveness of modern media give extraordinary power to the intellectual (as technology gives power to experts in general) that he can only exercise along narrow channels; the more widely consumed and technically sophisticated the medium, the more tightly regulated is the intellectual's access to it.[20]

A wide variety of personal reasons drew intellectuals to Communism—it is almost a platitude that personal troubles stimulate some individuals (which ones?) to work for structural transformations.[21] An emphasis on the neuroticism of intellectuals, their disdain for the middle class *from above* which carried over from the '20s, their alienation and loneliness, their search for strength and *machismo* and so on—none of these explanations will get us very far. Intellectuals by definition are aware of and frequently critical of the social order; in the 1930s the Communist Party seemed to be a realistic vantage point for changing the society. That this belief proved to be mistaken, that the Communist Party not only proved weak and unrealistic but also authoritarian, is as much a cognitive as a psychological problem. Historical knowledge cannot save us from psychological weaknesses—which are perennial and universal; but perhaps it can prevent the repetition of cognitive error, of following a party line that is unrealistic and authoritarian, both of which are cognitive as well as moral judgments.[22] We cannot keep our readers (or ourselves) from being neurotic, snobbish, lonely or *macho*—we *can* offer them the example of a historical mistake to prevent its repetition for cognitive reasons.

By 1935, a shift in the party line—Stalin's announcement of a new popular front period for Communism—opened the way to abandonment of dual unionism and consequently to strenuous efforts to participate in the ongoing industrial union drives.

We must now backtrack a little and discuss the beginnings of this phase of the American labor movement. From a variety of beginnings—which included Trotskyists and Socialists but can perhaps be fairly summarized as *spontaneous*—an industrial union movement which organized semi- and unskilled workers outside of the AFL was taking shape. The important events of these initial drives included the San Francisco general strike of 1934, the teamster strikes in Minneapolis led by the Dunne brothers (two Troskyists), the two-day battle at the Toledo AutoLite plant between the National Guard and the workers and unemployed, wildcat strikes at Toledo Chevrolet and Cleveland Fisher Body, and the first great sit-down strike at the Akron Goodyear plant.[23] The last event is especially important because in the other strikes, a substantial number of strikers had been killed; workers understood quite clearly that their safety depended on holding hostage company property—hence the unique effectiveness of the sit-down strike, which was essentially a temporary seizure of the plant. Until 1936, many of these strikes were called by workers themselves; when John L. Lewis left the AFL vice presidency in 1935 and established the Committee for Industrial Organization, a variety of leftists were accepted as union leaders and organizers. When Lewis was chided for this (by Hillman and Dubinsky) he grinned, "Who gets the bird, the hunter or the dog?" [24] Probably the most important victory of the CIO was won by the Reuther brothers —Socialists rather than Communists—against General Motors; court injunctions, vigilantes, police, and the National Guard all were ineffective against the sit-downers in the key Flint, Michigan plant. By 1937 both General Motors and Chrysler workers were organized as were millions of workers in other enterprises, especially steel, textiles and electrical equipment.[25] Several of these strikes—the efforts to unionize Ford and Republic Steel—resulted in the deaths of strikers; as usual real violence was still monopolized by the armed representatives of owners.

The Communists at their peak probably led unions representing about one fourth of the CIO's four million members and included supporters in a number of other unions.[26] (By 1945 about one third of American blue-collar workers were unionized.) Communist strength is summarized by Howe and Coser:

> For the most part, they were allowed to consolidate their grasp over the unions in which they had won leadership—though there appears to have been a tacit understanding that they would not disturb the Lewis machine in coal or the Murray machine in steel. By the summer of 1939, just before the Hitler-Stalin pact, the Communists had established themselves as one of the important blocs within the CIO. Their agents were firmly planted in the CIO national office; they had taken full control over a number of important unions and had established strong bases in other unions.
>
> By 1939 the following unions were under effective CP control: Maritime Federation of the Pacific; United Electrical, Radio and Machinists; State County and Municipal Workers; International Longshoremen and Warehouse; Mine, Mill and Smelter; Fur Workers; American Communications Association; United Cannery, Agricultural, Packing and Allied Workers. In the Transport Workers Union, the American Newspaper Guild, the Furniture Workers Union and the Teachers Union the CP shared control with cooperative fellow travelers. It also had control of strong sections of the auto and shoe workers' unions.[27]

These generally very hostile commentators grudgingly compliment the Communist Party in explaining its success in the CIO.

> But the main and new source of CP strength in the CIO was the participation of thousands of its members in the organizing drives of the late thirties. The Communists won power and trust by the traditional methods of winning power and trust in American unions: they became the organizers. If there was dirty work to do, they were ready. If leaflets had to be handed out on cold winter mornings before an Akron rubber plant or a New York subway station, the party could always find a few volunteers. If someone had to stick his neck out within the plants, a Communist was available. And the Communists were indefatigable meeting-goers, caucusing before each meeting, ready to sit out their opponents into the early hours of the morning, working together with a religious fervor. They knew little things, like parliamentary procedure, which quickly won them an advantage over ordinary trade unionists, and they knew other things too, things that for a while they kept to themselves.
> The point should not be exaggerated. Never were the Communists more than a minority among the CIO organizers, and often a disruptive and distrusted minority. Plenty of other people, ranging from run-of-the-mill unionists to left-wing Socialists, worked hard and took chances. But the Communists were the best-organized political group within the CIO, despite—or perhaps because of—the fact that at the beginning the party national office provided very little guidance and the local comrades had to fend for themselves. The moral is that, even when a political movement is slow in reacting to major events, it can still capitalize on them if its membership has been trained and disciplined.[28]

A rough justice was done in that Communist strength in unions corresponded to the degree to which Communist Party organizers gained support by democratic mobilization of workers as opposed to manipulation of union officials. The more Communists worked among the rank-and-file the more loyal the rank-and-file remained to Communism in the lean years of the forties (in electrical and auto unions for example). Where Communists gained control of a union by developing leaders (such as Joe Curran of the National Maritime Union) or depending on the patronage of a strong official (for example, Mike Quill of the Transport Workers) they were very rapidly and unceremoniously booted out when the unions turned anti-Communist.[29]

By the end of the decade the Communists had some reason to believe that their policies would be productive; they seemed to have a firm union base. That many Jewish and intellectual sympathizers dropped away after the Stalin-Hitler pact was seen as regrettable; but to some extent these losses were compensated by official support for the Soviet Union before the pact and again when Russia was invaded.[30]

A brief discussion of party structure is in order. Official membership lists remained small; voting turnouts for the Communist presidential candidate were meager. It is estimated that only 5 percent of college and high school students were involved in party protests.[31] Turnover was phenomenally high; one interesting index of it is the item that by the end of the thirties, eleven of the twenty-one former major contributors or editors to the *New Masses* were cited by the party as "enemies of the people"—a measure of turnover among intellectuals, a particularly fickle and independent group, perhaps.[32]

The strength of Communism in America lay not in its professional esoteric inner core but in its large penumbra of rank-and-file organizers, sympathetic intellectuals, and millions of blue and white-collar workers who were quite willing to accept Communist aid for an improvement of their fate under capitalism. Its weakness was in the disdain of the core for the penumbra, manifested in a variety of ways:

1. It was manifested *structurally* by a lack of upward channels of information flow and decision-making. As a matter of fact, the major feat of the CP—its involvement with the CIO—came only because rank and file organizers for once took the initiative locally, regardless of the vacillations and lag of the central line.[33]

2. It was manifested in the Communist Party's consistent subservience to and reliance upon an exrevolutionary movement in a country that was structurally completely different from the United States.

3. It was manifested in the weakness of the Communist Party's efforts to propagate a new cognitive order among its most important

potential support base, namely manual workers. It failed to educate (or indoctrinate—as you please) American workers, so that in the end workers returned to the supposed advantages of capitalism. This failure is related to its deafness to local conditions and rank and file attitudes. If it had been listening, the Party would have heard the same silence Frances Perkins did, who even at the height of the union drives "heard no statement that a man had property rights in his job."[34] That no worker came to believe in his right to control his labor suggests that the CP had been neither able nor willing to present to Americans the central principle of Marxism.

FOREIGN ENTANGLEMENTS AND THE QUIET GENERATION

The period from the late thirties to 1960 can be described as an era in which the main ideological focus of movement were events abroad: the Spanish Civil War, World War II, and the hostility of the two great powers—the United States and Soviet Russia. American movements of course continued to have class, regional and ethnic bases but the fears and discontents of these groups were transposed to the international setting. These formulations cannot be dismissed as a displacement of domestic difficulties onto a world arena; the growth of American and Russian economic and military power, the breakup of the Western European colonial empires, and the introduction of the jet and the television did indeed make us all citizens of the "global village." It is thus not the international focus per se of movements of the mid-twentieth century that makes them so frequently irrational. Rather, the problem lies in the fact that the more distant the events the more difficult it is for the individual to judge them, the more he must rely on the media and the more susceptible he is to perceiving them only after they have been cognitively distorted by the filter of ideology. One of the corollaries of this shift of focus has been that movements from 1936 to 1960 were heavily middle-class movements (that is, among salaried and entrepreneurial strata) since the mystique of expertise has brought with it the widespread belief that the middle class is more capable of judging distant events.[35]

The Late Thirties

The Communists must share the blame for the doctrine that competence in foreign affairs existed only among the few, informed by esoteric doctrine and sufficiently tough-minded. But as was the case with other Communist tenets, in the transition between the core and the penumbra perspectives on foreign affairs became tender-minded, humanitarian and even romantic; the result was the involvement—and death—of hundreds of young Americans in the Spanish Civil War.[36]

A different approach to events abroad was taken by a scattering of antiwar groups on the eve of American participation in the war. Several motives were involved in this uneasy alliance. Two were pro-German sentiment of a number of German-Americans and a handful of pro-Nazis (in the Deutschland-American Bund) and the feelings of some businessmen opposed to the imminent rapprochement with Russia and/or committed to business-as-usual with the Axis powers (including GM, Standard Oil of New Jersey, Alcoa, Dow Chemical, and U.S. Steel).[37] A third motive was that of midwestern isolationism, carrying on the Populist tradition of opposition to American adventures abroad (in America First, for one). A fourth source was traditional frequently non-Communist left-wing pacifism (among the Wobblies, the Trotskyists, some Socialists). This peculiar collection—it can hardly be called a coalition—did not last long; it succumbed to its own cleavages, to the American passion for entering wars (perhaps a result of the nationalist heritage of revolution), and to the circumstances that produced Pearl Harbor.

The Hunter Gets the Bird

> The English proletariat is becoming more and more bourgeoisie, so that this most bourgeoisie of all nations is apparently aiming ultimately at the possession of a bourgeois aristocracy and a bourgeois proletariat *as well* as a bourgeoisie. For a Nation which exploits the whole world this is of course to a certain extent justifiable.
>
> ———Engels

The first movement phenomenon of the post-war period, the purge of Communists from the CIO, appears to be a largely domestic affair; but it is merely the first of a series of events that can only be understood against the background of the Cold War.

The purge of Communists from the only American institution in which they had a realistic, useful base (control of approximately one-fourth of the membership by 1945) was initiated in 1946 and was essentially completed in 1949. Depending on the choice of explanatory level, one can find several reasons for this collapse. At the broadest—virtually tautological and useless—level, it happened because American ideology insulated the rank-and-file from acceptance of radical class consciousness. Thus when the leadership expelled Communists, the rank and file saw no reason to risk anything to stop the proceedings. But the statement that American workers remained convinced by a bourgeois ideology needs to be qualified; it is true that for historical reasons Americans had little experience with, and little interest in, any but a liberal (bourgeois) cognitive order,[38] but on the other hand, the Communists made no serious effort to offer such an alternative or use the cooperative collective action of strikes to create a model for the cooperative basis of behavior in a noncapitalist social order. As we have already noted, this failure to present new ideas about social order and to develop democratic proletarian institutions was inherent in Communist ideology, in party structure and in organizing tactics. But even with a receptive ideational system and an open movement structure the task of building a continuing democratic class conscious movement among workers is exceedingly difficult; the IWW, which was much more committed to this end also failed to sustain the organization beyond the crisis periods of the strikes. It is not surprising that the Communists, with no commitment to rank-and-file participation, failed to maintain rank-and-file support.

Thus when individual union leaders for a variety of reasons turned on their Communist secondary leadership, the purge of these officials generally took place as a routine intra-union power struggle with little broader import for the rank-and-file. The leadership's reasons for ousting Communists were varied—intra-union struggles; intra-party struggles and the changed nature of the party (reflections of the party purges, particularly the ouster of popular-front representative Browder and the correlated swing away from rapprochement with Western elites); the growing hostility between the USSR and the USA; the effective end of the Depression in America during the war and a consequent ebb of interest in "the social question"; and perhaps most important of all, the post-bellum reaction, a repetition in greatly altered form of the post-World War I reaction. As we have already noted, wars include two components that produce post-war antiradicalism—a mass *nationalist* mobilization and an exhaustion of ideological impulses (we are familiar with these phenomena as early as the post-Revolutionary war period!). A final factor is the life cycle, especially when it is tied to a period of rising prosperity, which resulted in the aging of radical and fellow-traveling union officials, their increasing integration into society through union jobs, family ties and so on. Under these conditions, the iron law of oligarchy (the concentration of power in the hands of an elite, even within formally democratic structures) took effect, and brought with it increasing conservatism because the newly entrenched officials did not want to risk their status by engaging in radical action. Thus they lost interest in encouraging Communists within the unions and even moved to consolidate their ties to societal elites by purging the Communists.

McCarthyism and the Return to Normalcy

Once the CIO was purged, the extirpation of Communists from the institutions into which they had bored became a mopping-up operation. The mechanism of this reaction, which, of course, suppressed not only Communism but also more democratic radicalism, was quite different from the mechanism of the post-World War I reaction. They have some points of similarity:

1. The general sentiment base of suddenly unfocused nationalism;
2. The refocusing of these sentiments onto events abroad—the Russian Revolution and the fate of Eastern Europe, respectively;
3. The development of an elite attack on radicals, partly exploiting the sentiment base for political power (that is, both Palmer and McCarthy were seeking campaign publicity), partly sharing these sentiments, and partly creating them—"sincerity" and cynical exploitation are here virtually inextricable,

4. The establishment of unofficial organizations, paralleling the official witch hunt; and

5. The spread of investigations and punitive acts from strictly radical movement organizations to reform movements, and the withdrawal of intellectuals from reform and radical politics.

Three elements of post World War I witch hunts were absent from the post-World War II period; gone were the violent attacks by vigilantes on alleged radicals, much diminished in scope was the patriotism-for-profit movement, and quite different was the response of intellectuals. After World War I, the formerly politicized intellectuals of both a radical and a Progressive bent responded either by continued efforts to implement Progressivism, by a withdrawal from politics into expatriation, Bohemianism, and literary attacks on American philistinism, and in a few cases, by commitment to the semi-clandestine activities of the new-born Communists. Virtually no intellectuals became spokesmen for "normalcy." After World War II, however, the reaction took a far more sophisticated form (with the absence of the crude vigilanteism of the earlier period), and the international situation was objectively more threatening and polarized; under these conditions a substantial number of intellectuals were able to celebrate pragmatism, the Free World, the psychological doctrine of "adjustment," anti-Communism as an end in itself, and in general, the whole ideational superstructure of the Cold War situation, the destruction of radical organizations, and the "return to normalcy" of the late forties and fifties. (One might add parenthetically that much of this uncritical antiintellectual ideology was inherited from the American Communist Party.) [39] This integration of intellectuals into the society was not strictly speaking a movement— the ill-fated CIA supported Congress for Cultural Freedom was as close as Cold War intellectuals came to a movement organization, and in any case, their impulse was toward supporting rather than changing current ideology and structure.[40] They shaped and articulated a variety of other movement-related phenomena—a revival of participation in existing religious denominations,[41] a retreat by women into homemaking,[42] and an application of adjustment as a norm to education and therapy. This activity does not constitute a movement in the strict sense because so much of it enhanced the cultural and political status quo, although one might almost go so far as to point out that it reversed some of the politicizing and secularizing trends of the prewar period.

A substantial portion of this uncritical antiintellectual ideology was inherited from the American Communist Party, as were a number of the Cold War intellectuals themselves; the Cold War blend of get-toughism and high-flown moralization was a rhetorical device that first appeared in Communist ideology of the thirties.[43]

A much more narrowly focused identifiable and obviously authoritarian phenomenon of the period was the crude and intense investigatory activity of Senator Joe McCarthy and the broad base of expressed support for him that together have been called "McCarthyism." It is as difficult to categorize this combination of an individual, a sequence of events, and expressed support as a movement as it is to categorize other phenomena of the period; it lacked organization beyond some massive letter-writing campaigns. There was little action component to McCarthyism at the popular level, and McCarthy-backed candidates did not fare particularly well in elections.[44] Thus, with slight exaggeration, one might summarize McCarthyism as opinion-poll-stimulated expressions of support for the anti-Communist activities of a senator who was sufficiently aggressive to receive much media attention. McCarthy did not become a fervent anti-Communist until late in life—during his 1946 campaign for the Senate and, more decisively, in 1950 in a general atmosphere of red-baiting in politics and on the basis of advice from conservative intellectual friends with whom he discussed the problem of campaign appeals.[45] His mass base, such as it was, consisted first of all of the traditional right wing of the midwestern Republican party, which produced his active campaign workers and combined support for his anti-Communism with economic conservatism (that is, opposition to welfare capitalism as well as to socialism)—"this was not a 'new' American Right, but rather an old one with new enthusiasm and new power." [46] A second, much more passive source of support were those individuals to whom Communism (and the Korean War) were especially salient—those mobilized on foreign policy issues. This ideological issue cross cut party lines and economic stands to some degree (for instance, among some working class Catholics, whom the church sensitized to the issue of Communism), although it was not in any way clearly reflected beyond the opinion polls. McCarthy was not widely supported among workers who backed welfare measures and/or took pro union economic stands, nor was he favorably perceived in the formerly LaFollette Progressive areas of the Midwest; thus traditions of working class consciousness and agrarian radicalism tended to protect against McCarthyism, as did education among middle-class subjects.[47] There is no evidence for and much evidence against any hypothesis of ideological or mass-base continuity between the protofascism of the thirties and McCarthyism.[48] In some localities (Vermont) expressed support for McCarthy was most widespread among a petty-bourgeois stratum of small entrepreneurs, who were both anti-labor and anti-big business;[49] nationwide this finding does not hold.[50] Psychologically, support for McCarthy correlated positively with the cluster of subclinical characteristics known as authoritarianism.

At the same time that scholars were so extraordinarily concerned with popular support for McCarthyism (which turned out to have little action component except among traditional right-wing Republicans) and with general American attitudes toward elites,[51] they devoted much less attention to the question of McCarthy's relation to elites and specifically the relationship between the McCarthy investigating team, the FBI, and other government intelligence agencies. What little evidence there is indicates that the FBI made its records indirectly accessible to McCarthy and, in turn, may have used the congressional committees to attack rival intelligence services and to circumnavigate loyalty boards and grand juries that "failed to take its informants seriously." [52] What is quite clear is that when McCarthy attacked the Republican Party and the Army, he was finally censured, silenced, and ignored in the media; in other words when he went beyond his aggressive, boorish, and exaggerated pursuit of a generally acceptable anti-Communism, and began to act as though he indeed hoped to create a mass reactionary movement, party and senate politicians and the Army turned on him.

I have spent much time in debunking McCarthyism as a mass movement not because it was harmless, but because it failed to develop into a movement. It was merely the extreme wing of an elite-sponsored witch hunt; when it threatened that elite itself rather than consolidating it in power (the function of a witch hunt), it was rapidly broken up by a more or less personal attack on the potential leader.

McCarthyism is also of interest in underlining the role of the media in developing these personality-centered largely unformalized movements. In a primitive way this media-dependent process was operative throughout American history, intensified during presidential campaigns and began to assume modern proportions with radio broadcasting and the proto-fascism of the thirties. McCarthyism does suggest how much greater is the potential for charismatic dictatorship in a period when the media are more pervasive, more technologically sophisticated, more oligopolistic, and less locally produced and oriented than they ever were. Nevertheless, the case of McCarthyism also suggests that media exposure without widespread movement organizing does not by itself produce a spontaneous movement.

The Right Wing in the 1950s and 1960s

As we just noted, the late forties and early fifties were not an active period for movements, by our rather strict definition, although there were broad cultural currents and elite-sponsored quasi-movements.

During reform periods (for example, 1900–1912, the 1930s and the 1960s), political movement activity took place "to the left" of the political center, while during the "quiet" postwar periods of reaction, it took place "to the right" of the center; the center itself shifted in a corresponding direction, partly as a cause of the movement activity.

The Progressive and New Deal eras and the 1960s were complex phenomena in which elite reforms, reform movements, and radical movements competed, cooperated, and exchanged goals; the postwar periods were ones in which a rather mild reaction among the elites had an extreme counterpart in the movements. In the Progressive and New Deal eras, one can identify elites more or less committed to political capitalism and movements some of which support elite reforms, some of which demand more welfare measures, and some of which actually attack the elites from a class-conscious position. In the postwar period, the elite remains more or less committed to political capitalism but deemphasizes its welfare aspects and attacks radicals; the movements are now on the "right," that is, specifically antiradical. Their positive features are more difficult to identify than are those of "left" movements (whether reformist or radical) because in America, they lack the intellectually sound conservative communitarian basis of European reaction.[53] Ideologically, right-wing movements in America (and I do not include the agrarian radicals among them) are extraordinarily primitive—generally centered on paranoid fantasies about Communist conspiracies, calls for law and order, and demands for a nationalist consensus. They fail to offer an intelligent conservative critique of political capitalism although they do have occasional telling criticisms—for instance, in their attacks on the media as contributing and producing the ideology of the new industrial state, on mental health rhetoric as suppression of socio-political deviation, on the growing power and centralization of the state and on American "materialism" (in other words, preoccupation with the disposal of the neocapitalist surplus). They are completely lacking in any coherent vision of alternatives; they lack a strongly differentiated substructural basis, such as provided southern ideologies like Fitzhugh's with a model of a possible alternative to the prevailing social order. With some exceptions, their intellectuals are not very intelligent (in a vicious circle, a mediocre ideology attracts only mediocre ideologues). Just as radical movements touch and even overlap reform movements, the "radical" right overlaps the conservative right —which emphasizes a revitalization of Lockeian-liberal capitalism.

I dislike the existing terminology intensely. The term "radical right" has partly been introduced simply to suggest that both it and the "radical left" are in *authoritarian* opposition to the status quo of a presumably democratic new industrial state—the authoritarianism of the Communist Party left has simply been used to smear the democratic left as well. I think at least five positions can be identified.

1. The "conservative" right, better termed the Lockeian-liberal position of laissez-faire capitalism and formal political democracy.

2. The "radical" right, which in Europe seeks a reconstruction of a corporate feudal order and in America, in a paucity of thought, calls for a nationalist consensus, some "conservative" right laissez-faire elements, and a large measure of anti-left-radicalism. In its European form, this ideology is by definition authoritarian; in its American form, it is too primitive to produce political programs beyond bourgeois political forms stripped of the bill of rights and a central focus on "law and order," military strength and suppression of "subversion" in life style and political activites.

3. The ideology of political capitalism (commonly known as "liberalism," rather misleadingly) with a commitment to oligopoly capitalism, a powerful state, some welfare measures, and a formal democracy with rather low levels of participation—authoritarian in fact, but not in theory. In its fascist forms, it abandons the commitment to democracy.

4. The authoritarian left, with a strongly class conscious analysis, but no political program for realizing the ascendancy of producers other than state socialism.

5. The democratic left, which also has a class analysis but seeks to combine it with an ideology of widespread participation in decision-making, that is, a dispersed, amorphous, and largely "withered-away" state. This position is Populist in character.

After this brief definitional excursus into ideational alternatives, we return to the American right. Its support base is disproportionately entrepreneurial middle class, elderly, college-educated, and Protestant (from a study of attendance at a meeting of the California Christian Anti-Communist Crusade), although some movement organizations seem also to have working class support as inheritors of the proto-fascist tradition, with the emphasis entirely shifted away from proto-fascist economic goals to political foci.[54] The middle-class base is especially strong in the movement organizations that fall in a borderland between the bizarre "radical" right and the conservative right. The extreme ideological primitivism of the right—its preoccupation with a Communist conspiracy—enables it to avoid the factionalism that plagues the left; where there are few tangible immediate rewards from organizational membership, factionalism is a potential problem unless the entire movement is focused on a single simple idea. Thus, there is some cooperation between movement organizations. The problem of tactics for changing the New Industrial State parallels the problem for "left" organizations for both must cope with the hegemony of political capitalism; right-wing efforts to solve tactical problems include paramilitary formations (the Minute Men, and its political arm, the Patriot Party), third-party efforts, efforts to capture somewhat more sober conservative bodies (such as the Wallace organization or the New York State Conservative Party), pressure group politics (the Liberty Lobby), boring from within in the Republican party (in attaining the nomination of Birchers for office), boring from within in the military, and largely educational efforts (the John Birch Society).[55] The last operates in a wide variety of forms—bookstores, radio and television programs, publicity attracting campaigns (such as the Impeach Earl Warren project of the Birch Society), infiltration of community organizations, study clubs, harassment of schools and election to school boards. One of the most important tactics has been efforts to establish contact with police departments and gain members from among policemen. It is difficult to estimate the success of the movement organizations—some exist primarily as mailing or periodical subscription lists and few have had many election victories, yet they do seem to have a degree of success with boring from within in police departments.[56] Success in this area could be an important factor in the fate of movements in America in the next few years. Second, these movements may be able to create a moderate penumbra sufficiently large to have an effect on American local and federal government policies. Although on the defensive in the late sixties, they remain a threat to both reform and left radical movements, less through their own independent activity than through pressures on existing elites.

The End of Ideology

By the late fifties, the storms of the Cold War had abated. Abroad, Stalin was dead, the Korean war had been brought to an end, Russia was thawing and the Polish and Hungarian resistance to the Soviet Union (as well as the less spectacular growing autonomy of Yugoslavia) indicated cracks in the Communist monolith. Domestically, dissent had been reduced to a very small scale by the investigations and organizational purges that left many jobless. Some of it was channeled into the Stevenson campaigns. The society seemed to be moving toward widespread integration into the central institutions. The manifestation of this societal integration included:

1. A widespread prosperity, despite the 1957–58 recession, which promised universal private affluence.
2. Integration in the usual sense—that is, what appeared to be the likelihood that blacks could become participants in educational institutions (and thus gradually, in the long run, in economic ones), that blacks themselves welcomed this integration, and that national

elites would encourage a pace of "deliberate speed" in these developments.

3. Automation and a boom in education that, together, promised an "up-grading" of the labor force, that is, a lower proportion of blue-collar workers, longer periods of training, more employment in business and government bureaucracies, and a more self-identified "middle class" (not class conscious) work force that would actively accept the prevailing ideology (as opposed to resignedly ignoring it) and participate in central institutions through legitimate channels of various types—including a politics centered on "issues." "Issues" became to the salaried strata in the political arena what wages and hours were to blue-collar workers in economic affairs, that is, a series of negotiable conflicts within the overall system of power.

4. An ideological shift from Cold War formulations to "end of ideology" ideology that emphasized technological solutions to more or less political problems, pragmatism, the conversion of intellectuals into "social engineers" and "scientific manpower" (correlated to educational trends triggered by Sputnik), and a consensus oriented mainstream in the social sciences.[57] These shifts were reflected in the language by the development of a superficial, morally neutral terminology for political and moral problems.

Perhaps for the first time in American history, large numbers of people were abandoning the ideology of individualism, self-reliance and unremitting toil and were ideationally accommodating themselves to bureaucratization and the fusion of private enterprise with the state into massive collective undertakings.[58] One sign of this ideological shift is the phenomenon of consumerism, which includes both ideational components and action. Consumerism has been defined as "the belief that each individual finds happiness in proportion to the amount of goods he buys and consumes." [59]

Against this background of massive structural and ideological integration, movements and movement phenomena seemed limited in power. In the late sixties, perhaps five were identifiable:

1. The "radical right," which we have already discussed as one effort to resist integration into the new industrial state.

2. Black movements—specifically, the Montgomery bus boycott—to accelerate the pace of integration.

3. A very small peace movement, almost reduced to its religious (frequently Quaker) core and concerned with disarmament and nuclear testing.

4. An unformalized Bohemian life style movement, the "Beat Generation," which formulated a cultural critique of America and lived its dissent through music, poetry, drugs, and voluntary poverty.[60]

5. A youth culture, not a true movement, and in many ways, an exaggeration and celebration of the prevailing culture more than an attack on it, although both elements are present. Cars, changing sexual mores and juvenile delinquency were the foci of popular interest in the proto-movement, which had both middle-class and blue-collar variants.[61]

Only the wisdom of hindsight can show how these innocuous currents were forerunners of another wave of turmoil in the sixties. We herewith end the historical section of our analysis with an apparent happy ending for movements in a period of quiet, of integration, of the end of ideology.

NOTES

[1] Eric Goldman, *Rendezvous with Destiny* (New York: Knopf, 1956), p. 248.

[2] Ronald Radosh, "The Corporate Ideology of American Labor Leaders from Gompers to Hillman," in James Weinstein and David Eakins, eds., *For a New America* (New York: Random House, 1970), pp. 125–52.

[3] Any comparison of an American institution to a fascist one is, of course, likely to arouse strong emotions. I wish to make it clear that I am using the term fascist here simply to mean a fusion of state and business elites (and possibly labor unions) in which the institutions of profit and private ownership are not abolished and in which there is continuity of the business elite (this last criterion distinguishes Liebermanism in the Soviet Union from a nascent fascism). Although the New Deal was more frequently charged with socialism than fascism, it made no explicit efforts to turn a class of employers into propertyless producers. Obviously, the analytic categories overlap to some degree. I certainly do not mean to imply that the New Deal was brutal, deliberately racist, destructive of formal democracy and/or im-

plemented by violence—the common associations of "fascism." I am confining myself strictly to categories based on class relations and the relations of the state to the productive system.

[4] Raymond Swing, *Forerunners of American Fascism* (New York: Julian Messner, 1935).

[5] Michael Rogin, *The Intellectuals and McCarthy: The Radical Specter* (Cambridge, Mass.: The MIT Press, 1967).

[6] Swing, *op. cit.*, pp. 98–99.

[7] Rogin, *op. cit.*

[8] *Ibid.*

[9] E. V. Walter, "Politics of Violence," in Robert Wolff and Barrington Moore, Jr., eds., *The Critical Spirit* (Boston: Beacon Press, 1967), p. 121; and Hannah Arendt, *On Revolution* (New York: Viking Press, 1965).

[10] Pluralists confusingly call these economically liberal.

[11] The reality of the fusion of state and capitalist enterprise and the illusion of laissez-faire rhetoric has produced some peculiar phenomena for example, Goldwater calling for more military expenditures and support for the SST, both "big government" stands. This shows that he at least knows where capitalism's interests lie, despite the "little government" rhetoric of some of his followers.

[12] Sheldon Messinger, "Organizational Transformation: A Case of a Declining Social Movement," *American Sociological Review* 20, no. 1 (February 1955): 3–10.

[13] Sidney Lens, *Radicalism in America* (New York: Crowell, 1966).

[14] Morris Janowitz, "The Black Legion," in Daniel Aaron, ed., *America in Crisis* (New York: Knopf, 1952).

[15] Kolko is among those who dismisses the CP as follows: "During the 1930's the majority of the Socialist Party's members were foreign-born or first generation, and this pattern of immigrant domination was even more widespread in the Communist Party. In this context both parties became a kind of fraternal center—the majority of the literature of the Socialist Party was not in English—for lonely migrants who might raise funds at banquets for the Scottsboro boys but were essentially adjusting as best they could to a strange, new life. What was ultimately more important to such leftists was the conviviality of the banquet hall and comrades who spoke the mother tongue. These activists might also finance the work of the more earnest younger men who were wholly committed to politics as they defined it and, especially in the case of the Communists after 1935, might be caught in the euphoria and passion of organizing the CIO, going to Spain or participating in student movements. Even when the Communists lost their capacity to attract the young and the earnest they could still, even in the worst days of McCarthyism, retain their banquet hall followers whose social roots were grounded in the activities of the IWO or other organizations—aging and bewildered people who were transformed in the social imagery into conspirators posing a serious danger to society.

"The intellectual problems of the Socialists and Communists in America were very much like those of their associates in Europe. Throughout the 1930's the European left was fighting a losing, rear-guard battle and drifting along with the capitalists toward a world conflagration. The left was characterized by futile efforts to respond to the initiatives of reaction." (Gabriel Kolko, "The Decline of Radicalism in America," in Weinstein and Eakins, *op. cit.*, p. 212).

This is too ready a debunking, I believe. Yet Kempton, who devoted a whole book to Communism in the thirties, wrote the following epitaph for the Old Left: "For most of the real history of the thirties went on outside while the committed were legislating an historical myth. The thirties met their problems, or at least beat them back a little while and held the door open. Hitler, unemployment, the crisis of capitalism—all the things the revolutionaries said could only be solved on their terms—the America of the thirties met and dealt with, to a degree at least, and with very little help from most of us." [Murray Kempton, *Part of Our Time* (New York: Simon & Schuster, 1955), p. 326.]

[16] Lens, *op. cit.*, pp. 308–9.

[17] Carol Bird, *The Invisible Scar* (New York: David McKay, 1966).

[18] Harold Cruse, *The Crisis of the Negro Intellectual* (New York: Apollo, 1968); and Lens, *op. cit.*, pp. 309–11.

[19] This claim about intellectuals' early dropping out is drawn from Murray Kempton and is not entirely satisfactorily documented.

[20] Hortense Powdermaker, *Hollywood: The Dream Factory* (Boston: Little, Brown, 1950).

[21] Gabriel Almond and Sidney Verba, *The Appeals of Communism* (Princeton, N.J.: Princeton University Press, 1954).

[22] Marcuse constructs a cogent argument to the effect that moral positions are also in long-run terms more rational. "In the interplay of theory and practice, true and false solutions become distinguishable—never with the evidence of necessity, never as the positive, only with the certainty of a reasoned and reasonable chance, and with the persuasive force of the negative. For the true positive is the society of the future and therefore beyond definition and determination, while the existing positive is that which must be surmounted. But the experience and understanding of the existent society may well be capable of identifying what is *not* conducive to a free and rational society, what impedes and distorts the possibilities of its creation. Freedom is liberation, a specific historical process in theory and practice, and as such it has its right and wrong, its truth and falsehood." Herbert Marcuse, "Repressive Tolerance," in Robert Wolff, Barrington Moore, Jr., and Herbert Marcuse, *A Critique of Pure Tolerance* (Boston: Beacon Press, 1969), p. 87.

[23] Irving Howe and Lewis Coser, *The American Communist Party* (New York: Praeger, 1962), pp. 369–70.

[24] Lens, *op. cit.*, p. 322.

[25] *Ibid.*, pp. 322–24.

[26] Howe and Coser, *op. cit.*

[27] *Ibid.*, p. 385.

[28] *Ibid.,* p. 375.
[29] *Ibid.,* p. 378.
[30] *Ibid.,* pp. 431–32.
[31] Bird, *op. cit.*
[32] Howe and Coser, *op. cit.,* pp. 296–97.
[33] *Ibid.,* pp. 370–71.
[34] Quoted in Bird, *op. cit.*
[35] Incidentally, contrary to stereotypes, the middle class has actually been more hawkish than the working class during both the Korean and the Vietnamese wars. I would like to draw the attention of my readers to the following two articles: Richard F. Hamilton, "A Note on the Mass Support for 'Tough' Military Initiatives," *American Sociological Review* 33, no. 3 (June 1968): 439; and Philip Converse and Howard Schuman, " 'Silent Majorities' and the Vietnam War," *Scientific American* 222, no. 6 (June 1970): 17–25.
[36] Kempton, *op. cit.*
[37] Gabriel Kolko, cited by Barton J. Bernstein, "America in War and Peace: The Test of Liberalism," in Barton J. Bernstein and Allen J. Matusow, eds., *Twentieth Century America* (New York: Harcourt, Brace & World, 1969), p. 352.
[38] Ely Chinoy, *Automobile Workers and the American Dream* (Boston: Beacon Press, 1965).
[39] Christopher Lasch, *The New Radicalism in America 1889–1963* (New York: Random House, 1965), p. 289.
[40] Christopher Lasch, "The Congress for Cultural Freedom," in *The Agony of the American Left* (New York: Random House, 1969).
[41] Will Herberg, *Protestant, Catholic, Jew* (Garden City, N.Y.: Doubleday, 1955).
[42] Kate Millet, *Sexual Politics* (Garden City, N.Y.: Doubleday, 1970); and Talcott Parsons and Robert Bales, *Family, Socialization and Interaction Process* (Glencoe, Ill.: Free Press, 1955).
[43] Lasch, *The New Radicalism in America,* p. 289.
[44] Rogin, *op. cit.,* p. 245.
[45] Eric Goldman, *The Crucial Decade, 1945–55* (New York: Knopf, 1956).
[46] Rogin, *op. cit.,* p. 247.
[47] *Ibid.,* p. 236.
[48] *Ibid.*
[49] Martin Trow, "Small Businessmen, Political Tolerance and Support for McCarthy," *American Journal of Sociology* 64 (1958): 270–81.
[50] Rogin, *op. cit.,* p. 236.
[51] Edward Shils, *The Torment of Secrecy* (New York: Free Press, 1956).
[52] I. F. Stone, *The Haunted Fifties* (New York: Random House, 1963), pp. 25–29. The quote is from p. 27.
[53] Louis Hartz, *The Liberal Tradition in America* (New York: Harcourt, Brace & World, 1955), part IV.
[54] Raymond Wolfinger, Barbara Wolfinger, Kenneth Prewitt, and Sheila

Rosenhack, "America's Radical Right: Politics and Ideology," in David Apter, *Ideology and Discontent* (New York: Free Press, 1964), pp. 262–93.

[55] Benjamin Epstein and Arnold Foester, *The Radical Right* (New York: Random House, 1967), pp. 45–50.

[56] *Ibid.*

[57] Daniel Bell, *The End of Ideology* (New York: Free Press, 1960), Chapter 14 and Epilogue.

[58] C. Wright Mills, *White Collar: The American Middle Classes* (New York: Oxford University Press, 1951); William H. Whyte, *The Organization Man* (Garden City, N.Y.: Doubleday-Anchor, 1956); Daniel Miller and Guy Swanson, *The Changing American Parent* (New York: Wiley, 1958); and John Seeley, *Crestwood Heights* (New York: Basic Books, 1956).

[59] Marvin Harris, *Culture, Man and Nature* (New York: Crowell, 1971), p. 262.

[60] Jack Kerouac, *On the Road* (New York: Viking Press, 1957); and Allen Ginsberg, *Howl and Other Poems* (San Francisco: City Lights, 1956).

[61] James Coleman, *The Adolescent Society* (New York: Free Press, 1961); and Arthur Stinchcombe, *Rebellion in a High School* (Chicago: Quadrangle Books, 1969).

9

The Present

> You can never have a revolution in order to establish a democracy. You must have a democracy in order to have a revolution.
>
> ———G. K. Chesterton

In this chapter we will consider movements after 1960, and will try to apply general perspectives derived from the historical data to present trends. This chapter must necessarily be an open-ended essay—we do not know what the outcomes of these movements will be, although we do know a little about their sources and can try to make some predictions.

CONCLUSIONS BASED ON THE HISTORICAL MATERIAL

In this section we will summarize propositions derived from the historical perspective.

1. Movements that have sought to reverse substructural trends —that is, to reconstruct an earlier economic, technological and socio-

political situation—have not succeeded in attaining their goals, unless they defined success as preservation of small communal subcultures.

2. Both radical and reform movements have succeeded best in programs of integrating groups into the central institutions, even though this result was an unanticipated and unintended consequence for radical movements.

3. Wars bring with them nationalist consensus and ideational exhaustion which contribute to an atmosphere in which class conscious radicalism is attacked and weakened and in which reform is also diminished; economic elites tend to assert stronger and more overt control.

4. Life style and religious movements may continue to exist even in these quiet periods and play a proportionately larger role in them relative to political movements; the non-political movements act as cocoons for political movements that emerge from them under more auspicious conditions.

5. It is difficult to establish any clear relationship between the business cycle and radical class conscious movements; the general tendency is for the latter to be stronger during depressions and weaker during periods of prosperity—this observation is by no means without exceptions and in some cases depressions destroy such movements by undercutting their bargaining power (which is based on a need for labor).

6. For reasons discussed in Chapter 2, movements of both the radical left and the "radical right" have been extraordinarily weak in America. Capitalist and neocapitalist hegemony have been correspondingly strong.

7. A number of religious groups whose historical roots antedate the establishment of America as a fragment of British liberalism have been important sources of radicalism (defined as a stand specifically opposed to prevailing ideology). Religious metaphors are a powerful vehicle of attacks on the prevailing social order.

8. Blacks, due to their unique history among American ethnic groups, have remained an unintegrable segment of the population (unintegrable even along the lines of the cultural integration and structural differentiation of other ethnic groups). Blacks and Indians are probably the only subgroups among whom a sizable proportion has never accepted the legitimacy of American central institutions.

9. America has experienced only two breakdowns of legitimacy: the Revolution (based on class coalition and nationalism) and the Civil War (based on ideological exacerbation of a substructural cleavage). American political legitimacy has sustained itself even in the face of massive economic breakdowns.

10. Third-party movements have been unsuccessful on their own terms, even if parts of their programs were adopted, because third parties cannot gain control of political elite positions and therefore can only have their goals adopted in fragmentary form. (The Republicans of the pre-Civil War period are an exception to this proposition.)

11. No movement or movement organization can consider itself revolutionary if it fails to develop a dual structure and to contest monopolization of the means of violence, be it by paramilitary units or infiltration of the police and armed forces. With the exception of the special case of the Civil War (special because of the unique situation of substructural and structural differentiation), there have been no serious instances of such a development since the adoption of the Constitution (the Dorr War in Rhode Island is not counted as serious).

12. Because of the general failure of American radicalism one can only speculate what kind of movement organization is conducive to movement success. In the case of reform movements a large penumbra of partially committed supporters increases the chances of influencing elites to adopt the reforms.

All movements must make a series of choices:

between single issue demands and multiple demands.
between radical demands and demands that do not attack the legitimacy of present distributions of wealth and power.
between influencing elites (or even incorporating movement members into the elite) and attempting to replace elites.

So far, reform movements—those with narrow goals that are implemented by influencing elites—have succeeded better than more radical movements in America. The latter have functioned mainly to impress elites with the relative mildness of reform movement demands. Thus, radical movements have in effect become a wing of reform movements in America, performing a function for them—which by definition implies failure for the radical movements. The Revolution and the Civil War are again the two great exceptions. The American case can be contrasted to that of France, for instance, where radicals have repeatedly breached the legitimacy of political institutions. In France the very power of the center has reduced the number of possible local and peripheral targets for movement activity, forcing it into radical attacks on the center itself; thus almost paradoxically, the power of the center has contributed to the repeated downfall of central elites.[1]

13. As a corollary of Proposition 12, we may note that while violence has played an important role in American movement history it has almost always appeared as a means of social control used by elites and their supporters against radical and on occasion, reform movements. Since movements in America have been unable to capture or independently create military forces they have not been effective users of violence.

This statement holds even if "violence" is speciously extended to include property destruction; American movements have generally not resorted to this tactic in contrast—for example—to British workers who used it as a routine bargaining tool in labor disputes during early industrialization.[2]

14. Further examination of the data suggests that Proposition 12 can be extended almost to its logical extreme. The *most* successful movements have been those that were created by elites, sometimes but not consistently under pressure from reform and radical movements. These elite-created movements have served several purposes:

(1) to improve and stabilize the economic climate, primarily for industrial capitalism.
(2) to reduce the strains and dislocations generated by political and economic modernization—especially depressions, rural-urban migration, and the decline of entrepreneurial opportunity.
(3) to foster societal integration by promoting channels of upward mobility (especially through education and "Anglicization" of immigrant culture.)
(4) to foster societal integration by improving living standards, directly or by supporting unions.

(5) to foster societal integration by increasing political participation.

There have been several major thrusts in these directions; Hamiltonian policy (concerned primarily with number 1), Jeffersonian policy (continuing number 1 but more enthusiastic for number 5), Jacksonian Democracy (numbers 1, 2 and 5), the Progressive Era (all), the New Deal (numbers 1, 2 and 4) and the post-war period through the present (all). These massive steps toward the integration of the state and civil society have many of the characteristics of movements in the strict sense. After World War II quasi-movements are specifically generated by elites to accomplish one or more of these tasks (Peace Corps, VISTA, OEO, and so forth) and in turn, formally independent movements are initiated simply to take advantage of the state's support of reform movements.[3] The appearance of large staffs of professional movement workers whose living depends on the relationship between the state and the quasi-movements and reform movements, began as early as the Progressive Era but only now has become a phenomenon of great importance.

There is a kind of mutual parasitism involved here, in which the movement professionals depend for their livelihood on the elite-sponsored movement while the state in turn gains legitimacy and mass integration from the movement. Obviously, this relationship places severe constraints on movement members' ability to act independently in any capacity. Enormous amounts of vested interest in the central institutions (as rewarders of the movements) and in the movement organizations themselves (as vehicles for obtaining these rewards) are built up. Only a few radical groups (for instance, the Black Panthers) and isolated reform movements (parts of the ecology movement, for instance) have been able to withstand this cooptation.

15. Because of the structural position of American intellectuals and the peculiarly overarching liberal tradition, American movements have been much less ideationally productive than European ones, both on the left and the right. (And this cognitive sterility and derivativeness, with its reliance on foreign models, has not prevented American radicalism from being factionalistic—perhaps has actually stimulated theoretical hairsplitting in the absence of a cogent analysis of American conditions.) Blacks—a group that is historically and structurally uniquely in a position to escape the cognitive monopoly

of the new industrial state—have also failed to develop an independent perspective, partly because of survival pressures and partly because of a long unproductive liaison with white reform and radical movements.[4]

16. A key problem for any movement is the sustaining of commitment (participation) beyond a crisis period. This is especially problematical in a society that is strongly structurally and ideationally integrated, in which there are relatively few marginal or deroutinized groups, a condition that increases with modernity (that is, in the new industrial state). Although America has a history of ethnic diversity and ethnic conflict, ethnicity has not provided the kind of deroutinizing marginality that leads to breaches of political legitimacy.

17. Youth, itinerant or isolated labor, status as an intellectual, and membership in a church whose teachings are extra-liberal all contribute to cognitive distance from the prevailing order. Poverty and ethnic minority status are more ambiguous, bringing with them *both* cognitive distance (which facilitates movement participation) *and* characteristics that inhibit movement participation (such as immediate survival problems, desire for "Americanization," etc.). Small entrepreneurship is a similarly ambiguous category. Employment as a white-collar worker in a large private bureaucracy, middle-age and family commitments, moderate to high levels of education with a large technical component—all these decrease cognitive distance from the prevailing order and lessen likelihood of movement involvement.

"Cognitive distance" is on a level of analysis different from "alienation" (a word that has been misused extensively) and "neurosis." In simplest terms, cognitive distance refers to the extent to which the prevailing ideology makes sense; that is of course partly conditioned by personality and life experiences as well as by structural position.

MOVEMENTS AFTER 1960: THE BEHEMOTH STIRS

Beginning as early as the 1955 Montgomery bus boycott but not fully underway until after J. F. Kennedy's election, were a series of movements that changed the political atmosphere and to some extent, the political realm of discourse in America.

The first of these was the civil rights movement, the movement for full legal equality for blacks in public accommodations and at the polls. The movement began innocuously enough as a thrust for full integration of blacks into the central political and consumer institutions of America—in other words, as a kind of mop-up operation against presumably premodern patterns of ascribed status in the South. The South was perceived as a region in which the formal equality guaranteed by liberal democracy had not yet been fully established; the tactics for establishing it were civil disobedience, the attraction of national publicity to what had been regional mores, and insistence upon formal rights (such as registering to vote) that had been informally denied. This movement was initiated largely by younger Southern blacks influenced by the Southern churches and based at the southern colleges; it was shortly joined by whites, often northerners, who helped to draw media attention to it and provided some technical (legal) skills to it. The civil rights movement can be described as a success; it achieved the Civil Rights Act of 1964, the end of Jim Crow statutes throughout the South, and the registration of many blacks and the consequent election of blacks to local office. Its constituent movement organizations—chiefly CORE, SNCC and SCLC—formed the basis of further movement activity among blacks. For it soon became apparent that the successes of the Civil Rights Movement—important as they were—were insufficient to raise the economically depressed status of the mass of blacks, both northern and southern. The successor movements of the civil rights movement therefore underwent three changes—a shift of focus from the South to northern urban settings, an easing-out of white members as essentially inappropriate for leadership positions in an ethnic movement and as irrelevant to the task of building institutions in black communities, and a change in goals from legal and formal political equality to political power and cultural influence. These shifts raised strategic problems and forced consideration of the question whether blacks could ever attain a sizable share of wealth and power under the present productive and ideological system. The former civil rights movement organizations in confronting these problems converged with nationalist groups whose sources were in the cultural separatist Black Muslim movement that expanded among urban blacks in the 1950s. By the late 1960s, these currents produced a new round of movement-phenomena and movement organizations: the urban riots, the politicized street gangs, the nationalist groups with a primarily cultural focus, a variety of community organization groups, and the Black Panthers with a strong Marxist emphasis and a definition of the American situation that links Afro-Americans to exploited colonial peoples. These groups varied tremendously in local strength, contact with the urban poor, attitudes toward the American polity and economy, and degree of co-optability by American central institution. At the time of this writing, black communities are the site of much movement activity but as yet no predictable directions of change.

The civil rights movement had an unintended spin-off in campus-based movements when students found that university administrators provided little support for movement activity, particularly when placed under adverse pressure by local elites; specifically, the University of California at Berkeley interfered with traditional student free speech rights when these were applied to recruiting for local civil rights protests and, thus, touched off the Berkeley sit-in and Free Speech movement. The Vietnam war, the draft, student participation in university decision-making, and the subservience of the multiversity to the "military-industrial complex" were added to relations with black neighborhoods as issues for movements directed against universities. Campus disturbances ranged from the highly dramatic multiissue Columbia uprising of 1968 to the rather modest demonstration at a southern college for the right to sit on the campus lawn. The chief tactic of the campus movement was the sit-in or building seizure. Although it is early to pronounce a final judgment on campus movements, one is tentatively tempted to assess them as failures in terms of their more specific goals. They have had little impact on de facto decision-making in universities even when they effected some de jure reforms; in this area they have been to a large degree counterproductive at public universities, inducing suppression and punitive fund-cutting by state legislators. They forced some of the overt arms of the military off-campus but have certainly not attained the goal of cutting the intellectual community off from its military patrons. They have had some impact on relations between urban universities and blacks, chiefly in the creation of black studies programs, a few open enrollment plans, and some symbolic acts; the black student movements—probably more properly viewed as black movement groups than as part of the student movement—have had the greatest impact on universities. Even when there was little identifiable movement activity, the challenge that urban proletarian blacks have posed to multiversity values, curricula, teaching methods, and "student affairs" has been formidable.

The most important contribution of the student movement as a whole, particularly where it was not confined to campus administrative reforms, has been a general re-politicizing of the society in the 1960s and a reinvolvement of American intellectuals in sociopolitical criticism. Even if individual members of the student movement withdraw to the suburban life style of the white collar proletariat, and even if the more radical groups are suppressed by court cases and police harassment in the next decade, the legacy of renewed political debate—the end of "the end of ideology"—will not be so rapidly destroyed and may provide some intellectual continuity between the radicals of the sixties and the next generation of American activists. One of the lasting aspects of this intellectual renewal is a revival of Marxist scholarship in the social sciences (primarily in history and sociology).

Organizationally, white student movements may have left less of a lasting contribution. The key movement organization of the sixties was the Students for a Democratic Society, a 1962 split-off from its parent organization, the League for Industrial Democracy (a holdover from the non-Communist old left). Until its faction-ridden demise in 1969, SDS was in the forefront of American radicalism and (like the pre-World War I Socialist Party) was able to develop strength in the Midwest as well as in urban areas and former old left strongholds. Although SDS as such no longer exists, some related organizations carry on its tradition of neo-Marxist ideology, organizational decentralization, and strong emphasis on activism and projects: among professionals, the New University Conference, Scientists and Engineers for Social and Political Action, and the Medical Committee for Human Rights; a number of working class youth organizations that developed independently of SDS organizers although politically awakened by them—for example, the (Appalachian) Young Patriots and "greaser" Rising Up Angry in Chicago; and underground media collectives.

A rather different strain in the student movement—although

doubtlessly overlapping in personnel—was the involvement of students in electoral politics in support of Eugene McCarthy (essentially a single-issue peace candidate) and Bobby Kennedy (who far from being a radical, seems to have stood for the politics of the New Industrial State—media-oriented and committed to full participation of ethnic and subcultural minorities in the central institutions). This current of youthful political involvement diminished after Kennedy's assassination and the debacle of the 1968 Democratic Convention but may have some long lasting effects in providing a base for reform movements.

By the late sixties and early seventies a note of despair was sounded in the Weathermen, one of the SDS successor groups, who pursued a heroic but necessarily doomed terrorist course—essentially a revival of anarchist "propaganda of the deed," a strong organization into collectives, and an abandonment of the white population as hopelessly bourgeois-ified—their struggle took no lives but their own. The other formal SDS-successor organizations, heavily influenced by the proletarian-oriented Progressive Labor Party, largely pursued a course of supporting the immediate demands of (chiefly unionized) workers—at the time of this writing not a visibly successful effort in terms of creating a mass movement organization.

In summary, then, at the moment, the white student movement has been most effective in restoring sociopolitical criticism among American intellectuals; the most promising organizational products are the decentralized and not doctrinairely-proletarian SDS successor groups, although their long term impact cannot now be assessed.

A rather different movement was (or is) the "hippie" movement with its components of drug use, communal experimentation and other life style phenomena, in many respects continuous with the Beat Generation. It is not a highly formalized movement—its identifiable bodies tend to be communes and "families"—nor has it produced a highly organized cognitive order. Where this new life style movement has become linked to radicalism—as the "cultural revolution"—it has created an extraordinarily democratic, not co-optable, decentralized and communistic threat to the New Industrial State— in the form of the Yippies, underground media collectives, and so on. It has been especially effective in exploiting one of the features of this society—the profit-making media's endless search for sensationalistic pseudo-news. But the same characteristics that have made this counterculture a refreshing additive for radicalism have made it susceptible to commercial exploitation, faddism, and resistance by partial incorporation. It has contributed to neo-capitalist hegemony the tactic of "repressive desublimation,"[5] the policy of encouraging sexual gratification and (to a lesser degree) drug use as long as these are not linked to radical analysis of and activity against the existing distribution of wealth and power. "Hip capitalism" has simply been a new form of consumerism, producing profits in the fashion industry and other areas. Similarly, the "encounter movement" and sexual experimentation have not markedly interfered with the operation of the large bureaucracies of modern society. Less legal but no more revolutionary is the use of marijuana by large numbers of younger people, occasional week-end trips and so on. The so-called countercultural life style can be transformed into a commodity whose enjoyment contributes to the stability of an advanced modern society.[6] The radical potential of these movement phenomena is realized only when links are created to political movements or, sometimes, to ongoing extra-liberal religious communities. Incidentally, groups of combined political and cultural form have been the victims of the most complete suppression in the late sixties and in the seventies, perhaps because their assault on the prevailing social order is so multi-faceted.

The political student movements and the counter culture have been treated together as a "youth movement." The interpretation of these phenomena as manifestations of a "generation gap" serves very definite ideological purposes—the label implies immaturity and transitiveness. It dismisses these movements as serious challenges to the status quo; it links them with "youth cultures," a mass media-consumerist phenomenon that exploits youth; it links them to the juvenile delinquency and youth culture of the fifties, which is historically valid but irrelevant to the critique of the social order that they present; it suggests roots in permissive child rearing, which may explain the phenomenon but does not therefore debunk it. The "generation gap" is not merely a recurrent life cycle phenomenon; it is also a historical phenomenon arising out of the dislocations of modern industrialism and aimed specifically at altering the social order of the new industrial state.

As we noted above, all post-World War II movements have some reference to events abroad and revolutions in the colonial and quasi-colonial countries are indeed important foci for the black and student movements. Very explicitly concerned with world events (and with their role in personal troubles) are the movement organizations concerned with the war in Vietnam, draft resistance, peace and American adventures abroad. In the early sixties most of these were directed toward nuclear testing and drew on a mixed Quaker and middle-class "conscience constituency" with some student affiliates.[7] As American involvement in Vietnam grew—especially during Johnson's presidency—this movement became broader and less genteel, with a turn toward larger demonstrations, draft resistance, and destruction of draft files among the most committed (especially in the churches). The most spectacular successes of this movement include forcing the withdrawal of Johnson from the '68 presidential race and creating a general lukewarmness toward the war in Vietnam among the American public. Few citizens really can be said to have participated in the movement but it created a penumbra of less support for the war than for any previous American war since the turn of the century. Hopefully, this dampening effect on mass mobilization on the "home front" will mean a smaller wave of anti-radical reaction after the end of the war.

The sheer size, the powerful lobbying and the enormous vested interests in the Pentagon, may however, produce further foreign military involvement even if the public fails to provide mass jingoistic support for it; this possibility becomes stronger if the anti-draft movement succeeds in establishing a volunteer army, for then the obstacle of low morale among draftees is removed from troop deployment. Even if there is no further foreign intervention, the dependence of 10 to 20 percent of the labor force on the Pentagon suggests that the influence of this institution will be difficult for any movement to reverse.[8] The antiwar movement produced analysis of America's de facto empire and helped to focus discussion on whether American intervention is a mistaken policy or an intrinsic feature of a neo-capitalist state; unfortunately this discussion may be muted and the penumbra drop away as America extricates itself from its infantry commitment in Vietnam.

Other important movements drawing on an even less radicalized constituency than the "conscious constituency" of the antiwar movement were the ecology and consumer movements. These had three identifiable wings—a culturally radical wing associated with communal experimentation, food faddism and return to nature; a middle-class base supporting legal and muckraking efforts personified above all by Ralph Nader; and a rather phony elite-sponsored wing for channeling student activism out of more manifestly radical movements. Like all movements of the sixties, the goals of these movements could be logically extended into a radical attack on social structure and ideology, centered on the consequences of neocapitalist commitment to profits and growth.

Also simultaneously potentially radical and potentially co-optable were a variety of community control movements; given the general loss of power of the local level in the United States their major targets were not national elites but the police, the educational system, and the welfare-health care system. Tactics for gaining these objectives varied from local elections to extra-legal direct action to pressure on elites to shift power from boards of experts to elected community based boards.[9] It is difficult to assess the overall impact of these movements—their major effect may be educational (to demonstrate how little is still locally decided in the society) and as a training ground for leaders of proletarian background.

Finally, an important movement of the post-consensus period is Women's Liberation. It emerged partly out of the experience of the persistence of sexist attitudes even in radical movements and the relegation of women in these movements to subordinate roles, as well as out of the general exploitation, neglect and subordination of women. The major objective foci of the movement are clear-cut: exploitation of women as employees and consumers; sexual exploitation of women, and the exploitation of women's sexuality by the advertising industry to promote consumerism; women's lack of control over the reproductive process; the use of women as a reserve labor force; men's refusal to participate in child-rearing; and at the ideational level, the stereotyping of women in a variety of ways. The movement organizations rage from specific goal reform groups to multiissue radical groups to women's caucuses within other movements, and tactics are correspondingly wide-ranging and include legal and legislative efforts as well as moral agitation ("consciousness-raising"). It is probable that Women's Liberation has touched only a small fraction of American women and that it must battle some of the most deep-seated aspects of ideology, not only among men, but, especially among women who have been socialized to accept exploitation as natural and becoming to the sex. Some key issues facing the movement are the problems of creating an alliance between poorer (and black) women and higher-income women, of the relationship to male-dominated radical movements, and questions of whether the demand for integration into the present structure is a bona fide goal or a strategy for attacking that structure. Allied with Women's Liberation in a struggle against rigid sex roles, the cult of machismo, and the involuntary socioeconomic marginality of sexual minorities, has been the Gay Liberation movement among homosexuals. These movements potentially can change the society in fundamental ways, through altered socialization experience and body-image. Women's Liberation in particular is perhaps somewhat immune to the suppression to which more narrowly political movements are now being subjected.

We may also briefly mention the movements within religious bodies—above all in the Catholic Church—toward diffusion of authority and even commitment to radical goals.

What do all these movements add up to, if anything? Let us try to draw some conclusions:

1. Each of these movements has a potential for completely destroying prevailing ideology. This is most true of the black and women's movements, whose constituencies are entirely outside the white-male created neo-capitalist hegemony. It is also true—although at a less fundamental level—of the explicitly radical political movements. It is even true of the more easily co-optable movements, such as ecology and consumers movements. Together these movements present a fundamental cognitive challenge.

2. Separately, each movement is subject to co-optation and incorporation, some more than others. Each one after all has some roots in the struggle of marginal and excluded groups for participation in the central institutions. To some extent, the neo-capitalist social order may prove incapable of meeting demands for full participation; but this remains an unexplored empirical question, and doubtless in a small scale and piece-meal fashion substantial integration can take place. For instance, it could take the following forms:

  (1) Creation of elite-sponsored movements to employ and constrain present movement leadership.
  (2) Acceptance of large scale employment at equal pay of

blacks and women; provision of day care centers—including expansion of the exploitive proprietary day care centers; a somewhat more than token involvement of women and blacks in electoral politics, as major party nominees; improved health care. Some doubt remains whether employment of blacks and women would seriously upset the very delicate unemployment equilibrium of neo-capitalism and consequently prove incompatible with economic stability.

(3) A shift to a volunteer army and diminished public concern for military intervention abroad, to "buy off" the anti-war movement.

(4) Ecology and consumer protection measures whose costs are largely borne by the consumer and the small marginal firm.

(5) Increased tolerance and "repressive desublimation" to accommodate Gay Liberation, communal experimentation, and drug users.

(6) De jure—and even de facto—changes in the *internal* distribution of power in universities and churches, and the retreat of military research off-campus into special institutes.

(7) Limited community control over schools, possibly over welfare facilities but probably not over police forces.

(8) Extension of unionization to presently unorganized workers.[10]

Substantial parts of this program of co-optation are underway. One might of course argue that such large scale co-optive change amounts to fundamental *qualitative* change. In some sense it does— just as the social order at the close of the Progressive Era and the New Deal *was* substantially different from the social order at the beginning of these periods. Given the co-optive program we have described there would indeed be changes in the distribution of American wealth and power. It is difficult but not impossible to distinguish massive co-optation-incorporation from revolution. As long as present elites are not dislodged (even if they have given up some prerogatives), as long as profit, organizational growth and efficiency are important goals, as long as consumerism is encouraged in a variety of ways and is essential to corporate and governmental planning and stability, as long as the military (and a variety of other governmental agencies) remain powerful, as long as unions do not seek ownership and control of the means of production—as long as at least these changes remain unaccomplished, it is not correct to speak of an ideological and structural revolution. Rather a co-optive program like the one outlined here would produce a more smoothly functioning, better integrated and more tolerant version of the new industrial state. One must conclude that this outcome would be preferable to a coercive society which uses large amounts of violence to keep dissatisfied groups in impoverished marginal positions—another possible alternative.

3. These movements arose from efforts at integration of and by (and initially, on behalf of) marginal groups. Much of the youthful fervor of the Kennedy administration was aimed at a pragmatic removal of poverty "pockets"; the administration encouraged the mobilization of idealistic middle-class youths in the civil rights movement and actually engaged in mobilization itself, through VISTA and the Peace Corps. Thus, inadvertently, it touched off movements whose analyses became increasingly radical and difficult to accommodate. These initial efforts at mobilizing the middle class on behalf of the poor gave the movements of the sixties their peculiar fragmentation into the poor and the affluent. For historical reasons blacks (as well as Chicanos, Indians and other groups that did not share the history of voluntary immigration from Europe) could not be as easily integrated into the society as optimists of the early sixties believed; therein lay the source of their increasing radicalization. Middle class youth on the other hand was susceptible to deroutinization and radicalism because of the affluence and "permissiveness" of their childhood environments; in these settings they had enjoyed: the leisure and intellectual training to question the prevailing ideology, parental support for cognitive liberation and experimentation; and exposure to unrealized parental hopes for alteration of the present social order. The potential consequences of the watered down Freudianism of earlier decades had finally been realized; the decline of instinctual repression in the postwar middle-class household brought about cognitive liberation from the prevailing ideology and a rebellion against authority.[11] Thus, two very distinct factors form the social psychological basis of current movements; on the one hand, Third World ethnic groups have been cognitively and emotionally distant from the prevailing order for historical reasons; on the other hand, many middle-class youths attained a self-conscious emancipation from it. The

distinctness of these motivating forces is responsible for the uneasiness of the alliance between white middle-class youths and Third World groups, which has presented serious obstacles to movement cohesion.

Even the antiwar movement (and its related groups) can be explained in terms of our model of pragmatic "end of ideology" integration suddenly run wild, for the war in Vietnam (and intervention elsewhere) represents an effort to subordinate other peoples to American central institutions and ideology, to include them in an international neo-capitalist economy, to "built their nation" according to a western liberal political model, and to convert them to a modern western value system as a condition for development. In this case, the effort to integrate the Vietnamese was met by Vietnamese resistance rather than by the ambivalence of Afro-Americans and other partially integrated peoples in the metropolitan country. And Vietnamese resistance to escalating American efforts at integration in turn touched off the anti-war movements in the metropolitan country.

4. American movements must also be seen in the context of worldwide unrest. Its sources are essentially similar: national liberation movements against large power economic and cultural hegemony (and in some cases, political and military domination)—in Czechoslovakia, in Mozambique and Angola, in Vietnam and in Cuba, in Algeria, in Peru and Chile, in Northern Ireland, in Biafra, and Bangla Desh, and so on. These movements generally fuse nineteenth century liberal concepts of nationalism with more or less Marxian views of social structure. They promise much: the only hope for an end to underdevelopment, which probably cannot occur without structural revolution and ideological transformation, and possibly also alternatives to the neo-capitalism and bureaucratic state Socialism of the United States and Soviet Russia.[12] For this reason, they have touched off sympathetic movements among Western intellectuals. In the United States which for historical reasons has captured quasi-colonial peoples (blacks, Chicanos, Indians and Puerto Ricans, primarily) they have also touched off a more direct response of solidarity and identification among such groups—what the fate of groups that are simultaneously ethnic minorities and "colonial subjects" within the United States will be remains unknown. The colonial analogy, although strained in terms of political structure, ge-

ographical location, and relative numbers, remains potent psychologically and ideationally; as we have repeatedly remarked, these groups have never been as fully incorporated in the American consensus as the European immigrants. Secondly, abroad as well as in America, there have been movements against the increasingly authoritarian and bureaucratized states and institutions. American movements must be understood within the context of the French worker-student movement of 1968, the Czech and Yugoslav experimentation with decentralized state socialism, the antiprofessional cultural revolution in China and the numerous student movements in Western Europe. It is still very unclear whether these movements will prove totally futile against the elites of the new industrial states; probably only in the smaller countries can antiauthoritarian movements assert themselves. Their future seems very bleak in the Soviet Union (where they can hardly be said to exist at all because of the lack of civil liberties and the enormous power of the central institutions) and at best doubtful in the USA. For this reason, support for national liberation movements against great power hegemony is vital because the smaller countries are more able to experiment.[13] And it is also essential that American civil liberties be supported because a movement of liberation against a large state without formal "bourgeois rights" is hopeless, whereas as long as these rights still exist to permit ideational and social zones of liberation to be created, it is merely difficult.

That American movements can now be understood in terms of worldwide currents indicates a political coming of age of America; to some degree of course American movements had already coincided with western European movements (labor agitation in the late nineteenth century, the "radical-liberal" reforms in pre-World War I Britain which parallel Progressive reforms, and so on) but the links have become more direct and self-conscious. Previously they were either general cotemporal products of substructural change as in the examples given or centrally dictated movements as with the Communist Party of the twenties and thirties. Now the relationships are explicit without being centralized and regimented.

One might venture to suggest that the main task for movements in the powerful countries must be to prevent their elites (by persuasion or diversion) from destroying sociopolitical experimentation in the smaller countries where liberation is possible.

5. Within America, the new wave of movements shows organizational and ideological promise. There appears to be less factionalizing over false dilemmas (the last SDS convention is a partial exception); there is a recognition that radical movement organizations must engage in a division of labor and that there can be no single "line" and no central co-ordinating body—that these would defeat the essential goal of democratic organization. Second, efforts are being made to analyze American society as a special case of a general theory, without doctrinaire application of the Procrustean bed of vulgar Marxism. In particular this must mean coming to terms with the following: the strength of neocapitalist ideology that has a not altogether irrational hold on the white working class which doubtlessly benefits from affluence and depends on corporate Capitalist growth; the role of the media; the failures of state socialism abroad, particularly its hardening into party rule and chauvinistic bureaucratization in Russia; the population explosion and ecological problems; the potential of the new technology of nuclear energy, cybernation and communication for creating freedom from scarcity.

SOME UNANSWERED QUESTIONS

I have left my reader with an open-ended report—because history itself is open-ended. But I would like to conclude with a series of questions which will hopefully direct current empirical work and which implicitly contain some predictions for the future of social change and social movements in America.

1. What is the future of New Politics in America—the legitimate electoral expression of the uneasy alliance of marginal groups (blacks, the very poor, and so forth), a white-collar and intellectual "conscience constituency" and politicians eager to use the potential of the media and willing to extend the welfare state? Can this coalition hold out against the large conservative business interests within the elite and their supporters among the population who still cling to an entrepreneurial ideology? Can the New Politics gain labor support and/or extend unionization and thus provide socioeconomic integration for poorer un-unionized workers? Can radical or even left-liberal elements in the alliance protect populistic demands against the image-politics, the reliance on media manipulation, and the faith in

expertise that currently characterizes "New Politicians"? If not, we will probably see a repeat of the Progressive Era—occasional populistic planks and welfare measures implemented within an anti–laissez-faire program that strengthens rather than weakens elite power, elite cohesion, and the role of expertise.

2. Is the new white-collar proletariat and intelligentsia in any sense a revolutionary class? At the moment adult employed members of it seem entirely symbiotically fused to economic and political elites—so much so, that distinguishing their upper echelons from the elites is actually quite difficult.[14] There is a lively debate in progress on what constitutes the most useful analytic approach to the strata of salaried professionals, technicians, middle-level managers and experts generally. Some theoreticians perceive the intelligentsia as a nascent ruling class in advanced industrial society whose control over information and decision-making has grown to the point where they are quietly displacing older elites from positions of power.[15] Others argue that they are a white collar proletariat, moving toward a consciousness of alienation and lacking control over fundamental decisions albeit providing information for trivial ones; for instance they choose the shape and color of cars but cannot halt the production of cars.[16] Still others see the intelligentsia as a stratum that shares the elites' dependence on the surplus value produced by workers, and that hence supports ruling class' power.[17] Yet each of these positions leaves open the question to what degree will a youth culture among the younger members and unemployment under present economic conditions pry these strata into

(a) cognitive liberation from and

(b) organizational efforts against the New Industrial State?

Will these organizations ever include more than the small proportion (probably under 10 percent of university and college students) of 1960s activists?

3. How likely are such organizations—if they arise at all—to be co-opted more or less as outlined above?

4. How likely is cooperation between these groups and Third World movement organizations?

5. Will black (and other Third World) movement organizations in the United States follow an ideological and structural course radically different from the differentiation/duplication course of the Eu-

ropean ethnic groups? Yet even for the latter, the differentiation/ duplication model of integration into the society is grossly oversimplified, for some of the groups have participated in the societal center by creating new institutions and new channels; thus, the modern political machine, the rackets and the growth of the cultural apparatus have been associated with the increasing power of the Irish, the Italians and the Jews, respectively.[18] Will black movement organizations create this type of institution, that capitalizes on changing substructural and structural features of the society? Will such new institutions and channels present fundamental challenges to the ideology and existing structure as have the new institutions and channels of other ethnic groups? Or will they be revolutionary in a more discontinuous and violent way?

At the moment, it looks as though the elite-supported welfare demands movement may become the vehicle of minority group collective advancement in the near future, just as the machine, the rackets and the media-educational sector were for the ethnic minorities of preceding generations; these movements may profoundly change American institutions without a real revolution.

6. What is the long-run impact of the life style movements— drugs, communal and sexual experimentation, new religious forms, and so forth? Are they simply the forerunners of a major shift in ideology away from the American Dream and the remnants of the Horatio Alger myth to a realistic acceptance of corporate capitalism, the welfare state, and consumerist abundance? In other words, will their potential for repressive desublimation and the extension of repressive tolerance be realized or will they contribute culture and life style to movements of opposition to the new industrial state?[19]

7. How precarious is the state of civil liberties in America today?[20] How powerful are "right-wing" authoritarian movements among the police?

8. What is the impact of a new technology of social control (surveillance, riot control, and so forth) on movements that attempt to seize control of territories within the society? Is a *revolution* in the usual sense of the word at all a possibility in an advanced industrial country, even if a movement creates a powerful dual structure and infiltrates the military rank and file?[21] The concentration of the technology of violence in a small military elite may have the consequence that mass infiltration of the armed forces becomes irrelevant to sei-

zure of political power; it may also have the consequence that the military itself becomes a potential movement, one that would probably choose to exert indirect power, via its influence over formal political elites.

9. Can a dual structure be built in a highly integrated, urbanized, bureaucratic affluent society?

10. What will be the outcome of the increasing confrontation between movements (or quasi-movements) of professionalization and expertise and the more populistic movements of community control? To what degree will radical professionals be able to use the issues arising out of their work as the "immediate demands" around which to organize themselves and their clients? To what degree will professionalization mean the introduction of more refined, more therapeutically-oriented, less violent and more technologically sophisticated means of social control, as in the professionalization of the police or prison guards?

11. Can American efforts at antirevolutionary intervention abroad be curbed? What would be the impact of such revolutions on the American economy? In other words, when a whole society is an exploiting bourgeoisie vis-à-vis the poor nations, perhaps long run as well as short run rationality requires American quasi-colonialism in the interests of national welfare and security.

12. Even if political and economic co-optation and incorporation of potentially radical movements is successfully accomplished, in what ways will future life style be altered, especially by the black and women's movements?

13. What role will the media play in movements? Specifically, will movements develop and control underground media organs, and who will exploit whom more effectively, the media the movements for sensationalistic stories, or the movements the media for gaining the attention of a potential mass base? [22] How do elites use media to generate elite-supportive movements?

My last question is the most important and the broadest of all. Can social movements contribute to the creation of a new social order that can satisfy basic human needs—material necessities, cognitive order, and individual creativity and affection—as well as provide a framework of political democracy that includes populistic participation and, thus, guarantees just distribution in the productive system? Can such a social order be built at all within the great powers? If not, can social movements within these states prevent the states from crushing the experimentation of the societies in which liberation is still possible? [23]

NOTES

[1] Brian Chapman, *Introduction to French Local Government* (London: Allen and Unwin, 1953); and Alexis de Tocqueville, *The Old Regime and the French Revolution* (Garden City, N.Y.: Doubleday, 1955).

[2] Eric Hobsbawm, *Laboring Men* (Garden City, N.Y.: Doubleday-Anchor, 1968), pp. 7–26.

[3] Mayer Zald, unpublished article (Nashville, Tenn.: Vanderbilt University, 1971).

[4] Harold Cruse, *The Crisis of the Negro Intellectual* (New York: Apollo, 1968).

[5] Herbert Marcuse, "Repressive Tolerance," in Robert Wolff, Barrington Moore, Jr., and Herbert Marcuse, *A Critique of Pure Tolerance* (Boston: Beacon Press, 1969).

[6] Aldous Huxley, *Brave New World* (New York: Harper, 1932).

[7] The term "conscience constituency" is used by Christopher Lasch, *The Agony of the American Left* (New York: Random House, 1969), p. 197.

[8] Seymour Melman, *Pentagon Capitalism* (New York: McGraw-Hill, 1970); and Jeffrey Schevitz, "Manipulation of Men for a War Economy," *Science for the People* 3, no. 3 (July 1971): 6.

[9] Francis Carney, "Radical Takeover in Berkeley," *New York Review of Books* 16 (June 3, 1971).

[10] Elinor Langer, "Inside the Hospital Workers' Union," *New York Review of Books* 16 (May 17 and June 3, 1971).

[11] Kenneth Keniston, *Young Radicals* (New York: Harcourt, Brace & World, 1968).

[12] Robert Heilbroner, *Between Capitalism and Socialism* (New York: Random House, 1970), Chapter 4, "The Anti-American Revolution."

[13] Hannah Arendt, "Thoughts on Politics and Revolution," *New York Review of Books* 16, no. 7 (April 22, 1971): 8.

[14] Zbigniew Brzezinski, *Between Two Ages* (New York: Viking Press, 1971); and John Kenneth Galbraith, *The New Industrial State* (Boston: Houghton Mifflin, 1967).

[15] *Ibid.*

[16] Keniston, *op. cit.*; and Richard Flacks, "The Revolt of the Young Intelligentsia: Revolutionary Class-Consciousness in Post-Scarcity America," unpublished paper (Santa Barbara: University of California, 1969).

[17] Martin Nicolaus, "Proletariat and Middle Class in Marx," in James Weinstein and David Eakins, eds., *For a New America* (New York: Random House, 1970).

[18] Daniel Bell, "Crime as an American Way of Life," in *End of Ideology* (New York: Free Press, 1960); and Christopher Lasch, "The Revival of Political Controversy in the Sixties," in Lasch, *op. cit.*

[19] Herbert Marcuse, *One Dimensional Man* (Boston: Beacon Press, 1964).

[20] Frank Donner, "Spying for the FBI," *New York Review of Books* 16, no. 7 (April 22, 1971).

[21] Barrington Moore, Jr., "Revolution in America?" in *New York Review of Books* 12, no. 2 (January 30, 1969): 6.

[22] Abbie Hoffman, *Woodstock Nation* (New York: Random House, 1970).

[23] Arendt, *op. cit.*

Appendix

Classes and Class Coalitions: A Model of American Politics

I would like to develop briefly a model for predicting the possible sources and outcomes of social movements in America in the next two or three decades. The model specifies groups and combinations of groups that could become important actors in the political arena; it also attempts to specify what the consequences of such action might be. Finally, it includes a consideration of the factors that might impel groups and individuals into a course of action, and a consideration of the probability of each action.

In accordance with the emphasis of the study as a whole, stress here will be placed on groups defined by *class*, by economic position. Each group may well also have ethnic, gender, or regional identifying characteristics; furthermore, these ascriptive categories may to some extent cross cut lines of class cleavage.

We must include in our model not only differences in the *amount* of wealth and power, but also differences in the *source* or *nature* of wealth and power. One of the characteristics of any complex society but especially of an advanced industrial one is that it includes a wide range of economic and technological subsystems differentiated by their distance from the frontiers of technology and by the types of production in which they are engaged. At one end of the spectrum we can identify an economy of abundance, sophisticated in its use of technology and the media, oriented toward the affluent consumer, and centered on large corporations and national political issues. This sector sets the tone for the new industrial state. At the other extreme is a cramped marginal sector, barely mechanized, physically located in the more underdeveloped parts of the country (be they the rural South or the inner city), and exerting power more at the local levels. In the affluent sector, social control and motivation are based on velvet glove techniques of identification with the firm, therapy for dissidents and the promise of an elegant life style. In the economy of scarcity, the threat of poverty, the fervent desire to make—rather than spend—money, and even the threat of violence motivate the owners and the work force.

The two sectors are by no means separate. For instance, the units of the economy of affluence have their roots in the economy of scarcity; the same firm that hires market consultants to attractively package its products may use migrant laborers to harvest these products. An institution of the society may overlap both sectors; thus for instance, "higher education" includes the great universities as well as the tiny struggling rural sectarian colleges and the legal system includes within it the alumni of the night schools as well as the alumni of the national law schools—and frequently, the former exercise power over the latter.

Let me specify more precisely what groups are included in each sector by introducing a diagram (see Figure 3). In Figure 3, symbols A_1 and S_1 represent the ruling class. The elite levels of the military-industrial complex, the executive branch of government and the top management of the 500 largest corporations (whether they are part of the military-industrial complex or not) are a good approximation to the ruling class. In addition, top managers and owners (major stockholders) of slightly smaller corporations as well as the more powerful senators, congressmen and local political figures may be included.

At the bottom level of this class, the boundary line with class A_2–S_2 is blurred.

A_2–S_2 represents individuals who do not set national political and economic goals but make decisions about the implementation of

Figure 3

AFFLUENT SECTOR		SCARCITY SECTOR
A_1 Ruling class	S_1	Ruling class
A_2 Managers, leading professionals	S_2	Self-employed: entrepreneurs
A_3 Producers	S_3	Producers
A_4 Dependents	S_4	Dependents

these goals. A_2 includes middle management of large corporations, and the cultural apparatus of academic and non-academic intellectuals (especially in the more prestigious institutions), mass media professionals, scientists and artists, and traditional professionals working in bureaucratic settings. S_2 includes the wealthier self-employed, local politicians without national power, and so on—in other words A_2 and S_2 represent the "upper middle class." The lower reaches of this stratum blend with A_3 and S_3, the mass of producers whether lower-level-professional and para-professional, white-collar or manual workers. Here the distinctions between the sector of affluence and the sector of scarcity become blurred, especially near the bottom reaches of this producing class where low income may force a life style of scarcity even on those who work in settings of affluence. A_3–S_3 includes the bulk of the nation's labor force.

A_4–S_4 are two distinct and large segments of society that neither control the means of production nor engage in labor. A_4 are the female, aged, and youthful dependents of the ruling, owning, managing and producing strata. They are analytically differentiable from these strata because they do not take part in production themselves, although as household members, they are practically and ideologically difficult to pry loose from their protectors' class position. The vital function of the women and youth in this category are to *consume*, rather than to produce. A variety of institutions, such as schools and universities, the monogamous neo-local family, youth culture, etc., function to prevent these groups from demanding producing roles which the economy cannot provide. Hence they are forced to picture themselves as spenders (as consumers and not as savers); thus even if they are dependent on members of the sector of scarcity, they are at least marginally members of the sector of affluence. Finally, S_4 shares with A_4 the dependent status of its members and their lack of a role in production; this group includes the long-term unemployed and underemployed, the poorer aged, and the institutionalized. In part, they function to provide employment for workers in social welfare organizations and to provide a raison d'etre for these large public and private organizations. In part they act as a reserve labor pool and as the "horrible example" that motivates workers to continue in their present roles.

Each of these strata are a potential source of instability, that is, of social movements or elite movements (in the case of the ruling class) that change the political and social structure.

The most likely sources of change are the producers and their dependents in the sector of affluence and the dependent impoverished population in the sector of scarcity (A_2, A_3, A_4 and S_4). These are the segments of the society that are not in the mainstream, that is, that are least locked into occupational (as well as familial and residential) roles and most easily deroutinized. Insofar as many of the producers in the sector of affluence are involved in the cultural apparatus, in creating the ideology, they are less trapped by ideology; they are more able to understand a system of values and norms as a human product, to wit, their *own* product which they have created and sold in order to gain their livelihood. For the upper levels of this group (A_2), a new source of discontent is appearing—namely, the belief that they are the actual decision-makers and goal setters in the society. This belief has several consequences: one is that this class may use its control over the discovery, production, and flow of information to enlarge its power and, thus, to become an actual threat to elites; second, it may find itself more and more in open conflict with the present ruling groups, and when its own myth of liberal technocratic rule is shown up to be an inaccurate representation of reality, it may begin to organize movements to gain more power.

Figure 4

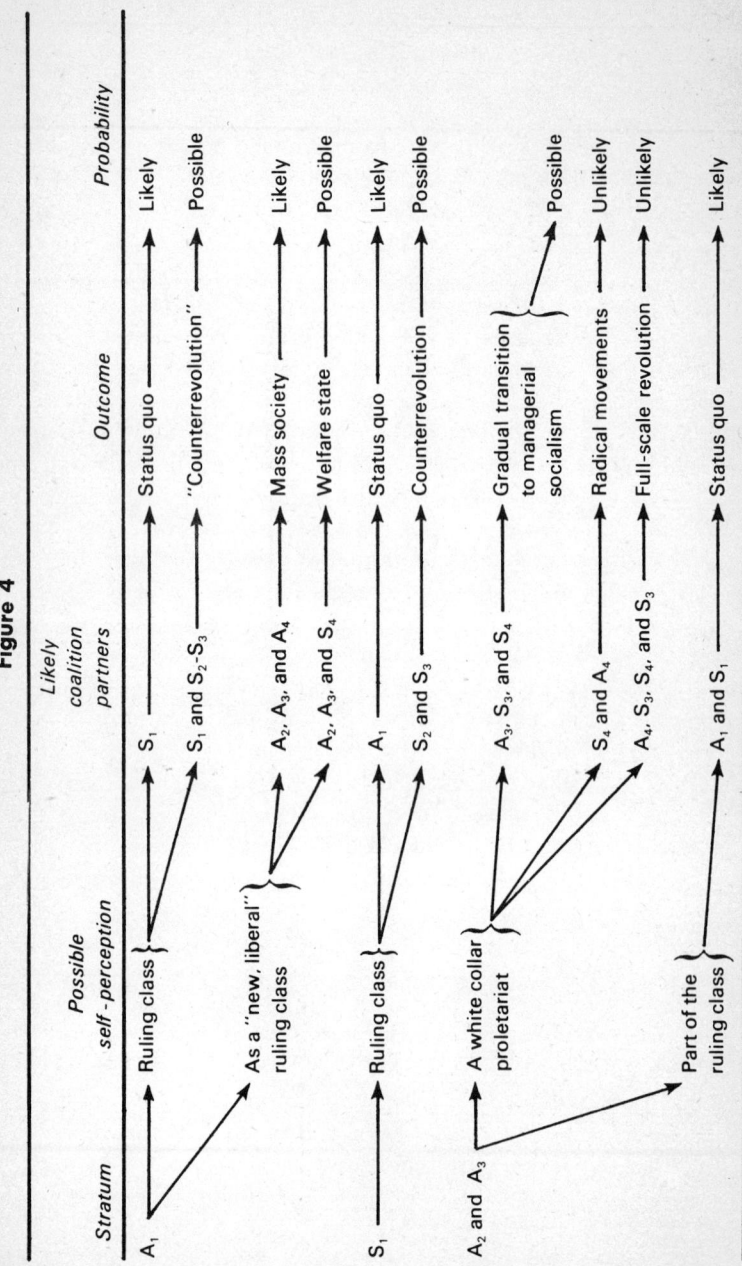

Stratum	Possible self-perception	Likely coalition partners	Outcome	Probability
A_1	Ruling class	S_1	Status quo	Likely
	As a "new, liberal" ruling class	S_1 and S_2–S_3	"Counterrevolution"	Possible
		$A_2, A_3,$ and A_4	Mass society	Likely
		$A_2, A_3,$ and S_4	Welfare state	Possible
S_1	Ruling class	A_1	Status quo	Likely
		S_2 and S_3	Counterrevolution	Possible
A_2 and A_3	A white collar proletariat	$A_3, S_3,$ and S_4	Gradual transition to managerial socialism	Possible
		S_4 and A_4	Radical movements	Unlikely
		$A_4, S_3, S_4,$ and S_3	Full-scale revolution	Unlikely
	Part of the ruling class	A_1 and S_1	Status quo	Likely

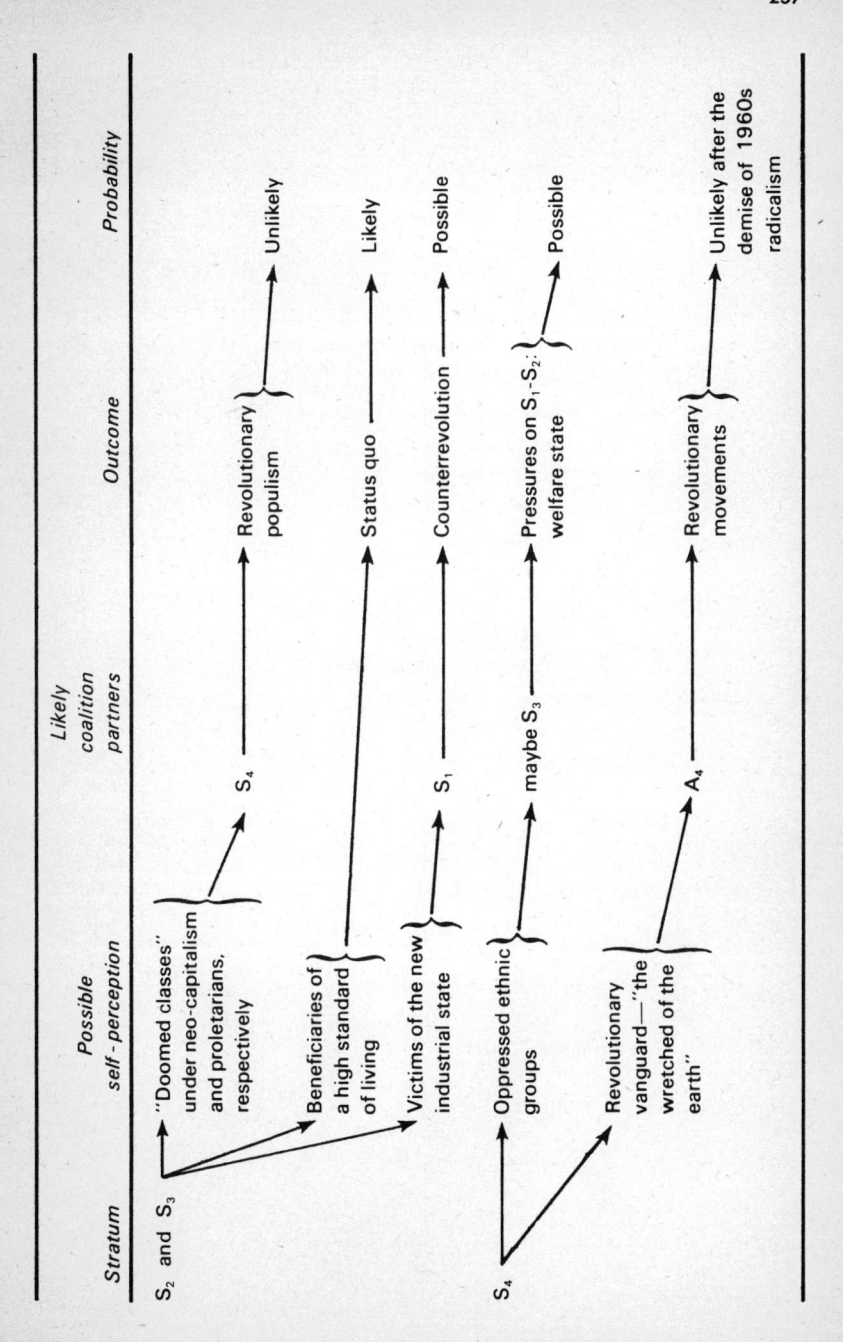

Stratum	Possible self-perception	Likely coalition partners	Outcome	Probability
S_2 and S_3	"Doomed classes" under neo-capitalism and proletarians, respectively	S_4	Revolutionary populism	Unlikely
	Beneficiaries of a high standard of living		Status quo	Likely
	Victims of the new industrial state	S_1	Counterrevolution	Possible
	Oppressed ethnic groups	maybe S_3	Pressures on S_1–S_2: welfare state	Possible
S_4	Revolutionary vanguard—"the wretched of the earth"	A_4	Revolutionary movements	Unlikely after the demise of 1960s radicalism

The disruptive potential of A_4 (especially youth) and S_4 (the underclass) is more obvious and has already been demonstrated in the uneasy affiliation of these groups in the sixties.

Each of these groups could also develop a self-perception that would inhibit rather than sustain movement formation.

For obvious reasons, the ruling class is not likely to launch full-scale social movements. But in efforts to co-opt or suppress movements launched by other strata (including its own youth), it may fundamentally change the social structure below it.

Finally, the producers and entrepreneurs in the sector of scarcity have proven to be sources of stability with occasional extensions of support to reactionary-right movement organizations based on the entrepreneurial stratum. Class consciousness among workers (S_3) has been absorbed by unions, obscured by ideology, and dampened by the exigencies of the strained but not desperate circumstances of everyday life. In this group, there is also a substantial resentment against the managers and intelligentsia (A_2), both in their role as supporters of the ruling elite *and* in their role as radicals.

This structure of strata and alternative self perceptions has a number of possible political outcomes depending on which of the alternative self-perceptions are acted upon by stratum members generally and by movement organizations associated with each stratum. The resulting model, Figure 4, is one with multiple-branching alternatives.

These seem to be the most likely and/or most interesting examples. Each outcome can be more fully described. For instance, *counterrevolution* might include the following elements:

1. Radicals in A_2–A_3, A_4 and S_4 may be killed or imprisoned, and A_2–A_3, A_4 and S_4 as entire strata will decisively lose power.

2. Members of A_2 will understand that they are *not* the ruling class and will lose some political power to S_2 while generally maintaining their economic roles (thus maintaining their potential for revolutionary action in the distant future).

3. S_2 (and S_1 and S_3 as well) will gain power at the expense of the above-listed groups and will be able to use it to protect incomes and to re-establish more traditional life styles as the norm.

4. The ruling class (A_1 and S_1) will gain some of the power lost by the suppressed groups. It may have to make a few minor life style concessions to S_2. In general its position will be much more secure

because the threatening strata (A_2, with its control over the flow of ideas, and A_4 and S_4 with their threat to core bourgeois values) are eliminated or neutralized.

The "mass society" "status quo" and "welfare state" outcomes—the most likely, given present circumstances—are respectively a more and a less extreme extension of the trends toward the new industrial state we have discussed earlier. They include the decline of the individual entrepreneur, tolerance for and experimentation with a variety of life style forms, mass integration of impoverished and isolated groups into the domain of the central institutions, refined, therapeutic and professionalized forms of social control, and the continuation of the power of the large corporations and the federal government. In the "mass society," the most prominent foci of activity would be life style experimentation and new forms of social control; in the "welfare state," "our priorities would be reordered" and more attention given to the integration of marginal and impoverished groups. Both of these can emerge with the pattern of co-optation outlined in Chapter 9.

The mere passage of time makes counterrevolution less likely and mass society/welfare state more likely, both for reasons of substructural trends (decreasing the power of S_2) and for generational reasons, as authoritarian patrifocal families and puritanism (both Protestant and Catholic) become less popular.

The more radical changes include the following: a gradual shift to a managerial state socialism as power is transferred to A_2—an unlikely, but not impossible, development given the strength of private corporations, and one that partly emerges out of semantic difficulties of distinguishing a frequently propertyless ruling class from a powerful stratum of managers and professionals; and more disruptive efforts at transformation involving social movements, such as populism, anarchism and Yippie-ism, anarcho-syndicalism, ethnic "liberation fronts" and so on. Each of these types of movement activity would of course touch off further rounds of responding activity, with outcomes that are increasingly difficult to catalog. We leave it to the reader as an exercise in sociological science fiction to imagine such a sequence of moves and counter moves. Suffice it to note that each pattern discussed here is an ideal type and in reality a combination of the more likely among them will appear in a weak and obscured form.

Index

Abolitionism, 37, 99, 100–7, 110: intellectuals, 107; success, 123. *See also* Slavery
Adams, Sam, 76
Addams, Jane, 180
AFL (American Federation of Labor), 121, 127: Communist Party, 178; IWW, 176, 177; Socialists, 167, 169–73, 175
Afro-American Realty Company, 185
Afro-Americans, 186, 187, 189, 235: colonial era, 51. *See also* Abolitionism; Blacks; Slavery
Agrarian movements, 127–34: communes, 10; political parties, 200; revolts, 42, 61–68; slavery, 38–39
Alcott, Bronson, 90: abolitionism, 103
Alger, Horatio, 118, 157
Alien and Sedition Acts, 84
Almond, Gabriel, 225n
Amana, 89
American Civil Liberties Union, 180–81
American Legion, 180, 181
American Party. *See* Know-Nothings
American Railway Union, 169
American Woman's Suffrage Association, 139
American Revolution, 47, 70–78, 82: agrarian revolts, 68; intellectuals, 33; legitimacy breakdown, 230
Americanism, 118, 149
"Amoral familism," 5
Anabaptist groups, 89
Anarchism: labor movements, 121, 122, 124. *See also* Radicalism
Ancient Order of the Hibernians ("Molly Maguires"), 119–20, 123–24
Antinomianism, 57

Antiradicalism: post-war, 214; War Department, 180. *See also* Rightwing movements
Antisemitism, 15: agrarian movements, 131
Anti-Slavery Society, 103, 104
Antiwar movements, 212, 223, 239, 244: status politics, 17; volunteer army, 242
Aptheker, Herbert, 46n, 69, 79n
Arbitration: labor movements, 119
Arendt, Hannah, 37–38, 46n, 224n, 250n, 251n
Army, U.S., 217
Arnold, Anthony, 66
Articles of Confederation, 82
Ash, Roberta, 28n
Attitudes: change without action, 2
Authoritarianism, 200–2: McCarthyism, 216–18
Authority: central value system, 8
Automation, 222

Babel, Isaac: anti-semitism, 15
Bacon's Rebellion, 64, 66
Bales, Robert, 226n
Baptist abolitionism, 100, 102
Baran, Paul, 46n
Bartlett, Irving H., 114n
Battis, Emery, 79n
Beard, Charles, 46n, 94n, 113n, 149n, 150
Beard, Mary, 46n, 94n, 113n, 149n, 150n
Beat Generation, 223: "hippie" movement, 237; prepolitical movement, 10
Becker, Carol, 79n
Bell, Daniel, 191n, 227n, 251n
Bensman, Joseph, 46n

261

INDEX

Berger, Peter, 26n–27n: existential phenomenology, 4
Berkeley, Governor Sir William, 66
Berkeley (Calif.) sit-in, 235
Bernstein, Barton J., 27n
Bimetallism, 132
Birch Society, John, 17, 221
Bird, Carol, 225n, 226n
Body of Liberties, 53
Bohemian movements, 162, 223: socialism and, 162; unformalized, 23
Boorstin, Daniel, 79n, 114n
"Black International" (International Working People's Association), 121
Black Legion, 204
Black movements, 37, 183–90: potential, 241; study programs, 235
Black Muslim Movement, 234–35
Black Panthers, 232, 235
Black Power, 188
Blacklist, 180
Blacks: American Revolution, 73; civil rights movements, 234–36, 241, 242; colonial era, 51; communism, 205–6; integration, 221, 222, 229–30, 243; IWW, 176; labor movements, 121; New Industrial State, 232–33; Populists, 131; post-Civil War, 111–13; racism, 14, 15; student movements, 236, 239; women, 139, 241. *See also* Abolitionism; Afro-Americans; Slavery
Blue-collar workers: communism, 208, 210
Bonus Marchers, 204–5
"Boring from within," 166: labor movements, 172, 204, 206; right-wing movements, 220–21
Boston Massacre of 1770, 74
Boston Tea Party of 1773, 74
Bourgeoisie: American Revolution, 70–71, 78; Civil War, 99; colonial era, 31; industrial, 85, 86; Jacksonian period, 93; Lockeian liberalism, 31; slavery, 37; status politics, 17. *See also* Petty-bourgeoisie
Bridenbaugh, Carl, 78n, 79n
Brook Farm, 89–90

Brown, John, 102, 105, 106
Bryan, William Jennings, 131
Brzezinski, Zbigniew, 250n
Bubble Act of 1720, 67
Burns, William, 180

Callahan, Raymond E., 191n
Calvinists, 100, 102
Capital punishment: Quakers, 54
Capitalism: agrarian movements, 129; beginnings, 83–84; Civil War, 98–99; development, 41, 42; fascism and, 201; "hippie" movement, 238; IWW, 177; Jackson, 93; middle-class movements, 140; populism and, 131, 133; slavery, 38
Capitalism, political. *See* New Industrial State
Carney, Francis, 250n
Catholicism: radicalism, 241; separatism, 182; war resistance, 11
Central institutions: co-optation, 241–43; elite movements, 232; integration, 221–22; the Left, 163–64, 165–66; Shils (Edward) on, 8–9; social movements, 12; urban proletariat, 125
Channing, William Ellery, 100, 103
Chapman, Brian, 46n, 250n
Charisma, 24
Chesterton, G. K., 228
Chicanos: integration, 243
Child labor, 122
Chinoy, Ely, 226n
Christian Science Movement, 24
CIO (Congress of Industrial Organizations), 178: communism, 204–11, 212–13
City-manager governments, 158–59
Civil Rights Act of 1964, 234
Civil Rights March (1964), 205
Civil rights movement, 234–35: Kennedy administration, 243; organizations, 2; political aspect, 10; post-Civil War, 112; status politics, 17; women, 138
Civil War, 97–113: legitimacy breakdown, 230; liberalism, 42
Claflin sisters, 138

INDEX

Class. *See* Elite; Lower class; Middle class; Poor, the; Social structure
Class conflict, 30: agrarian revolts, 61–68; American Revolution, 75, 77; ethnicity, 14; Federalists vs. Jeffersonians, 85; interchurch conflict, 59; liberalism, 32
Class-conscious movement, 9, 10, 11: AFL, 171–72; business cycle and, 229; cognitive liberation, 21; rank and file, 213; slavery, 38; violence, 69
Clayton, Horace, 192n
Clayton Act of 1914, 160
"Cognitive distance," 233
Cognitive liberation, 20–21
Cold War, 215–16
Coleman, James, 227n
Collective action, 40: phenomenology, 18–22
Colonial Dames of America, 138
Colonial era, 47–48: agrarian revolts, 61–68; delimitation, 48; Indian resistance, 60; religious movements, 51–60; social structure, 49–51; uprisings of the poor, 68–70
Columbia University: blacks, 14; uprising, 165, 235
Committees of Correspondence, 76
Common Sense, 75
Communal experiments (utopian experiments), 89–91: cognitive liberation, 21; co-optation, 242; "hippie" movement, 237
Communication, 24. *See also* Mass Media
Communism: agrarian movements, 129; blacks, 188; Christian norms and, 52; CIO, 166, 204–11, 212–13; McCarthyism, 216; 1930s, 200–1; socialism, 169, 175
Communist Labor Party, 170, 175
Communist Party, 170, 175: intellectuals, 207; CIO, 209–10. *See also* Communism
Community control movements, 240
Company unions, 177
Competition: ethnicity, 14; farming, 131; immigration, 40; movement organizations, 167
Conscription. *See* Impressment

Conservatism, 24: postwar, 214
Constitution, U.S., 82: political constraints, 33–34; social movements, 31
Consumer movements, 241, 242
Consumerism, 43, 222: "hippie" movement, 238; Women's Liberation, 240
Continental Congress, 75, 76
Converse, Philip, 226n
Conversion experiences: Indians, 142
Cooperatives, 91: agrarian movements, 129; black, 186; labor movements, 119, 120
Co-optation, 13, 23, 232: blacks, 235; forestalls revolution, 77; social movements, 241–43
CORE (Congress of Racial Equality), 2, 234
Corporations, 154
Corruption: agrarian movements, 129; government, 154, 159
Coser, Lewis, 191n, 208–9, 225n, 226n
Cotton gin, 86
Coughlin, Father Charles E., 197, 200–1: status politics, 17
Counterculture: "hippies," 238
Counter-Reformation, 8
Craft unions, 119, 120–21: AFL, 178
Crevecoeur, St. Jean de, 94n
Crime: politicization, 72; the poor and, 68–69
Cronon, Edmund, 192n
Cruse, Harold, 188–89, 192n, 225n, 250n
Cultural apparatus: dissident intellectual, 206; Jews, 248
Cultural movements, 153, 190, 223: post-World War I, 182
Cultural pluralism: ethnic cleavage, 14, 15; Progressive Era, 157
Curran, Joe, 209
Currency Act of 1764, 70, 71

Dahl, Robert, 46n
DAR (Daughters of the American Revolution), 138
Darwinism, 118

Davenport, James, 59
Davies, Samuel, 59
Debs, Eugene, 123, 169, 170
Declaration of Independence, 74
Degler, Carl, 113n, 150n
Delany, Martin, 186
DeLeon, Daniel, 169, 172
Democracy: fascism and, 201; frontier, 35, 36; jingoism, 148; New Industrial State, 152, 153; postrevolutionary, 81–83; professionalism, 159; rural community, 129; totalitarianism and, 202–3; Williams, Roger, 56
Democratic Clubs, 112
Democratic Party, 87: agrarian movements, 131; antiwar faction, 34; blacks and, 184
Democratic societies, 84
Depression: communism, 214; farmers, 130–31; Great Depression, 164, 165; jingoism, 149; labor movement, 87, 88; post-revolutionary, 82; revolts of the poor, 69
Deroutinization, 164–67: elderly, 203; middle-class youth, 243–44; modernity, 233; wartime, 179
de Tocqueville, Alexis, 250n
Dickens, A. G., 79n
Dillon, Merton L., 114n
Direct primary, 162
Divine Light of Christ, 54
Division of labor: movement organizations, 166, 246
Dollard, John, 28: black oppression, 14
Donner, Frank, 251n
Dorr uprising, 88
Douglass, Frederick, 160
Draft resistance, 239. See also Antiwar movements
Drake, St. Clair, 192n
Draper, Theodore, 191n
Dream Dance of the Menomini, 145
Dreamer movement, 144
Drug use: co-optation, 242; "hippies," 237, 238; postpolitical movement, 10; psychedelic, 22
Dual political structure: American Revolution, 74, 76; labor movements, 123, 124; revolution, 230; southern counterrevolution, 112
Dual unionism, 172: abandonment, 207; IWW, 176, 178
Dubofsky, Melvin, 191n, 192n
DuBois, W. E. B., 185, 187, 188, 189
Dupee, F. W., 191n
Duverger, Maurice, 45n

Ecology movement, 241, 242
Education, public: "adjustment" norm, 215; boom, 222; cult of efficiency, 159; labor movement, 88
Edwards, Jonathan, 59
Elderly: social movements, 203
Elite movements, 2, 12–13, 231–32: co-optation, 241; status politics, 17; welfare, 248; witch hunts, 57–58
Elites: agrarian revolt, 66; American Revolution, 82; antiradicalism, 214; colonial era, 49–50; fascism, 201; goal displacement, 24; initiate changes, 2; manipulation of, 9; New Deal, 196; postrevolutionary, 26; Progressive Era, 156, 160; Puritans, 52–53; Quakers, 54–55; revolts of the poor, 69; revolutions and, 77; rural community, 129; social structure, 6–9; socialism and, 174; violence of, 231; war effort, 179, 180; witch hunts, 217
Emancipation, 111
Emerson, Ralph Waldo: abolitionism, 102, 103
"Emics," 19, 21
"Encounter movement," 238
Epstein, Benjamin, 227n
Equal Rights Party, 88
Equality: frontier myth, 36; immigrants, 40; Puritanism, 55; Quakerism, 54
Ethnicity, 14–16, 30, 39–41: deroutinization, 233; foreign influence, 244; labor movements, 124, 176; 1920s, 182; Progressive Era, 157
Ethnocentrism, 202
"Etic" analysis, 19, 21
Evangelism, 59

Factionalism, 25: labor, 173; radicalism, 170

INDEX

Factory system, 85
"False consciousness," 16
Farmers: colonial era, 50, 51; frontier, 36; populism, 200; smallholders, 127, 130. *See also* Agrarian movements
Farmers' Alliances, 131
Farmers Holiday Movement, 196
Farmers Union, 200
Farming, commercial, 41
Fascism, 201, 202
Federal government. *See* National government; New Industrial State
Federalist, 83
Federalists: bourgeoisie, 32; Jeffersonians vs., 84–85
Feminist movement. *See* Women's Liberation; Women's movements
Flacks, Richard, 250n
Flying saucer cults, 21
Foester, Arnold, 227n
Foreign affairs. *See* Internationalism
Formalization of movements, 23
Fossilization of movements, 35
Foster, William Z., 191n
Fourier, Francois, 90
Fox, George, 54
Fragmentation: movements, 33–34, 35; Protestantism, 52
Franchise, 42
Free Speech movement, 235
Freedom of worship: Quakers, 54; Williams, Roger, 55; witch hunts, 57
Freeholders, 50, 51
Free Soil Party, 104, 105, 106
Frelinghuysen, Theodore, 59
French and Indian War (Seven Years' War), 71
Fries, Amos, 180
Frontier, 35–37: class conflicts, 30; closing, 74, 117; Indian resistance, 60, 141; safety valve, 31
Fugitive Slave Law, 104, 105

Galbraith, John Kenneth, 4, 27n, 46n, 250n
Gangs: politicization, 72
Gara, Larry, 114n
Gardner, Lloyd, 151n
Garrison, William Lloyd, 114n: abolitionism, 100, 101–2, 103–4, 106

Garvey, Marcus, 186–87
Garveyism, 186, 187, 188
Gates, Paul W., 45n
Gay Liberation movement, 241: co-optation, 242
"Generation gap," 238
Genovese, Eugene, 4, 27n, 44n, 113n, 114n
George, Henry, 122
Ghost Dance movement, 142, 144–47: cognitive liberation, 20; prepolitical movement, 9
Ginsberg, Allen, 227n
Gitlin, Todd, 191n
Goals of movements: displacement, 24; realization, 25–26
Goldman, Eric, 150n, 192n, 223n, 226n
Gompers, Samuel, 121, 170, 171, 173
Granger movement, 130
Grant, Joanne, 192n
Grantham, Dewey W., Jr., 192n
"Greaser" subculture: premovement phenomena, 10
Great Awakening, 58–59
Great Depression, 164, 195: communism, 214
"Greenbacks" (Independent National Party), 130
Greenwich Village, 162
Guerrillas, 106, 124
Gusfield, Joseph, 28n
Gutman, Herbert, 150n

Hacker, Louis, 79n
Half Way Covenanting, 53
"Ham and Eggs" movement, 204
Hamilton, Richard F., 226n
Hamiltonian policy: elite movements, 232
Handlin, Oscar, 46n
Handsome Lake movement, 143
Harlem, 185
Harlem Renaissance, 189
Harmony (community), 89, 91
Harris, Marvin, 27n, 227n: social structure, 4, 5
Hartz, Louis, 44n, 94n, 114n, 226n
Hayes, Max, 170, 173
Haymarket incident, 122, 127

INDEX

Hays, Samuel P., 191n
Heer, Friedrich, 45n
Heilbroner, Robert, 250n
Hell's Angels: premovement phenomena, 10
Herberg, Will, 226n
Heresy: Hutchinson, Anne, 57. *See also* Witch hunts
"Hippie" movement, 182, 237–38
Hobsbawn, Eric, 28n, 250n
Hoffman, Abbie, 251n
Hofstadter, Richard, 45n, 46n, 95n, 190n
Hollander, Nanci, 191n
Homestead strike, 122
Homosexuals. *See* Gay Liberation movement
Hoover administration: Bonus Marchers, 205; unemployment, 195
Horatio Alger myth, 118: Progressive Era, 157
Howe, Irving, 191n, 208–9, 225n, 226n
Hudson Valley tenants uprising, 67, 68
Huntington, Samuel, 150n
Hutchinson, Anne, 53, 56–57
Huthmacher, J. Joseph, 190n
Huxley, Aldous, 250n

Ideology, 4, 5: changes in, 26; charisma and, 24; collective action, 18, 21; dearth of alternatives, 32; medieval societies, 5; Protestantism, 51–60; southern, 107–8. *See also* specific ideologies such as Communism; Democracy; Fascism; Socialism
Immigrants, 30, 39–41, 117: cognitive liberation, 20; colonial era, 51; integration of, 155; Know-Nothings, 135; liberalism, 32; political capitalism, 161–62; socialism, 175; urbanization, 42
Imperialism, 148
Impressment (Conscription): colonial era, 50; draft resistance, 239; revolts of the poor, 69, 70
Indentured servants: colonial era, 51; revolts, 68

Independent Labor Party of New York, 122
Independent National Party ("Greenbacks"), 130
Indian Ghost Dance. *See* Ghost Dance movement
Indians: ethnicity, 15; genocide, 30; Ghost Dance movement, 9; integration, 229–30, 243; manifest destiny, 148; Quakers and, 54; resistance, 91, 141–147; Williams, Roger, 55, 56
Individual, role of: collective action, 19–22; labor movements, 121–22, 123, 127; motivation, 23, 25; religious enthusiasm, 59; social movements, 18; utopian experiments, 90, 91
Individualism, 40: frontier, 37; New Industrial State, 22
Industrial capitalism. *See* Capitalism
Industrial Workers of the World (IWW, Wobblies), 165–66, 167–68, 170, 173, 174, 175–79: class-conscious movement, 10, 213; liberalism, 32
Industrialization: agrarian movements, 128; based on British, 31; goal displacement, 24; history of, 41–42, 117; labor movements, 124–25; post-revolution, 84–86; Progressive Era, 154; railways, 117, 118; slavery, 38. *See also* New Industrial State
Inflation: agrarian movements, 128; bimetallism, 132; "Greenbacks," 130
Inquisition: intellectuals, 33
Integration, 231–32: blacks, 186, 188, 189, 221, 222, 234; marginal groups, 243; women, 241
Intellectuals (Intelligentsia), 30, 189: abolitionism, 103; and change, 2; Civil War, 107, 108; Cold War, 215; communism, 204, 206–7, 210; cultural movement, 182; deroutinization, 165; future of, 247; hostility to foreigners, 39; industrial economy, 5; isolation of, 31; New Industrial State, 43; opposition to professionalism, 159; socialism, 175; structural position,

232; student movements, 236; two-party system, 34–35; underdevelopment, 32–33; utopian experiments, 89; women, 137
Interest groups: political decision, 12
International Ladies Garment Workers, 173
International Working People's Association ("Black International"), 121
Internationalism, 194–95, 211, 212: civil rights movement, 239; farm trade, 130–31; U.S.-Soviet hostility, 211, 213–14
Interregnum, The, 81–83
Interstate Commerce Act of 1887, 118
Intolerable Acts, 74
Irish: anti-black riots, 184; Know-Nothings, 135; labor movements, 120, 123; machine politics, 248
Isatai's movement, 145
Isolationism: midwestern, 212
"Issues," 222
Italian-Americans: and blacks, 14; rackets, 24
IWW. See Industrial Workers of the World

Jacksonian Democracy, 93: elite movements, 232; Progressive Era vs., 156
Jamestown colony, 48
Janowitz, Morris, 79n, 224n
Jeffersonians, 84: bourgeoisie, 32; elite movements, 232
Jews: agrarian creditors, 128; communism, 210; cultural apparatus, 248; separatism, 182, 183
Jingoism, 148–49: Pentagon, 239
John Birch Society, 221: status politics, 17
Johnson, James Weldon, 190
Johnson, Lyndon, 239
Juvenile delinquency: premovement rebellion, 2, 10, 11; youth movement, 238

Kanter, Rosabeth Moss, 95n
Kaplan, A., 26n

Kelly, Abby, 104
Kempton, Murray, 225n, 226n
Kennedy, Bobby, 237
Kennedy administration: integration, 243
Kenniston, Kenneth, 250n
Kerr, Clark, 149n
Kerouac, Jack, 227n
Kickapoo, 144
"King Philip" (Metacom), 60
Knights of Labor, 119, 120–21, 127, 169
Know-Nothings (American Party), 135: nativism, 39; status politics, 17
Kolaskin's movement, 145
Kolko, Gabriel, 46n, 150n, 190n, 224n, 225n, 226n
Kraditor, Aileen S., 150n
Ku Klux Klan, 112, 179–80

Labor Day riots, 2, 10
Labor movement: co-optation of, 242; history, 86–88, 119–27; institutionalization, 24; tactics, 165. See also specific labor unions
La Follette, Robert, 181
Laidler, Harry, 191n
Laissez-faire, 31: concentration of power, 203; New Industrial State, 160–61; populism, 134; Progressive Era, 155
Land bank, 67
Langer, Elinor, 191n, 250n
Language community, 19
Lanternari, Vittorio, 150, 151n
Lasch, Christopher, 4, 27n, 45n, 150n, 190n, 191n, 226n, 250n, 251n
Lasswell, Harold, 26n, 28n: elites, 4, 6; partial incorporation, 13
League for Industrial Democracy, 236
Lechford, Thomas, 53
Left, the, 163–67, 220: IWW, 175–79; the "right" vs., 218–19; Socialists, 167–75
Legal system: agrarian revolts, 67–68; colonial era, 52–53
Legitimacy: breakdowns, 230; institutions, 82; mobility, 40; post-

revolutionary elite, 26; social movements, 9; societal perception of, 2
Leisler's Revolt, 65, 66
Lemisch, Jesse, 4, 27n, 78n, 79n
Lemke, William, 199, 200
Lens, Sidney, 95n, 114n, 149n, 191n, 224n, 225n
Lerner, D., 26n
Lewis, John L., 207–8
Liberalism, 41: Civil War, 42; (1800–1850), 92; frontier, 35; immigration, 40; labor movement, 88; Lockeian, 31, 219; party system, 34; political capitalism, 220; Progressive Era, 155; social movements, 31
Liberal Party, 104, 106
Life style movements, 229. *See also* Bohemian movement; "Hippie" movement
Lifton, Robert, 151n
Link, Arthur S., 192n
Lipset, Seymour Martin, 45n, 46n
Litwack, Leon F., 114n
Lobbying: labor movements, 123
Local government: frontier, 36; professionalism, 158; social movements, 12; socialism, 173
Lockeian liberalism, 31: capitalism, 219
Long, Huey, 17, 198, 199
Lowell, James Russell: abolitionism, 103
Lower class: colonial era, 50; factory laborers, 42. *See also* Poor, the
Loyalists, 75–76
Loyola, St. Ignatius, 22
Luckmann, T., 27n
Lundy, Benjamin, 103
Luther, Martin, 22
Lynd, Staughton, 4, 27n, 79n, 94n, 114n

MacArthur, General Douglas, 205
Machine politics: Irish, 248
Magico-religious ideology: social movements, 10; witch hunts, 58
Malcolm X, 188, 192n
Manabozo, 143–44

Manifest destiny, 91: Jingoism, 148
Marcuse, Herbert, 4, 27n, 28n, 225n, 250n, 251n: repressive desublimation, 44; repressive tolerance, 13
Marijuana, 23, 238
"Maroon" settlements, 69
Martineau, Harriet, 92–93, 95n, 137
Marx, Karl: cognitive competition, 99
Marxian Workingmens Party, 121
Marxism: elites, 7; ideology, 8; liberalism, 32; ruling class, 9; social process, 4; student movements, 236
Mass action, 165
Mass culture, 182
Mass markets, 85
Mass media, 163; civil rights movement, 234; communism, 206; defusion techniques, 13; "hippie" movement, 237–38; ideology technology, 41; personality-centered movements, 218; and the poor, 69; Progressive Era, 155; Progressive organizations, 171; radio, 200; the "right," 219; two-party system, 34–35
Materialism: collective action, 18; the "right," 219
McCarthy, Eugene, 237
McCarthy, Joe, 216–18: bourgeoisie, 17
McCarthyism, 181, 216–18
McPherson, James M., 115n
Medieval societies, 5
Meier, August, 192n
Melanesian Cargo Cults, 10
Melman, Seymour, 250n
Messinger, Sheldon, 224n
Metacom ("King Philip"), 60
Methodist abolitionism, 100, 103
Middle class: central institutions, 222; colonial era, 50; development, 43; labor movements, 125; 1920s, 181–82; Progressive Era, 156–57, 158–59; the "right," 220; social movements, 135, 141, 211; socialism vs. progressivism, 174; status politics, 17; utopian experiments, 90; war effort, 181; youth movements, 243–44
Migrant workers: IWW, 176, 178

Militants: American Revolution, 72; OEO, 2. *See also* Riots; Violence
Military power: dual structure, 76, 77; Indian wars affected, 60; right-wing movement, 221; social movements, 231; urban guerrillas, 124
Miller, Daniel, 227n
Miller, John C., 79n
Millett, Kate, 226n
Mills, C. Wright, 46n, 227n, 191n
Miners: labor movements, 120, 123
Minute Men, 220
Minutemen, 74, 76
Mobility, geographical frontier, 36
Mobility, social, 17: American Revolution, 82; blacks, 187; frontier, 36-37; illegal institutions, 40; immigrants, 155; labor movement, 88; rural community, 129; utopian experiment, 91
Mobilization, 171
Modern Times, 90
Modernization: social movements, 10
"Mohawks" (Sons of Liberty), 72
Molasses Act of 1733, 71
"Molly Maguires" (Ancient Order of the Hibernians), 119-20, 123-24
Monopoly, 118: small farmer and, 129. *See also* Oligopoly
Moore, Barrington, Jr., 4, 27n, 46n, 113n, 115n, 251n
Mormons, 89; Indians, 145
Motivation: movement participation, 21-22, 23, 25
Movement organizations. *See* Organizations, movement
Murphy, Paul, 192n

NAACP (National Association for the Advancement of Colored People), 183, 185
National Association of Manufacturers, 162
National government: and big business, 41; industrial capitalism, 118; social movements, 12. *See also* New Industrial State
National League for Social Justice, 198
National Maritime Union, 209

National Organization of Women, 34
National Recovery Plan, 203-4
National Woman's Suffrage Association, 139
Nationalism: Afro-American, 186-87; blacks, 204; labor movements, 125; northern, 37; postwar, 214; wartime, 179, 229
Nativism: agrarian movement, 131; middle classes, 136; populism, 133; Progressive Era, 156-57; war effort, 179. *See also* Racism
Neocapitalism: political elite, 6
Neo-Marxism: elites, 7
New Deal: communism, 204; New Industrial State, 41, 43; social change, 2; as social movement, 195-96; substructural shift, 93; welfare, 204
New Industrial State, 152-90, 193-223: co-optation, 243; deroutinization, 233; development, 41, 43; "generation gap," 238; youth movement, 237
New Left: class-conscious movement, 10; intellectuals, 33
"New Lights," 59
"New Side," 59
Niagara Movement of 1904, 185
Nicolaus, Martin, 250n
Nixon, Richard M.: "New American Revolution," 2
NLU (National Labor Union), 119, 120
Norms: social structure, 3
North, the: abolitionism, 110; black migration, 184; civil rights movement, 234; Civil War, 97-99; colonial era, 49, 51
Noyes, John, 103

Oath-taking: Quakers, 54; Williams Roger, 55
OEO (Office of Economic Opportunity), 2
Oligarchization, 24
Oligopoly, 117: development, 41, 42
Oneida, 90
O'Neill, William L., 150n
Organizations, movement, 1-2, 234. *See also* specific organizations

INDEX

Owen, Robert, 90
Owen, Robert Dale, 90

Pacifism: Quakers, 54, 223. *See also* Antiwar movements
Paine, Thomas, 48, 75
Palmer era: status politics, 17
Parsons, Talcott, 226n
Party system. *See* Political parties
Patriot Party, 220
Paxton Boy's revolt, 67
Peace and Freedom Party (1968), 34
Peace Corps, 243
Peace movement, *See* Antiwar movements
Penumbra: communism, 210; radical movements, 171
Pentagon: foreign involvement, 239; political elites, 6
"Peoples Constitution," 88
Peoples' Party (Populists), 131–34
Perkins, Frances, 211
Petty-bourgeoisie: American Revolution, 70; frontier, 36, 37; Jackson, 93; Ku Klux Klan, 179; labor movements, 121; nativist hostility, 39; populism, 132; Progressive Era, 159. *See also* Bourgeoisie
Peyote Cult, 147
Phenomenology: collective action, 18–22
Phillips, Wendell, 100, 102, 106
"Pigmentocracy," 98
Pilgrims, 52
Police: anarchists and, 122; IWW, 176; massive breakdown, 124, 125; right-wing movement, 221
Political movements, 9, 10: social structure, 3; success, 12–13. *See also* specific movements
Political parties: abolitionism, 104; labor movement, 127, 172; two-party system, 34–35; workingmen's parties, 87–88. *See also* Third-party movements; and specific parties
Political system, 93–94: agrarian revolts, 61, 66; American Revolution, 74, 76; autonomy, 7; Civil War, 99; labor force, 88; post-Civil War, 112; power, 5; revolutionary movements, 9; women, 138
Poor, the: communism 205; crime, 72; Long, Huey, 199; Protestantism, 52; uprisings among, 68–70; women, 241. *See also* Lower class
Populism, 202: farmers, 200; Jingoism, 149; Progressive Era, 159, 161; progressivism vs., 156; socialism, 167
Populists (People's Party), 131–34
Postpolitical movements, 10
Poverty. *See* Poor, the
Powderly, Terrance, 120
Powdermaker, Hortense, 225n
Power: definition, 3; threatened, 12
"Power elites," 2, 6, 43. *See also* Elites
Prejudice: ethnicity, 14–16. *See also* Nativism; Racism
Premovement phenomena, 9, 10
Prendergast, William, 68
Prepolitical movements, 9, 10
Pressure groups, 92
Prewitt, Kenneth, 226n
Production, 4, 6: agrarian movements, 128; change in relations, 11; elites, 6; IWW, 176; labor movements, 122; middle-class women, 137; political change, 26; socialism, 174; wartime, 82
Professionalism: public administration, 154–55, 158–59, 162
Progressive Era, 153, 154–62: elite movements, 232; substructural shift, 93
Progressivism: intellectuals, 33; middle-class, 174; New Deal vs., 196
Prohibition: middle class, 162; success, 25; unformalized movement, 23; WCTU (Women's Christian Temperance Union), 11–12
Proletariat: Darwinism, 118; IWW, 177; labor movements, 121; revolts, 68, 69, 70; status politics, 17; urban industrial, 86, 125
Propaganda: American Revolution, 76–77
Property: institutional change, 12; Martineau on, 92–93; slavery, 100

Protestantism: abolitionism, 102–3; colonial era, 51–60; nativism, 136; populism, 133; Progressive Era, 156
Proto-fascist movements, 196–204
Provincialism, 32
Pullman strike, 123
Pure Food and Drug Laws, 160
Puritans, 52–53, 54, 55: ideology vs. power, 56

Quakerism, 53–55: abolitionism, 100, 102–3; ideology vs. power, 56; war resistance, 11
Quasi-movements, 232: Indian religious movements, 141–47; left-wing, 17

Racism: Indians, 60; slavocracy, 98. *See also* Nativism
Racketeering, 40, 248
Radical movements: cognitive liberation, 20; division of labor, 246; goals, 13, 24; intellectuals, 33; investigations, 215; labor, 124–25; the Left, 163–67; perspectives, 229, 230; psychedelic drugs, 22; single-issue reform, 131; slavery, 38–39; Women's Liberation, 240–41
Radical Republicans, 110, 111, 112–13
Radicalism: abolitionism, 106; agrarian revolts, 61; American Revolution, 75, 82; class oppression, 92; "hippie" movement, 237–38; Hutchinson, Anne, 56–57; labor movements, 123–25; middle-class youth, 243; opposition to, 214; post-WW I, 181; rank and file, 213; SDS (Students for a Democratic Society), 236; violence, 162. *See also* Anarchism; Radical movements
Radosh, Ronald, 192n, 223n
Railways: industrialization and, 117, 118
Randolph, A. Philip, 187
Rank and file: goal displacement, 24; radicalism, 213

Recall, 154, 162
Reconstruction, 113
Red Shirts, 112
Referendum, 154, 162
Reform movements, 9: cognitive liberation, 20–21; investigations, 215; Jacksonian period, 93; labor movement, 88; perspectives, 229, 230–31; post-WW I, 181; single-issue demands, 13; Women's Liberation, 240
Reformation, 33
Regulator movement, 67
Religion: abolitionism, 100, 101, 102–3; blacks, 186; central value system, 8; class movements, 10; colonial era, 31; intellectuals, 33; medieval societies, 5; radicalism, 241; utopian experiments, 90
Religious movements, 229: colonial era, 51–60; social structure, 3, 61
"Repressive desublimation," 44
"Repressive tolerance," 13
Republican Party: blacks and, 184; McCarthyism, 216, 217; right wing, 220; the South, 107, 110, 112
Return to normalcy, 179–83, 214
Reuther brothers, 208
"Revolt of the common man," 42
Revolutionary movements, 9: co-optation, 242; elements, 77, 123; goal realization, 26
Right-wing movements, 17, 218–21
Riots: civil rights movements, 235; post-Civil War, 112; premovement phenomena, 2, 10; Stamp Act, 72–73. *See also* Violence
Rise of Anthropological Theory, The, 5
Rising Up Angry, 236
Robespierre, Maximilien, 203
Rogin, Michael, 224n, 226n
Roosevelt, Theodore, 122
Rosenhack, Shelia, 227n
Ross, Arthur, 149n
Rossiter, Clinton, 78n, 79n
Roszak, Theodore, 27n
Rothenberg, Jerome, 151n
Rousseau, Jean Jacques, 203
Rudwick, Elliot, 192n
Ruling class. *See* Elites

Rural society: colonial era, 49, 50; social mobility, 129

Salvation Army, 136
Scapegoating, 201. See also Witch hunts
Schevitz, Jeffrey, 250n
Schneider, Jane, 27n
Schuman, Howard, 226n
SCLC (Southern Christian Leadership Conference), 234
Scott, Orange, 100, 103
SDS (Students for a Democratic Society), 236
Secession, 99, 107, 108, 109–11
"Second American Revolution." See Civil War
Secularization: Puritans, 55; social movements, 10, 48; Williams, Roger, 55, 56; witch hunts, 57–58
Securities and Exchange Commission, 196
Seeley, John, 227n
Segregation. See Separatism
Seneca Falls convention of 1848, 91
Separation of church and state. See Secularization
Separatism, 37, 183, 189
Seven Years' War (French and Indian War), 71
Sexuality: "hippie" movement, 238; women's movements, 138, 139, 240
Shakerism, 89, 145
Share the Wealth Movement, 17, 198
Shays's Rebellion, 83; bourgeoisie, 32
Sherman Anti-Trust Act of 1890, 118
Shils, Edward, 26n, 27n, 191n, 226n: elites, 4, 7; central value system, 8–9
Siegel, A., 149n
Sinclair, Upton, 204
Single-issue demands, 13: populism, 131
Sit-down strike, 207, 208
Sit-ins, 235
Sklar, Martin, 191n
Slater, Philip, 46n
Slavery, 183, 188: American Revolution, 73; Civil War, 97–113; cognitive liberation, 20; colonial era, 51; cotton gin, 86; Loyalists, 76; revolts, 68, 69; Williams, Roger, 56. See also Abolitionism
Slavocracy, 98–99
SLP (Socialist Labor Party), 169, 170, 177
Smith, Gerald L. K., 198
Smohalla, 144
SNCC (Student Non-violent Co-ordinating Committee), 2, 234
Social bandits, 18: cognitive liberation, 20
Social controls: U.S. vs. U.S.S.R., 5
Social Democracy Party, 169–70
Social mobility. See Mobility, social
Social movements, 1–11: abolitionism, 100–7; black movements, 183–90; collective action, 18–22; colonial era, 31; Constitutional constraints, 34; Constitutional convention, 83; co-optation, 241–43; determinants, 13–18; effects, 11–13; foreign influences, 193–93, 244–45; Indian resistance, 141–47; Jingoism, 148–49; middle-class movements, 135–41; New Deal, 195–96; 1960s, 233–46; perspectives, 228–33; right-wing movements, 218–21; secession, 108; slavery and, 37; transformations, 22–26. See also specific movements
Social structure, 3–9, 93: American Revolution aftermath, 82; based on British, 30–31; Civil War aftermath, 111; collective action, 18–22; colonial era, 49–51; religion, 60; threatened, 12, 13. See also Elites; Lower class; Middle class
Socialism, 167–75: agrarian movement, 131; blacks, 188; political elites, 6; Socialist Party, 169–70, 174–75; blacks and, 184–85; deroutinization, 164; IWW and, 175, 178
Society of Friends. See Quakerism
Sons of Liberty ("Mohawks"), 72, 73, 76
South, the: civil rights movement, 234; Civil War, 97–99, 107–10; colonial era, 4, 9, 51; counterrevolution, 110–13
"Spider Web Chart," 180

Spoils system, 42
Stamp Act of 1764, 71: riots, 72, 73
Stanton, Elizabeth Cady, 138
Starkey, Marion, 79n
State government, 174
Status quo: factionalization, 25
Status politics, 16-18
Status revolt, 156
Stinchcombe, Arthur, 127-30, 131, 150n, 227n
Stone, I. F., 226n
Strikebreakers, 122
Strikes, 87, 207-8: deroutinization, 165; IWW, 176; labor movement, 119-25
Student movements, 235-37, 239
Substructural level of society, 4, 6: changes, 83-86, 117-19; Civil War, 98. *See also* Production
Suffrage: blacks, 111; labor movement, 88; women, 137, 138, 139, 140
Superstructural level of society, 4, 5. *See also* Ideology
Suppression of movements, 23-24. *See also* Co-optation
Suttles, Gerald D., 28n: ethnicity, 14
Swanson, Guy, 227n
Sweezey, Paul, 46n
Swing, Raymond, 224n

Tammany Hall, 86-87
Taxation: Long, Huey, 198, 199
Tea Act of 1773, 71, 74
Technocrat Movement, 204
Tecumseh, 144
Temperance movements, 136. *See also* Prohibition; WCTU
Tenant farmers: colonial era, 51
Tennant, William, 59
Tenskwatawa, 143-44
Theresa of Avila, 22
Third-party movements, 92, 230: agrarians, 131; class conflicts, 30; difficulty of establishing, 34; labor, 122; populism, 133-34; Progressives, 170; right-wing, 220; Union Party, 199-200. *See also* specific parties
Third World groups, 243-44

Thompson, Leonard, 113n
Torres, Camillo, 11
Totalitarianism, 202
Town meetings, 74
Townshend, Dr. Francis, 203
Townshend Act of 1770, 71, 74
Transport Workers, 210
Trevor-Roper, T. R., 79n
Trow, Martin, 28n, 226n: bourgeoisie, 17
Tuskegee Institute, 185
Two-party system, 34-35. *See also* Political parties; Third-party movements

Underground Railway, 104
Union Party of 1936, 199
Unitarians, 100
Universal Negro Improvement Association, 186, 187
Universities: founded, 33; power structure, 242; student movements, 235-36
Upper class. *See* Elites
Upward mobility. *See* Mobility, social
Urbanization, 130: American Revolution, 70-71; Civil War aftermath, 42; colonial era, 50, 51; proletariat, 68, 69, 70, 125; Utopian experiments. *See* Communal experiments

Value system, 3, 4: Shils on, 8. *See also* Ideology
Verba, Sidney, 225n
Vidich, Arthur, Jr., 46n
Vietnam war: antiwar movement, 244; youth movements, 139
Violence: abolitionism, 105, 106; agrarian revolts, 61; against blacks, 183, 184; elites, 69, 231; IWW, 176; labor movements, 120, 123; legitimacy, 3; military elite, 248; revolution, 82; slavocracy, 98; against strikers, 208. *See also* Riots
VISTA (Volunteers in Service to America), 243
Volunteer army, 239, 242

INDEX

Wallace, Anthony, 150n
Wallace, George, 17
Walters, E. V., 224n
War and social movements, 229
War Department: antiradicalism, 180; civil liberties, 181
War on Poverty, 34
Washburn, Witcomb, 79n
Washington, Booker T., 185, 186, 192n
WASP nativism, 39–40
Watson, Tom, 151n
Ware, Caroline, 191n
WCTU (Women's Christian Temperance Union), 138: ideological change, 11–12; status politics, 17; success, 25
Wealth, distribution of, 5, 6: colonial era, 50
Weathermen, 34, 237
Weaver, General James, 131
Weber, Max, 26n
Weld, Theodore, 102
Weinstein, James, 4, 27n, 191n, 192n
Wharton, Vernon L., 115n
Whiskey Rebellion, 84
White-collar workers: communism, 210
White Leagues, 112
Whitefield, George, 59
Whites: black movements, 183–90; civil rights movement, 234; Indian resistance, 60, 141–47; racial supremacy, 186; radicalism, 37; student movements, 236–37
Whyte, William H., 227n
Willard, Frances, 138
Williams, Roger, 53, 55–56
Wilson, Jack (Wovoka), 22, 145
Witch hunts, 201, 215: elite movements, 57–58; McCarthyism, 217
Wobblies. See Industrial Workers of the World

Wolf, Eric, 79n
Wolfinger, Barbara, 226n
Wolfinger, Raymond, 226n
Women: abolitionism, 104; as a class, 16; equality, 34; Know-Nothing Party, 135; labor movement, 121; middle-class movements and, 136; Progressive Era, 155; Protestantism, 57; the South, 109; Spider Web Chart, 180. See also Women's movements
Women's Liberation, 138–40, 240–41
Women's movements, 136–40: co-optation, 242; goals, 25; Seneca Falls convention, 91; Women's Liberation, 240–41
Working class: frontier, 37; Progressive Era, 156, 158, 159, 162; radicalism, 72; the "right," 220; socialism, 173–74; status politics, 17; utopian experiments, 90–91; women, 139. See also Labor movement
Workingmen's Clubs, 86–87
Workingmen's movements. See Labor movement
World affairs. See Internationalism
World War I, 179
Worsley, Peter, 151n
Wounded Knee Massacre, 142

Yippies, 237
YMCA, 24, 136
Young Patriots, 236
Youth culture, 43, 223
Youth movements, 238, 243–44. See also "Hippie" movement; Student movements

Zald, Mayer, 28n, 250n